One Customer, Divisible

One Customer, Divisible

Linking Customer Insight to Loyalty and Advocacy Behavior

Michael W. Lowenstein

THOMSON

Australia · Canada · Mexico · Singapore · Spain · United Kingdom · United States

THOMSON

Composed by: Cadmus Communications Corp.

Printed in the United States of America by
R.R. Donnelley, Crawfordsville

1 2 3 4 5 08 07 06 05

This book is printed on acid-free paper.

ISBN: 0-324-30129-4

This publication is designed to provide accurate and authoritative information in regard to the subject matter covered. It is sold with the understanding that the publisher is not engaged in rendering legal, accounting, or other professional services. If expert assistance is required, the services of a competent professional person should be sought.

For more information about our products, contact us at:

Thomson Learning Academic Resource Center 1-800-423-0563

Thomson Higher Education
5191 Natorp Boulevard
Mason, OH 45040
USA

Library of Congress Cataloging-in-Publication Data

Lowenstein, Michael W., 1942–
 One customer, divisible : linking customer insight to loyalty and advocacy behavior / Michael W. Lowenstein.
  p. cm.
 Includes bibliographical references and index.
 ISBN 0-324-30129-4 (alk. paper)
 1. Customer services. 2. Customer loyalty. 3. Customer relations. I. Title.
 HF5415.5.L68 2005
 658.8'12—dc22

                                    2005012411

To my family, and especially Susan.

The best way to put distance between you and the crowd is to do an outstanding job with information. How you gather, manage, and use information will determine whether you win or lose.

—Bill Gates

Profit in business comes from repeat customers, customers that boast about your product or service, and that bring friends with them.

—W. Edwards Deming

Some people see things that are and ask, Why? Some people dream of things that never were and ask, Why not? Some people have to go to work and don't have time for all that.

—George Carlin

CONTENTS

FOREWORD

Companies fail that don't understand their customers. Yet most firms don't methodically collect and leverage available customer intelligence.

Customer service departments are a good example. More customer touches occur in the customer service department than any other group in a company. Plus the phone transcripts and email logs they store contain a permanent record of all their customers' wants and desires. But, at most firms, marketing and sales departments don't have access to this intelligence.

In fact, many companies still treat their customer service operations as some sort of "necessary evil" or "complaint department" in spite of the fact that customer service understands customers so well. This attitude must change. Valuable customer intelligence cannot be discarded or sequestered, because leveraging this customer knowledge results in dramatically higher-quality service at significantly lower costs and also in immediate revenue increases. These results occur over and over again.

At RightNow Technologies, we have completed more than 2,000 deployments of customer service systems around the world for companies in all industries. We have seen the impact that a coordinated knowledge base-centered strategy for customer care can have on an organization. By systematically tracking all customer touches, companies can uncover ways to exceed their customers' expectations with proactive support while lowering costs, and anticipate customers' product and service needs to increase their revenue.

The days of blast and pray marketing are gone. Shotguns have been replaced by rifles. But to be effective in this new world we must first understand our customers—individually—or we miss the target.

One Customer, Divisible gives us hope. This book presents the array of specific methodologies being applied today by forward-looking firms across the globe to increase customer loyalty and lifetime value. *One Customer, Divisible* addresses the important issues of data quality and our dissatisfaction with CRM; but, most valuably, it provides practical, real-world examples and techniques.

Departments within corporations cannot exist with separate silos of data. No longer can sales not know what is going on in service, or marketing not know what issues are being raised by customers. A much more holistic, cross-department approach is required, which we refer to as Customer Lifecycle Care. It provides for the systematic design of customer touches throughout the customer purchasing lifecycle and also the comprehensive collection and analysis of the records that result from those interactions. Amazing insights are revealed as thousands of customer interactions are assessed and made actionable, many examples of which appear in *One Customer, Divisible*.

The disappointing results of the CRM era might encourage some to say, "Isn't this just warmed over CRM?" Well, yes and no. Previous CRM initiatives were primarily driven from an Enterprise Resource Planning (ERP) or Sales Force

Automation (SFA) perspective, not from a customer or service orientation. When CRM strategy is led from an ERP perspective, customers get treated like widgets. When CRM strategy is led from an SFA perspective, customers get treated like transactions. It is only when CRM strategy is approached from a customer service and value delivery perspective, that customers are treated like customers, experience by experience, to optimize their loyalty and advocacy potential.

Furthermore, as markets mature, all products in all industries tend to commoditize. The result is that one of the few remaining points of differentiation between these products and services, and those offered by competitors, is the quality of customer interactions. We have two choices. First, we can treat all our customers with the same broad and indiscriminate brush, satisfying some and alienating many. This passive, nondifferentiated approach attempts to force all shapes and sizes of customers into one-size-fits-all offerings, resulting in the disappointment that can lead to defection.

Or second, we can choose to collect and analyze what customers are already telling us about themselves and apply automated processes to treat them as individuals. Products, messaging, services, and support offerings are personalized to various customer segments in order to reach them effectively and ultimately satisfy them on an individual and experience basis. In other words, one customer, divisible.

One example Michael Lowenstein highlights in this book is British Airways, a long-time premier airline of the United Kingdom. Saddled with large overhead costs, they had come under heavy pressure from the airline industry upheaval and attacks from upstart low-price airlines. It is hard to imagine a more difficult position for a company. In order to reverse the consequences of this tough economic environment, British Airways adopted a strategy of "retain, invest and prevent" to insure they kept their customers. They restructured and introduced new services, even their own low-priced offerings. The result? A quote from *The Times*, summarizes this airline's dramatic turnaround: "British Airways has recorded encouraging results for the year ending March 31, 2004. The company reported a pretax profit of $372 million, a 70% jump when compared to 2003. Following a difficult period in the wake of September 11, BA has achieved a remarkable turnaround."

Understanding how and when we touch our customers, and systematically collecting and analyzing the resulting intelligence in order to personalize those interactions, is becoming the new minimum bar for corporate performance. A company's failure to effectively implement this new standard will result in their customers leaking away to competitors. At best, this defection will result in a mediocre corporate existence. At worst, it will lead to a slow and painful death of many small wounds.

I encourage you to read and apply the concepts and examples Michael Lowenstein presents in *One Customer, Divisible*. They represent a monumental opportunity for a company's clear market differentiation and corporate success, as competitors continue to suffer along in their old indiscriminate ways.

Greg Gianforte, CEO and Founder
RightNow Technologies
rightnow.com

PREFACE

While a few smart companies around the world are making dramatic strides in building customer value, keeping customers, and generating lots of money and profits, CRM is pretty much treading water, both as a concept and in applications for enhancing communications and relationships with customers. General estimates are that 60 to 80 percent+ of IT-based CRM programs fail to meet objectives. Too many companies, executives, and managers have gotten burned out and disappointed with CRM due to misunderstanding and misapplying techniques thought to be relationship focused and leveraging of customer loyalty behavior and advocacy.

Companies that were early big investors in CRM have largely gone the way of re-engineering a decade ago: They've thrown vast sums of money into the creation of relationship systems without considering how, strategically, this builds customer value and loyalty on a microsegment, if not an individual customer and experience, basis.

Further, there has been a strong technical- or IT-driven approach to CRM, rather than a forged partnership between IT, marketing, sales, and service. Additionally, there has been a fairly profound objectives definition disconnect between clients and their CRM software solutions providers and consultants.

A marketing director at a major wireless telecom supplier in Venezuela complained she had been restricted from executing loyalty programs for over 18 months while IT management and an outside CRM software vendor worked through their massive customer database problems. In the meantime, the telecom had suffered classic "leaky bucket" loss, with established customers rapidly defecting to telecom suppliers that offered better value and regular communications with them. Sad and unnecessary.

A lot of companies have soured on CRM as a result of stories like this, but a select group are gathering, managing, and using customer data in a positive, holistic manner. Executives and professional staff want to know, and need to know, how this happens. At every CRM conference around the world, these questions are asked over and over by attendees. Tell us how to fix what we're doing. Tell us what works and who is doing it. Help us make the best use of our resources.

In this book, there's going to be minimal discussion of CRM. In fact, almost all of the references to CRM will be in this preface and in the introduction.

CRM isn't dead, but neither is it a panacea. What CRM is, or ought to be, has been, for me, nicely defined by Alyssa Dver, Chief Marketing Officer of software and solutions provider Sedona Corporation: "The ability of an organization to effectively identify, acquire, foster and retain loyal, profitable customers."[1]

---

[1] Alyssa Dver, "CRM: May the Sales Force Be with You," www.realmarket.com, October 27, 2002.

We're going to explore the essential underpinning of business: *Customer data*. Our focus will be on understanding how it's identified and gathered; stored and managed; and shared, analyzed, and applied for creating the highest levels of perceived customer value, and loyalty behavior and advocacy, experience by experience.

An example of a company that knows how to generate customer data and how to apply it for optimal effectiveness is Royal Bank of Scotland. Building on groundbreaking customer loyalty research several years ago, they began applying value-centric relationship programs that were largely simple, hands-on telephone and personal communications protocols by bank service and sales staff.[2] Royal Bank has about 6 million customers, so there are definite scale challenges to use of such labor-intensive approaches.

Another challenge was their discoveries about the customers themselves. Through further research and analysis, they've found that their customer base doesn't break out into neat segments. As a consequence, Royal Bank has modified typical one-to-one approaches to build customer groups from an individual interest basis. Their head of marketing operations, Ian Wilson, said: "We think customers fall into groups on certain things but can be in more than one group at any one time."[3]

As suggested by the title of this book, Royal Bank's customers were divisible, that is, capable of being in multiple segments at any point, depending upon how the company was categorizing them for loyalty building. Many other organizations, if they had better, more comprehensive data about their customers, would draw the same conclusion and design customer programs and protocols accordingly.

These facts—the intensive use of staff for customer loyalty purposes and Royal Bank's insights regarding customer segmentation—required still further innovation to build on their early relationship successes. Royal Bank has used a software solution that enables their marketers to execute personalized, multichannel offers to individual customers. They can automate event-driven campaigns. First, they test creative material on representative customer groups. When trigger criteria have been met, they can send out a print campaign to relevant customers within 48 hours.

Three or four years ago, most of their mailings were to 300,000+ customers per program: Now the average print run is 20,000. For event-driven promotions, as few as four or five customers can be included in a mailing.

Wilson has found that their most effective and timely campaigns now elicit previously unheard of response rates in excess of 75 percent. He's concluded: "We are trying very hard to move from a traditional product push to a customer requirement approach."[4]

Ian Wilson's statement is, in essence, what this book addresses: effectively getting close to customers and providing perceived value on an individualized basis, message

[2] Michael Lowenstein, "Reaching for Divisible Customers," www.crmguru.com, October 24, 2002.

[3] Michael Lowenstein, "Reaching for Divisible Customers," www.crmguru.com, October 24, 2002.

[4] Michael Lowenstein, "Reaching for Divisible Customers," www.crmguru.com, October 24, 2002.

by message and experience by experience, through the use of the best available customer data. This is not the often theoretical and cosmetically appealing ideas that some one-to-one marketing has proven to be, but the practical, successful approaches being applied by companies like Royal Bank on a daily basis around the world.

Customer experience management has evolved to the point that micro-segmentation, customer data integration, and personalized software is both available and affordable, even for smaller and mid-sized companies. Yet it's clear that few organizations have taken the right course. Many CRM programs have crashed or receded due to data quality issues, taking with them the opportunity for closer customer relationships.

Alison Bass, the senior editor of *CIO* magazine, said, in an editorial entitled "The Perils of Personalization":

> Forget trying to increase your market share in this economy. It costs too much, and returns can be elusive. In these fiscally tight days, the thing to do is squeeze more profit out of your best customers and persuade them to spend more money with you. But before you pursue that strategy, you have to know how to massage your customer information. Therein lies the tricky part . . . the path to customer segmentation is strewn with mines, which could easily blow up in your face.[5]

She's nailed it.

In discussing how banks, for one group, approach high-, moderate-, and low-volume customers through segmentation and personalization, Bass concluded: "Thus, the moral of CRM might be: Don't even bother to think about doing it until you understand exactly who your customers are, how they drive your business, and what you want to do with the information you've collected. Otherwise, you could lose your shirt without even trying."[6] Banks, which are by admission too often ineffective at creating value-based customer relationships, ought to pay particular attention to statements like that; but her perceptions really apply to companies of any size and in virtually any industry.

For smaller and medium-sized businesses, known as SMEs, the challenge is particularly daunting. Frequently lacking the resources or the knowledge to gather, store, and apply even the most basic customer data puts incredible pressure on them. They often realize the importance of having current, applicable customer information, but realization alone is not nearly enough. They fail to act, and that equals disaster.

Consider these results from a study of 1,000 SMEs in the UK, conducted by Sage, a supplier of customer data management software to this market:

- Forty-six percent rely on verbal customer feedback, while only 7 percent say they've used the results of customer research or complaints to help improve their service levels; and 12 percent do nothing at all.

---

[5] Alison Bass, "The Perils of Personalization," www.cio.com, December 11, 2001.
[6] Alison Bass, "The Perils of Personalization," www.cio.com, December 11, 2001.

- Over half of the SMEs—54 percent—have no record of new or lost customers; and, of those who do, 40 percent keep this information on a manual basis.[7]

Commenting on these results, Clive Gray, Sage's general manager, said:

In the current economic climate, keeping your customers happy and attracting new customers has never been more important, particularly to small businesses, who cannot afford to lose customers. We are concerned that a significant number do not seem to actively seek out new customers or make the most of new technology to stay in contact with, and react quickly to, existing customers.[8]

This book is about generating quality data and applying it for optimal customer relations and delivery of perceived value. To paraphrase Alison Bass, unless a company can effectively practice CRM fundamentals such as defining and understanding customer segments, gathering and interpreting customer needs, and learning how to collect, clean and qualify, store, collate, manage, and apply customer data, and target the data appropriately, success will be elusive. Conversely, doing it well can differentiate any company, positively and strategically, with customers.

According to Jeremy Braune, Head of Customer Experience at Detica, a marketing communications consulting organization in the UK, "[O]rganizations need to adopt a more structured and rigorous approach to development, based on a real understanding of what their customers actually want from them. The bottom line must always be to start with the basics of what is most important to the customer and build from there."[9] The vital nature of having the right customer information, and using it to create advocacy, can't be overstressed.

In *Gorgias*, one of Plato's lesser-known morality plays, he stages a debate (featuring Socrates as moderator) on the nature of rhetoric, or public speaking. The questions Socrates poses: Is public speaking art or science? Is it good or evil? Through Socrates, Plato concludes: "Not an art but a knack gained by experience."[10] Those who take the best of art and science are like gourmet chefs.

They know what they are doing and why it works, and they can distinguish between good and bad results. They succeed in delivering the best, most lasting value possible for the customer. That is what we will endeavor to do with customer data for everyone who reads and uses the material and ideas presented in *One Customer, Divisible.*

---

[7] "SMEs Value Customer Service, But Still Don't Put It into Practice," www.crmforum.com, June 17, 2002.
[8] "SMEs Value Customer Service, But Still Don't Put It into Practice," www.crmforum.com, June 17, 2002.
[9] Jeremy Braune, "Customers Say CRM Is a Letdown," www.crmforum.com, March 6, 2002.
[10] Charles Griswold, "Plato on Rhetoric and Poetry," in *Stanford Encyclopedia of Philosophy*, edited by Edward N. Zalta, http://plato.stanford.edu/archives/sum2005/entries/plato-rhetoric.

ACKNOWLEDGMENTS

In one of my earlier books, I quoted seventeenth-century Japanese poet and Zen master Basho, who once said: "Do not seek to follow in the footsteps of the wise. Seek what they sought." I still believe that, perhaps now more than ever, and particularly in customer management where the only constant is change and continuous learning is a basic requirement. I'm inspired by new-age thinkers and doers in this field, like Philip Kotler, Lester Wunderman, Clive Humby, JoAnna Brandi, Gary Hawkins, Feargal Quinn, Gary Loveman, Mary Naylor, Michael Price, Robin Clark, Brian Woolf, Adrian Payne, Ruth Stevens, Malcolm Gladwell, Greg Gianforte, and Gerald Zaltman to cite just a few among the many. Some of these names are better known than others, but all have been innovators in understanding and managing customer behavior.

One Customer, Divisible? It's (Almost) All About the Data

Much of what I've learned over the years about sales, marketing, and customer service has to do with the critical importance of customer data. It's how smart, well-led, customer-centric companies generate the right customer data, manage data the right way, and use it at the right time and to best effect to optimize loyalty and profitability, that makes them successful, or not, on an individual customer basis. Culture, leadership, and systems will facilitate effective information gathering, storage, and application; and, CRM, ERP, or other acronyms notwithstanding, it's impossible to be successful without having as much relevant insight about customers as possible.

One of my key sources for the uses of information gathered by customer clubs and loyalty programs, for instance, is my friend and colleague, Brian Woolf (brianwoolf.com). Brian is president of the Retail Strategy Center, Inc., and a font of knowledge and insight about how companies apply, and don't apply, data generated through these programs.

In a Peppers & Rogers newsletter, for example, Don Peppers quoted Brian in his article, "The Secrets of Successful Loyalty Programs":

> Loyalty program success has less to do with the value of points or discounts to a customer, and much more to do with a company's use of data mining to improve the customer experience. Top management hasn't figured out what to do with all the information gleaned. You have all this information sitting in a database somewhere and no one taking advantage of it.
>
> You need to mine the information to create not only relationships but also an optimum (purchasing) experience. The best loyalty programs use the customer data to improve not only promotions, but also store layout, pricing, cleanliness, check-out speed, etc. Firms that do this are able to double their profits. When these elements are not addressed, all you're doing is teaching the customer to seek out the lowest price.[1]

Most companies fit within a narrow spectrum that extends from mediocre to downright awful in how they approach the data need identification/development/storage/application process. In fact, it's a worldwide epidemic of inefficiency and ineffectiveness.

Poor customer data development and application negatively impacts customer loyalty efforts for companies of any size. According to a 2001 survey of 506 global

[1] Don Peppers, "The Secrets of Successful Loyalty Programs," *Inside 1 to 1*, October 22, 2001.

CEOs by The Conference Board, these execs ranked customer loyalty and retention as their #1 management challenge.[2] That challenge and need have driven some companies to invest as much as $30 million or more to install CRM systems and to invest even higher amounts in frequency marketing programs. But we know there's widespread frustration among execs because 1) CRM systems aren't being used with nearly enough effectiveness to optimize customer loyalty; and 2) frequency marketing programs tend to reward customers who are already loyal, and don't cover other customers very well.

There is little or no attempt, within either CRM systems or frequency marketing programs, to either generate information about what customers consider as having tangible or intangible value and then use that insight for leveraging loyalty behavior. That's the pivotal cause for the high failure rates of these systems and programs.

Even companies that properly introduce a CRM system often underutilize its full information-gathering and application capabilities. "Businesses are often limiting the scope of information that they attempt to capture in their CRM environments," says Karl Büttner, president and CEO of 170 Systems, Inc., a systems application provider.[3] Büttner says he sees many companies mistakenly focusing only on contact information, thereby passing up the opportunity to capture a broader, "360-degree" view of the customer.

Here are study findings, for instance, showing that very few UK businesses are collating or exploiting their customer data adequately, according to the results of research carried out by UK CRM consultancy firm, Detica.

The research report, *Converting Customer Data into Effective Decisions*, shows that only 13 percent of companies can be categorized as leaders when it comes to collating customer data and subsequently using it to improve customer relationships. Another 32 percent were classed as the "followers," having good data in certain areas but only using it to support a limited number of business functions. Another 15 percent of companies were classed as "under-achievers," having some good customer data but making very little use of it; and the remaining 40 percent were categorized as "strugglers," having very little good data and limited ability to exploit what they do have.

Colin Sheppard, strategic business development director at Detica, said:

> The research highlights the challenges businesses face in developing a good understanding of their customers, and in using the resulting insights effectively across the enterprise.... Our research shows significant differences across different markets. In particular, telecommunications and utility companies have

---

[2] Michael Lowenstein, "It's Really Almost All About the Data: Optimizing Loyalty Initiatives," www.searchcrm.com, February 7, 2003.
[3] Michael Lowenstein, "It's Really Almost All About the Data: Optimizing Loyalty Initiatives," www.searchcrm.com, February 7, 2003.

been shown to be lagging well behind those in the financial services and travel, transport and leisure sectors.[4]

When it comes to the types of data being used, most companies are good at capturing the basics, such as contact and billing details, but few use additional descriptive information such as demographic or lifestyle data. When asked if their business had a good single view of the customer, no industry sector performed well. Just 17 percent of travel, transport, and leisure companies said they did, compared to 27 percent of utilities, with telecommunications (55 percent) and retail banking (60 percent) performing the best.

Here is a graphic depiction of Detica's key findings:

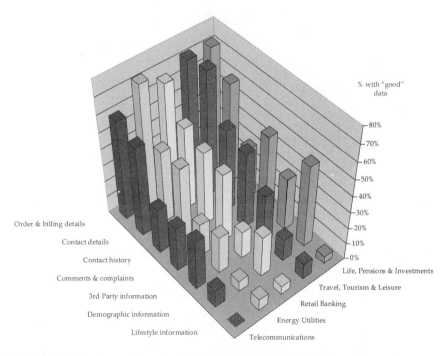

Figure I.1 Customer Data Availability and Quality by Industry Sector
Source: "Converting Customer Data into Effective Decisions: The UK Leaders and Followers," Detica Research Report (Guildford, UK: Detica, Ltd., May 2002), p. 6.

Clearly, while some industries are generally capable of generating in-depth customer information, most are not. Generating the right data, however, is only the beginning of customer insight challenges for most companies.

---

[4] Colin Sheppard, "Businesses Not Making Good Use of Customer Data, Says Detica," www.crmforum.com, May 15, 2002.

According to Sheppard, creating a single view of the customer is a key business requirement that very few companies have truly achieved. This problem hampers the effectiveness of marketing, sales, and customer service operations alike. And when asked how their customer data are used, companies in all sectors were strong in using it for acquiring new customers (if fact, many cited this as a reason for developing a database in the first place). Yet few are using it to target cross-selling, retention, and win-back campaigns or to reinforce relationships with customers.

Detica has created a model, which we actively support, for the continuum of generating, storing, sharing, and applying in-depth data for customer value optimization:

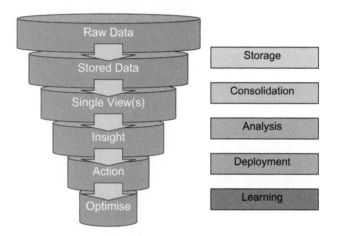

Figure I.2 Customer Data Value/Stages
Source: "Converting Customer Data into Effective Decisions: The UK Leaders and Followers," Detica Research Report (Guildford, UK: Detica, Ltd., May 2002), p. 6.

This model is really pretty straightforward. It provides a disciplined, sustainable process for moving from data collection to creating customer advocacy and commitment. Like most elegantly simple approaches, however, completing the journey has been a challenge for most companies, as borne out by the results of the Detica study.

The underlying reason study findings like this keep surfacing is that companies, in the main, do not identify what customers want. In addition, these companies do not become customer-centric, using their learning to build stronger relationships with customers, in spite of all the CRM system and loyalty program investment we've witnessed.

A good analogy, or model, for CRM and loyalty program effectiveness or ineffectiveness may be what can be termed the "car-fuel relationship." A car, no matter how attractive, powerful, and technically sophisticated, can't go anywhere without fuel. Not only that, to reach a desired destination, the car must have the right fuel for its engine, and in the right quantity. For customers, the car is CRM, and its key data-related systems components (data gathering, integration, warehousing, mining, and application). The destination is optimized customer lifetime value and profitability. The fuel is the proper octane and amount of customer data.

One of the key elements in the Detica model is Deployment, the internal movement of customer data for action. A recent British Telecom study showed that managers are often suspicious of sharing information, with almost one-third keeping customer information within their groups and another tenth keeping data on paper-based systems. As a BT executive concluded: "Sharing the right information at the right time is crucial to getting the best results, but it seems that too few businesses are encouraging their staff to do so."[5] This is equivalent to keeping fuel from getting from the tank to the pistons.

Leading-edge companies are focusing on real and projected customer lifetime value, and the creation of felt loyalty and customer advocacy, as a destination. They are collecting the right data and using the right skills, processes, tools, and customer data management technologies to make sure that key customer insights are available wherever they are needed, in all parts of the enterprise. Dave Cox, managing director of Swallow Information Systems, a customer support software provider, believes that service and use of customer data are what positively, and strategically, differentiates one company from another:

> Customer information held in databases in the service department provides the clues that sales, marketing and development are looking for to understand their customers. So share it. Integrate the systems and let everybody listen to what customers are telling you. Bottom-up, customer-led, service-driven, call it what you want, but customer feedback must be included in the strategic decision-making process for any hope of continued success.[6]

He concludes: "Good service isn't just about providing a helpline or a support desk any more. It's about gathering the information, disseminating it throughout the company, and considering customers' opinions in corporate decision-making." We completely agree.

---

[5] "Sloppy Businesses Losing Sight of Customers," www.thewisemarketer.com, February 12, 2004.
[6] David Cox, "Taking the 'R' Out of CRM," Swallow Information Systems White Paper, *CRM Today*, 2000.

A Few Historical Perspectives, Basic Ground Rules, and Looks into the Future Never Hurt Anybody. . . .

How Well Do Most Companies Understand Their Customers?

Not so very long ago, life and relationships with customers were much simpler for just about all businesses.

Customers didn't have the choice, mobility, and information available to nearly everyone today. The local retailer or tradesperson, or business-to-business supplier, had in-depth knowledge of all his or her customers' needs and wants through their purchase activity; and, frequently, that business knew even more about their customers' demographic and lifestyle profiles through direct interaction. Typically, that information was stored and managed in his or her head, which served as random access memory before we had personal computers.

The reality for most businesses today is that customer loyalty is in decline, threatening not only their success but their basic ability to stay competitive. Customers *do* have more choice, they *do* more have mobility, and they *do* have access to much more information.

Customers also have a "need for speed," where time-pressured lives have caused them to be more fickle and demanding of performance with their suppliers. On-line, for instance, an e-tailer is always little more than one click away from losing a customer, probably for good.

At the same time customer needs are changing, we're also seeing a general decline in the perception of service, so important in helping retain good customers. The technological service tools, such as IVR and ACD (Interactive Voice Response and Automatic Call Distribution, the telephone menus and non-interactive features so many of us find annoying) and greater incidence of customer self-help have tended to drive suppliers further away from their customers. Add to that the costs associated with staff training, or even getting and keeping capable staff in the first place, and you have a multilayered threat to customer loyalty and commitment to any supplier.

Customer studies show that, while consumers want more *value*, suppliers struggle to break out of the perceived sameness, or parity, that characterizes many of them. In other words, one local butcher shop, computer maker, cleaning service, airline, deli, remodeling company, distributor, or card store looks pretty much like all the rest. The products and services from one type of business seem identical to the same kind of business on the next block or in the next town. They're replaceable and interchangeable. Businesses don't make the effort to differentiate themselves in ways that are important to their customers. This is partially because they don't know how, partially because, even if they know, they don't execute. Mostly, however, it's because they don't know their customers well enough to understand what can positively, successfully, differentiate them from their peers. They often realize the impact of having current, applicable customer information, but realization alone is not enough. Failing to act can mean disaster.

There are a lot of names given to tools and systems, and the people who use them, in companies that have embraced a customer-centric approach to business. Relationship, service, and marketing management can perhaps best be positioned as the acts of using these tools and systems to provide customers with greater perceived value. In much of the discussion about customer management and CRM, the emphasis has tended to become disjointed, focusing on the technology rather than the customer, missing how insight into the customer, and the customer's needs at each supplier transaction and decision point, can deliver that value.

Customer-Wise, How Did We Get to This Point . . . Or, at Least, How Did Lester Wunderman Help Marketers Make It to the '90s?

Perhaps there will be some benefit in tracing the roots of modern customer management for perspective in how to optimize individual customer value. At least we think so, and we're devoting some of the first chapter to doing this.

The roots of being customer focused can be traced to the Industrial Revolution, beginning with the more scientific approaches brought into the factories and greater use of mechanization in producing basic goods—glass, clocks, textiles, chemicals, etc.—perhaps culminating with the steam engine (Thomas Newcomen in 1705, James Watt in 1763), broad-scale use of electric power in the latter nineteenth century, and the concomitant growth of railroads and other forms of transportation.

The Industrial Revolution changed much of the world from an agrarian, rural life to a concentrated workforce, principally located in cities and suburbs. It also created new social classes within the populations of the United States and Europe, with enough spending power to be somewhat discerning in their purchases.

During the mid-1800s, a German customs union, the Zollverein, began a movement to make products designed more to meet customer needs than simply to take advantage of manufacturing efficiencies. Although the Zollverein is seen today as little more than a German plan to more effectively manage their country's economy, it nonetheless contained some of the seeds of what we now understand to be "mass customization." or producing for more individualized needs. In that period, Germany was competing for customers mostly with England, the other European manufacturing powerhouse; and German companies understood, on an elementary level, that they could generate more customers and sales if they created products and services more along the lines of expressed customer requirements instead of merely competing only on availability and price.

At about the same time, communications were changing, never to step back. Regular, low-cost mail, the telephone, and wireless telegraph made the world shrink, capped off by radio in the early twentieth century and television in the mid-twentieth century, all of which served to speed communication and the pace of life. Consumers could now have access to more information than ever before, along with the emerging desire for more customized products and services. Through World War I and the Depression in the U.S., communications continued to improve. Following World War II, pent-up demand for consumer and business goods led to more sophisticated sales and marketing approaches with customers.

It was in the late 1940s that marketing and advertising pioneer Lester Wunderman, constantly looking for new ideas to present to his clients, encountered the Jackson & Perkins Company of Newark, New York, the world's largest marketer of rose plants. His work with Jackson & Perkins would be the embryonic foundation of individualized customer management.

Jackson & Perkins, through its advertising, was generating over 100,000 prospects a year, principally through print advertising and mailings. Only about 10 percent, however, became customers; and the company was also losing a good share of customers due to non-purchase. This was the classic leaky bucket syndrome. Although Wunderman didn't have the advantage of segmentation modeling or computers, he recognized that Jackson & Perkins had a deficiency of actionable customer data. As he says, "Our mailings were not relevant to many of the customers because we didn't know what they had already bought and what, if anything, they were likely to buy again. Nor did we know the size of their gardens or what was already planted in them. We were marketing in the dark."

Wunderman first began to classify customers by type, size, frequency of purchases, and the date and size of last purchase. He quickly determined that, after four inactive purchase seasons (two years), customers were considered defectors. Next, he turned his attention to category of purchase, i.e., roses, perennials, fruit trees, and so on. As this elementary segmentation began, Wunderman determined that the more finite buyer identities he could create, and the more he could learn about each customer, the more profitable their marketing campaigns could be. The customer learning quickly became what we would today call "interactive communication."

Jackson & Perkins embarked on a "Rose of the Year" campaign, and created a fee-based membership club of customers to select it as a massive panel. Now, instead of sending an expensive catalog to inquiring prospects as they had done prior to the segmentation exercise, Jackson & Perkins sent a letter telling them when the Rose of the Year would be available for purchase. Almost 10 percent of inquirers ordered it from the letter, sight unseen. Additionally, later, when the catalogs were sent out, the company was still generating 10 percent in new cash sales. Thus, not only did Wunderman discover just how curious and interested the prospects were, but he also learned how the prospect and customer list could be mined for greater revenue.

Within ten years of Wunderman's initial segmentation of Jackson & Perkins' list, an array of segmented promotions and offer approaches ensued, and the company had increased sales to the "average" customer by 300 percent. Beginning with roses, Jackson & Perkins had become the largest seller of mums, lilies, and tulip and other bulbs from Holland. More important, the company became a prime source of information for home gardeners, increasing their level of engagement, commitment, and loyalty. This learning became the foundation for decades of success, expertise that Wunderman subsequently applied to scores of his company's clients in the years since his initial work with Jackson & Perkins.

It's The Dawning of the Age of Relationship Marketing and Customer Management (Not Necessarily to Be Confused with Database Marketing, Loyalty Marketing, One-to-One Marketing, Permission Marketing, or CRM)

Wunderman has defined marketing, particularly direct marketing, as having a "front end" and a "back end.". The front end is the initial sales result from identifying, and communicating with, prospects and moving them to action. The back end is determined by the number of customers who buy multiple times, how much they spend and on what, how frequently they buy, how strongly they are committed to the supplier, how long they remain as customers, and their likelihood to return if they do stop buying. What Wunderman describes as the "fundamental franchise" of suppliers is the nature of the relationship they build. As he concludes, "The quality of the relationship is what motivates customers to buy repeatedly over long periods of time. When the relationship is good, a special bond of loyalty develops between buyer and seller."

Since Lester Wunderman first coined the term "relationship marketing" at a presentation to the Boston chapter of the American Marketing Association at M.I.T. in 1967, companies have been building on his ideas. Perhaps the best, most salient definition of relationship marketing comes from Ian Gordon, an author and management consultant from Toronto:

> Relationship marketing is the ongoing process of identifying and creating new value with individual customers and then sharing the benefits of this over a lifetime of association. It involves the understanding, focusing and management of ongoing collaboration between suppliers and selected customers for mutual value creation and sharing through interdependence and organizational alignment.[1]

If this definition seems abstract and somewhat esoteric, here are the basics about relationship marketing:

- It acknowledges the importance of individual customers, both as purchasers and as definers and arbiters of value in products and services. Previously, suppliers were engaged in "push" approaches, first developing a product or service and then aggressively marketing it, with little customer input or choice. As Henry Ford once remarked with regard to his Model T, customers could have any color they wanted—as long as it was black!
- Companies, if they are to remain, or become, successful, will need to design and align all business processes—communication, technology, and people—around the value customers want.
- It recognizes the value customers represent on a lifetime basis, as individuals and on a purchase occasion by occasion basis. As an extension of this awareness that customers do indeed have a life cycle, an objective of relationship marketing is to build more relevance and engagement opportunities for customers, enhancing the bond.

These are three of the key elements that will be explored in *One Customer, Divisible*.

Relationship marketing also seeks to build, as Gordon defines it, a chain of involvements and engagements on behalf of the customer, within the organization to build the value customers desire, and also between principal stakeholders, including suppliers, distribution channels, shareholders, the financial community, and the general public. This will be considered at various points throughout the book; however, it could be the subject of an entire book by itself.

Gordon has also been careful to define what relationship marketing *is not*, which is as important as what it is. It isn't, for example, another iteration of marketing, but it is a new discipline that can help create value for customers. As Gordon sees it, the marketer is the advocate of the processes that deliver that value.

---

[1] Ian Gordon, *Relationship Marketing* (Mississauga, ON: John Wiley & Sons, 1998), p. 9.

It's not *database management,* because those involved with this aspect of customer infrastructure are principally focused on profiling, predictive modeling, and other forms of analysis, while relationship marketing and customer management employ the fruits of what database managers produce.

It's not *loyalty marketing,* which is usually another term for encouraging more frequent purchases. Sometimes value is created for customers along the way, sometimes not; but the principal objective is to create more active purchasing.

It's not *partnering,* or *PRM,* because, while companies are interested in creating alliances and alignments between customers, employees, suppliers, and channels, this is rarely, if ever, achieved in a way that creates value for all.

It's not *permission marketing,* which was touted as the tool for marketers to shape customized messages for customers and prospects so that they would be willing to accept them. Unfortunately, much of permission marketing has devolved into fairly mundane one-way communication, rather than the learning relationship that was envisioned. Companies too often have not proven disciplined enough to deepen the permission-based communication platform with customers.

It's not *one-to-one marketing* as an end goal. There are many situations where one-to-one marketing is highly appropriate, such as where customer needs are diverse and customers have high value. This can be seen in industries such as airlines and lodging. But even in businesses with seemingly undifferentiated needs and uniform customer valuations, such as service stations, there is tremendous opportunity to customize both the experience and communication needed to increase commitment levels. Unfortunately, relatively few companies are applying the techniques necessary to enhance perceived value. For every Dell, FedEx, BellSouth, and American Express that have employed advanced approaches to understand individual customer value, develop customer data, measure results customer by customer, and target communication, thousands of companies, as identified by Detica and other studies, have failed to make much progress here.

Finally, it's not *customer relationship management,* or *CRM,* at least not directly. While CRM as a discipline struggles to define and redefine itself, it's still principally about the IT aspects of customer data development and systems, with IT personnel too often taking the majority of the direction and responsibility without meaningful collaboration by other major stakeholders. Although there are varied definitions of CRM, fundamentally it's the use of software to create an integrated customer contact approach and greater efficiencies through sales, marketing, and customer service. It is a set of data-driven techniques used to leverage past purchasing behavior to determine the types of future communication that should be undertaken. Ultimately, it has everything to do with behavior leverage and little to do with establishing a relationship, or emotional bond, of customer advocacy.

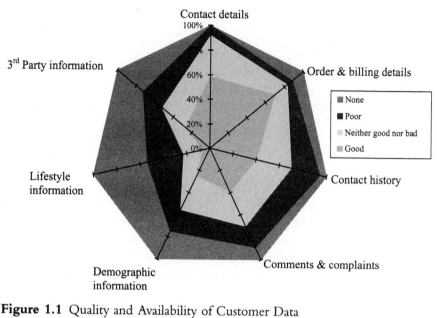

Figure 1.1 Quality and Availability of Customer Data
Source: "Converting Customer Data into Effective Decisions: The UK Leaders and Followers,"
Detica Research Report (Guildford, UK: Detica, Ltd., May 2002), p. 5.

A principal objective of CRM is to increase customer value by becoming more customer focused across the organization. Effective CRM requires an in-depth understanding of customers, and it's fair to say that there are many who are still looking for the "customer" in customer relationship management.

Required: More Effective Approaches in the Art of Customer Insight

Companies have challenges in every pivotal area of customer insight development: what types of information are generated; how the data are gathered and stored; how individualistically companies are able to identify and address each customer (and also how that capability supports their strategic customer-related planning); how these insights drive marketing, sales, and customer service operations and processes and new product, service, and channel management; and, finally, what performance metrics are developed, and how they are communicated across the organization. The Detica study presented in the Introduction addressed every facet of insight creation, and found the vast majority of companies deficient in multiple areas.

In each area where companies could create a resource of data that would help generate customer value—demographics, lifestyle information, even comments and complaints (because of the high frequency of unregistered complaints that exist with customers)—few companies perform even adequately (see Figure 1.1).

While most businesses are aware of the necessity of generating good-quality customer data, the need to have a single, organization-wide view of the customer, and the value of monitoring the dynamics of customer changes over time, very few were capable of doing it. While businesses recognized how segmentation, microsegmentation, and even individualized understanding of customer needs were valuable for planning and objective setting, and most did some rudimentary customer segmentation, over 40 percent admitted that their segmentation approaches were not effective or actionable.

The study also found that there was a lack of consistency between industries even in how customers are segmented. For example, Detica learned that retail banks, telecoms, and travel and leisure companies actively use demographics and/or lifestyle data, while utilities rely more heavily on research-based attitudinal information.

Customer data, ideally, can be applied to improving the customer's experience, eliminating the necessity for customers to repeatedly provide details about their needs and requirements, having a complete picture of the customer at every contact point and situation for differentiated service and support, and personalizing communication to enhance the relationship throughout the customer life cycle. Additionally, it helps insure that development of products, services, and messaging is focused on individual customer requirements. A component of Detica's study was to ascertain how well the deployment of customer insight was being accomplished, and the degree to which performance objectives and metrics were being applied.

Detica learned that most customer data is generated during acquisition, because companies tend to be overly focused on this phase of the customer life cycle. Far fewer focus on upsell, cross-sell, win-back, new product/service development or referral, lasering-in on market share rather than value optimization or share of wallet. Finally, the study found that under half did not use any customer-based performance metrics to guide and manage the business; and of those that did use these metrics, fewer than one-third could affirm that the measures were well communicated within the organization.

As stated in the Introduction, 39 percent of the companies Detica studied were labeled as *Strugglers,* having very little good data and little capability of applying it. This was a shocking 55 percent in telecoms and 56 percent in utilities. Another 15 percent were labeled *Under-Achievers,* businesses with some good customer data but with poor processes for effectively utilizing it.

Also, increasingly companies are going to have to deal with unstructured data, such as the text-based information that resides in Microsoft Word and PowerPoint files, emails, and Intranet newsletters; as well as the structured data on which the Detica study has focused. This is going to require investment in skills and technology in new areas such as "content analytics" to look for patterns and anomalies in text and "information visualization" to reveal hidden meanings. While these terms and capabilities are unknown to many companies, some experts have estimated that up to 80 to 90 percent of the customer information residing within an organization may be in text form. Due to sheer volume alone, this will have to be addressed.

So the stage is set. What must companies do as customers become less loyal, their needs more immediate and complex? One of the first, and maybe most important, things companies have to address is data quality.

Critical Data Quality Issues, or Don't They Know Who We Are?

Data quality is much more than simply knowing that my name is Mr. Michael Lowenstein and not Mrs. or Ms. It means eliminating "stale" entries, incorrect addresses, and duplicate records. It also means vetting customer data sources for accuracy. Poor data quality results in both higher communication costs and the strong possibility of misunderstanding customer profiles.

Clean and current data are but two aspects of data quality. According to the Navesink Consulting Group, data are of high quality "if they are fit for their intended uses in operations, decision-making, and planning."[2] That means the data:

- Are free of defects: accessible, accurate, timely, complete, consistent with other sources, etc.
- Possess desired features: relevant, comprehensive, proper level of detail, easy to read and interpret, etc.

Using these criteria, no customer database is error free, and the high level of erroneous data has become a high-cost problem for suppliers and an annoyance for customers. In a recent study, close to 80 percent of consumers polled said they dislike receiving duplicate pieces of mail for the same promotion. But also names can be misspelled, or mail pieces can be sent to former residents or the wrong address. High-quality data and the sophisticated statistical techniques to analyze this information are absolutely essential for successful customer programs and processes. Everything is potentially important in customer relationships—historical purchase data, essential demographics, and lifestyle characteristics—so suppliers are becoming increasingly concerned.

A recent Detica-sponsored study among 200 senior marketing and CRM executives drawn from Europe's top companies showed that 41 percent identified duplicate customer data and incomplete customer records as a major problem and a principal impediment in creating a single, organization-wide customer perspective. Part of the challenge, the study found, was that data quality issues can arise in almost any area of the business—sales, finance, customer service, marketing—but that

---

[2] Thomas C. Redman, "Data: An Unfolding Quality Disaster," *DM Review,* August 2004.

"ownership," or responsibility, for data quality and business processes, and an unwillingness to invest in strategic technology solutions, were the key contributors.

The range of estimated errors in most databases is quite broad. Studies reveal percentage figures that go from the low single digits to 40 percent and higher. One such study, conducted by British Telecom among marketing and business development managers, found that 25 percent had wrongly recorded crucial customer data. (Additionally, 40 percent revealed that they don't share customer data with colleagues, or across departments. These are structural, systems, and cultural issues that can be as damaging and dangerous as incorrect data.)

Errors can come as a result of keying mistakes, misheard names and addresses, or straightforward multiple entries of the same data. They can come when companies merge two or more disparate information sources. They can also arise from poor list merge-purge programs, errors when data streams are integrated, infrequent cleaning, and so on.

Costs associated with poor data quality go well beyond the easily identifiable, and obvious, waste from mailing duplicate merchandise catalogues. They include dealing with customer complaints caused by data errors, and the staff costs involved in checking databases, finding missing data, and fixing incorrect data. Order entry staff, for example, may spend up to 25 percent of their time performing these tasks. In a company with 40 staff members, that would equal 10 effort-years annually. Further, if the loaded cost for each of these staff members is $50,000 per year, the annual cost associated with data errors—in just this one area—would be $500,000!

This is a pervasive and troubling issue for suppliers. A study of 500 European marketing directors from an array of industries revealed that two-thirds believed inaccurate and incomplete data impact both company profitability and customer-perceived performance. Another study, this one conducted in the U.K. among 120 marketing, CRM, and database managers, found that almost 40 percent had no standard policies on data quality. A study of 600 U.S. companies by PriceWaterhouseCoopers found that 75 percent thought that defective data was having a negative financial impact, and only 37 percent were very confident in the quality of the data they developed. It's little wonder, then, that data quality, often involving customer data from third-party sources, remains such a challenge. Some companies, however, have found ways to emerge from data quagmires.

Lutheran Brotherhood, a member-owned fraternal benefits organization (mutual funds and annuities, insurance, estate planning, college and retirement programs, etc.), has over 2 million member names and addresses spread across several product and service line databases. In addition, they have 6 million names in their prospect database. They often ran into customer service problems, one of which centered around delivery of their bimonthly magazine. If a household had multiple members, and they requested multiple copies, there were questions about why they were getting only one copy. The same member might get multiple copies of the magazine even if they should have received only one.

The organization was principally using front-line staff to rectify member data quality problems, but this was both expensive and inefficient. Lutheran Brotherhood undertook a process to centralize all member information into one database (customer data integration), so that employees would have a complete view of their members. This was a proactive and positive first step, but it didn't eliminate the bigger problem of duplicate names and addresses. Staff were still responsible for the searching and matching process, functions that were costly, time-consuming, and negative for morale. According to JoAnne Gibbs, business analyst for Lutheran Brotherhood, "We were spending too much time entering and cleaning duplicates."

Lutheran Brotherhood solved this issue by using advanced linking software, in this case provided by Innovative Systems, Inc., to de-duplicate member and prospect names from the database. Their entire file of 8 million names can now be cleaned for duplicates in four hours; and, as Gibbs concluded, "Our use of the product saved us from duplicating a total of 482,000 customers and prospects." Much of the problem surrounding magazine delivery evaporated as a result.

Data quality upgrade efforts such as these are usually transparent to customers, and they should be. The real rewards of higher-quality data, however, are improvements in areas of customer relationships such as service and market research, and greater efficiency in marketing and other customer-related processes, making CRM activities more productive and consistent. Harrah's Entertainment, for instance, runs manual database checks every night to merge any duplicate records that might be created in its customer rewards program. This not only saves on communication costs but helps insure that customers receive both the credit and individualized treatment they've earned.

The Data Warehousing Institute has estimated that data quality problems cost U.S. businesses more than $600 billion a year, yet most executives are unaware that these challenges—accuracy, integrity, consistency, completeness, validity, timeliness, and accessibility—are impairing both their bottom lines and ability to sustain relationships with customers. One data quality expert estimated that missed revenue opportunities, layered onto the non-recoverable costs associated with correcting customer data, may represent between 10 percent and 25 percent of an organization's total revenue.

If companies are to effectively engage customers on a one-to-one, and purchase scenario, basis, they will need to apply a bit of discipline and rigor in the following ten areas:

1. *Get senior management support.* This begins at the top, with senior executives establishing and enforcing rules regarding parameters for the gathering,

storage, and application of data. This means, among other things, communicating that data quality is a strategic program, rather than something that's dealt with on a tactical, or occasional, basis.

2. *Create partnerships, and teams, between business functions and IT.* Companies tend to have some proficiency at collecting and storing data but have problems in gaining access to, and sharing, it. Partnerships and teams can help make certain that systems are in place to make data availability as real-time and consistent as possible. Virtually everyone in the organization is a customer data "customer," so their teamwork is essential.

3. *Identify which group or groups has data quality responsibilities.* Companies must make absolutely clear which group or groups have stewardship regarding data management. Data management responsibilities, between and within the technical and business (sales, marketing, and customer service) departments, should be as clear as possible, and accountabilities should be established. If data quality responsibilities are outsourced, they should have very specific internal contacts, with analysis and reporting on a regular basis. Some larger companies form data quality departments, which may be part of the overall IT department or within individual business units. If this is done, their accountabilities across departmental lines should be well understood.

4. *Make certain data quality is a corporate value.* Companies, in their search for self-knowledge, must incorporate data and data quality in that search. As such, the cultural aspects of data quality—i.e., making data advocacy a shared value—should be emphasized.

5. *Appropriately train personnel.* Data have to be well documented as well as gathered, managed, and distributed, which requires specialized training. Customer data management, like other business functions, can be considered as a set of processes; and like any processes, they can be defined, standardized, improved, and optimized through training. Personnel responsible for data quality have to be trained in both management architecture and the tools needed to comb through data as they assure data quality.

6. *Understand and communicate the causes of poor data quality, and their virtual and real costs to the organization.* Data quality experts have identified quality as contributing to warehouse failure rates of up to 70 percent, so this is extremely serious. Ultimately, the costs of insufficient data quality are played out in suboptimal experiences at the individual customer level. This needs to be formally conveyed, and reinforced, across the organization.

7. *Apply a consistent, disciplined approach for ensuring data quality.* Establish milestones, dedicated resources, and measures that identify whether data

quality levels are being met. Data audits, generating statistics about the content of each field, should be conducted on a regular basis, with verification (matching, consolidation of records, correction, and augmentation when necessary) routines as a key element. For example, when looking at consumers, many companies standardize their customer files against the Postal Service national database.

8. *Build data quality incrementally across the organization.* If organizations try to build out their databases too quickly, they encounter one of the most common problems—data integration failure. Companies must, from the beginning, make certain that data from multiple sources are well integrated so that they have a realistic, single, and complete view of each customer. Phasing rollout of data quality initiatives enables companies to build on small successes.

9. *Track the ROI of data quality monitoring and enhancements.* When companies know the costs of failing to meet objectively set customer service levels, or loss of business because of bad data, or gains—such as shorter processing times, tightened sales cycles, better customer analytics, and more effective cross-sell, upsell, and referral programs—this helps to establish the benefits of improving data quality across the organization. Surveying customers can also help increase the "soft" measures of performance, which leverage engagement and commitment.

10. *Treat customer data as a corporate asset.* Data may be the most important resource a company has. It is everyone's job to insure data quality.

Data quality has everything to do with going to, and beyond, addressing customers on an individual basis. More accurate data means that billing and purchase records will be freer of inconsistencies, omissions, and inaccuracies, avoiding issues that can undermine customer commitment. It can make customer service response faster and more specific, because customer histories will be complete and current. With reliable intelligence within the customer's record, this also means that customers can be more readily upsold and cross-sold, deepening the relationship and helping insure that it remains intact.

Finally, it definitely helps to create the single customer view and greater unity within companies. When data redundancy, inaccuracy, and inconsistency can be reduced to the point of elimination, multiple business units, often serving the same customer, can speak a common language. This has both productivity and strategic impact. Companies must have assessment processes for analyzing and interpreting the effect of data quality issues; and when there are problems, these processes must be able to identify potential remedies to rectify them as quickly as possible.

Applying Data for Customer Advocacy: The View from 30,000 Feet

The importance of developing a database that has a depth of customer information, and putting in place methods to insure its quality, continuous flow, and movement within the organization, cannot be understated. But it's not enough. Companies need to set the strategies and apply the tools to make the best use of the data to create advocacy.

First, building a customer commitment plan should incorporate desirable success factors, whether they are customer service levels, revenue goals, performance metrics, or time periods. These should be defined at the beginning of any customer initiative, rather than trying to find the goal once an effort or program has begun. As much as possible, this needs to be done on a micro-segment level, down to the individual customer and purchase scenario.

Next, everyone using the customer data should be schooled in analytical methods, going beyond basic interpretations. Users must be able to gain optimum insight from customer information, whenever they need to use it. Predictive models, looking at which customers are profitable or not and which customers might churn, can help interpret the impact of response, transaction, volume, and revenue, and also chart the prospective results of changes in communication, process, or program.

Companies should endeavor to "democratize" customer data. Today, customer data will be drawn from multiple channels and collection points; and users should be equipped with code-breakers to help them synthesize and incorporate data from disparate sources into their decision making.

Customer definitions should be relevant, helping facilitate more effective engagement, value delivery, and creation of commitment. While data software sophistication has advanced to the point where it's possible to generate hundreds of customer segments and subsegments, only if the definitions are meaningful, business-wise, will companies be able to gauge their own progress and success.

Some customers are purchasing at maximum levels, some will never create greater value for the organization no matter how much attention and support they receive, and some are truly "growable." Customer data should be applied to create profiles of these potentially high-end customers, so that the company can determine which of its customers are worth the investment of resources against future revenue. Organizations like Harrah's, for instance, will continually experiment with offers designed to build the volume of customers seen as having growth potential based on distance from the casino; likelihood to participate in gaming; interest in casino, restaurant, or entertainment facilities; and other information they may collect on an individual basis. This approach extends to prospects as well, because Harrah's will also actively invest in marketing and promotion to profile-matching households in targeted geographic areas that have high concentrations of active patrons of their casinos.

Understanding customer behavior and needs also means that companies must look at declining purchase activity and the back end of the customer life cycle, recognizing when customers are at risk, or have been lost and might be won back. Examination of customer turnover, reports of negative service or transaction experiences, or rejection of offers can often provide as much value as learning about successes. Optimizing customer advocacy means addressing the bad as well as capitalizing on the good.

Evolving Toward Customer Divisibility, Part I: Examples of What Some Advanced Companies Are Doing

Companies now have the means to identify their best, most valuable customers, and at increased levels of detail, using data warehouses. For example, a 2003 study among 6,000 retail executives by software firm Blue Martini showed that almost 60 percent could do so, an increase over just 40 percent in 2002.

Evidence of this greater ability to communicate with each customer on a divisible basis can be found in applications used by companies, irrespective of size, in multiple industries, as shown in the following scenario.

Adam's Mark, a hotel chain with about 25 properties, continuously collects information about its online customers, establishing detailed new profiles at a rate of about 100 per day. They are able to customize web site pages, messaging and promotion down to the customer, location, and lodging scenario level by looking at individual demographics, purchasing habits, reservation history, and loyalty-program membership. Adam's Mark can further tailor communication based on knowledge of customer needs and previous experiences, such as use of hotel facilities and amenities, and any customer comments or service issues. Since they began doing this, reservations have increased substantially and cancels have, correspondingly, declined.

Capital Concierge, which provides personalized services to companies and individuals in scores of Washington, DC buildings, and its sister company, VIPdesk, delivering "live" web-based concierge services in the same market, are strong believers in the concept of customer divisibility and using a data warehouse as the engine to accomplish it. As noted by Mary Naylor, Capital Concierge's CEO:

> A solid database solution is invaluable for making sense of your learning and for reaching your ultimate goal of developing unique service and marketing plans for your best customers. The bottom line: no company should be

without a customer database, no matter how elementary. If you don't have an automated solution, you're at a competitive disadvantage because any company can afford a contact manager these days. Even the corner florist has one.

Capital Concierge believes in creating "customer chemistry," which they define as a customer-centric approach to optimizing sales and profitability by concentrating on creating unique relationships, for each customer, and for each purchase scenario. This begins with capturing data for individual customers and with frequent customer surveying and other listening tools, melding these results with customer purchase profiles and demographics, analyzing the results, and applying them through customized messaging on a personalized basis. As they conclude: "Companies are turning to data warehousing, automated call centers, websites, and integrated applications. Now small to medium-size companies can harness the power of the web by mining pieces of data—surveying customers and gathering information about them—in order to prompt customers to buy more and to tailor services that will keep them coming back."

Feargal Quinn, CEO of Superquinn, Ireland's leading grocery chain, is known as the "Pope of Customer Service" for his humility and his fanatical devotion to providing the most outstanding "destination experience" available for shoppers. Superquinn offers some of the most advanced retail technology in the world, including self-scan shopping, multifunction kiosks, digital shelf labels, and mobile checkout. But it's his focus on listening to customers that sets the company apart. With a foundation belief that his customers and employees know more than he does (his most oft-repeated phrase is "I listened, I learned, I discovered"), his company uses highly unusual and creative methods of adding to the customer information database and applying results. Store managers are required to spend substantial time each month experiencing the store as customers do, shopping, waiting in line, lodging complaints, and talking to customers. The company, in addition, uses multiple methods to capture customer data: comment forms, a service desk at the entrance to each store, customer panels, and formal market research. Also, every quarter, managers personally call upwards of 100 members of Superquinn's loyalty program.

Every Superquinn employee has access to store and chain weekly results, including sales, store-by-store and department-by-department performance, year-to-year changes, and the percentage of total customers who have made multiple purchases in a week. Employees are expected to build loyal households for their portion of the business.

British Airways uses a number of data generation approaches that are unique to the airline industry. One distinctive method is their data collection feedback kiosks used in principal hubs to get fresh experience information from arriving passengers. They have multiple touch points for anecdotal and formal data collection.

Unlike most other airlines, their Customer Service operation plays an integral role in helping create customer commitment. They've made the prevention of customer defection a corporate goal (they say "retain, invest, and prevent"). This has been built into their staff training programs, coaching sessions, and performance criteria.

British Airways has what they call the Marketplace Performance Unit. This group is responsible for monitoring all customer data gathering efforts in the company, and evaluating the company's performance, using 300 unique measures. They interact with senior company executives, proactively recommend areas of service for further study or upgrade, identify problem areas, and recommend new dimensions of brand equity. The Marketplace Performance Unit makes certain that British Airways remains a data-driven, customer-centric company.

At the back end of the customer life cycle (see Chapter Five), data innovators like Baptist Health Care look at each patient issue, or incident, as an opportunity to learn, share, build loyalty, and improve customer processes. Baptist Health Care is very unusual among health-care providers. They have a truly holistic view of all their customers, and they consider every interaction an opportunity to create equity. What they do with problems and complaints through HealthSource, their Contact Center, they are doing equally well from the time the patient and his/her family first enters one of their facilities.

In 2000, Baptist Health Care won the prestigious USA Today/RIT award for the quality of their customer service; were named #10 on *Fortune* magazine's "100 Best Companies to Work For in America" in 2002; and won the Malcolm Baldrige National Quality Award in 2003. This is a culture that's built on gathering, sharing, and applying data for performance optimization; and they've been studied and benchmarked by hundreds of health-care and other organizations from around the country, so they're doing something right.

Evolving Toward Customer Divisibility, Part II: What Companies May Be Doing in the Future

It's likely that not too far into the future, even the most sophisticated data gathering, management, and application will need to be enhanced in order to more effectively approach customers on a divisible basis. One of the probable techniques for harnessing the power of customer data, will be to create a "persona" for each customer.

What is a persona, and why should we care about it? As we will explore in Chapter Six in understanding how companies can develop individual customer commitment, personas are based on what is known as ethnographic customer data. Ethnography is, simply, the creation of a profile of a customer's unconscious attitudes, perceptions, goals, and behaviors. While there may be demographic variables that impact behavior, the more abstract elements of ethnography will predominate.

Ethnographic techniques focus not on stated customer wants but on actions, areas of frustration, aspirational life objectives, and areas of positive and reinforcing result. Companies are, to the extent possible, looking for methods of identifying and patterning behavioral and attitudinal elements. In retail shopping situations, for example, variables might include shopping frequency, sections or departments patronized, the customer's level of disappointment and enjoyment with the shopping experience, and whether the customer has a stronger orientation toward price or service. Ethnographic research combines both observation, often in an actual usage context, and in-depth interviews. If time and budget allow—as they should—observation and in-depth qualitative data should be verified with quantitative research to dimensionalize the ethnographic learning.

Once all of the attitudinal, goal-based, and behavior variables are developed, it's possible to plot, or map, each customer relative to all others. Most companies will look for attitudinal, goal, and behavioral clusters down to the microsegment level, but it is possible to consider customers on an individual, and even purchase scenario, basis.

At this point, it should be explained that traditional market segmentation and personas are two different, though complementary, tools. Market segmentation is built on models such as we've seen developed over recent years—demographic and geographic variables, psychographics and lifestyle, values, approaches to risk, and decision-making patterns. Other profile and classification systems, such as PRIZM clustering, can make these models even more focused by incorporating consumer purchasing power, sets of motivations, and available resources. Segmentation tools are what many companies apply to their databases to help interpret why customers purchase as they do.

Personas, however, are a tool that companies are likely to be using with some frequency before too long, to help understand what motivates each customer to purchase, situation to situation and product by product, relative to all other customers. Personas can be used for product and service design, campaign and communication planning, and upgrading customer processes. One of the advantages is that, for every descriptor used to create a persona characteristic, there are both real and profile data to support it.

To continue looking into the future of customer data application, it's also likely that personas will be applied in combination with microsegment definitions, rather than as a replacement. Both provide suppliers with useful direction. Both can provide a set of customer models.

Personas are ideally suited to reveal motivations and potential usage patterns, and motivations have a great deal to do with creating commitment. As a practical example of persona application, consider how an automotive company might design its storage systems in a minivan or SUV. A 30-something stay-at-home mom with young children, who does a lot of carpooling and local driving for after-school activities, might want a lot of storage within easy reach of her seat, even on the dashboard and sun visor. For the same vehicle, a regional sales manager in her fifties who's doing a lot of long-distance driving between territories, making a lot of customer presentations, and traveling for several days at a time may want greater storage capacity around the entire vehicle. Once these features are designed-in, the automotive company and its dealerships can market and sell-in vehicle storage around individual customer needs and usage scenarios. As this highly simplified example suggests, the learning and opportunity have only begun to be realized. They represent the next logical step in going beyond loyalty to create true commitment and advocacy.

2

IS VIRAL MARKETING AN EPIDEMIC?

IF SO, WHAT'S THE CURE?

The Spreading Infection

In a recent edition of *The Philadelphia Inquirer*, there was a disturbing story about how a mortgage loan company in Phoenix, Arizona had sent "spam" advertising messages that appeared on the screens of thousands of wireless phone customers. Not only were the messages not requested, but these customers had to pay to retrieve them. Ouch![1]

In the United States, phone numbers are allocated to wireless companies in blocks of 9,999, all beginning with the same three-digit prefix following the area code. The text messaging address for each mobile phone is derived from the phone number assigned to each customer's handset and the wireless company's name. This means that an advertiser can simply choose any three-digit prefix in an area code and send a message to 10,000 people by changing the last four digits after the prefix.

One industry analyst noted that this is just the tip of the iceberg. This type of spam is cheap and easy for advertisers to use. Wireless text messaging is growing rapidly in the U.S.; and, while some carriers are taking precautions to protect their customers from text message advertising, so far neither the direct marketing industry nor the federal government has been able to control this form of spam. As the president of the mortgage company noted, the advertising had brought in new clients and "There still isn't any rule against e-mailing." Online, the concept of "permission marketing" is similarly tossed aside each day with the receipt of unsolicited promotional emails. There is blocking, or firewall, software to suppress some of them, but inboxes are still becoming bloated with unwanted, unrequested messages.

We call this indiscriminate solicitation of prospective customers the "Casanova Complex," reflective of the 18th-century Italian adventurer, perhaps best known for his many female "conquests." In the haste to bring in customers, companies can often forget to court the *right* customers, those who represent the best long-term

---

[1] Michael Lowenstein, "Has Viral Marketing Gotten Out of Hand—and Out of Touch?" www.searchcrm.com, September 26, 2001.

revenue potential, or who won't overtax the company's customer service and support structure.

If offline instances of the Casanova Complex are a disease, then it is an epidemic among Internet companies. Many online retail sites have engaged in sweepstakes programs. Their objectives, they say, are to create "viral" promotions that generate excitement for their sites and build their databases of available names both inexpensively and quickly. In one instance, 4anything.com, a portal site that runs more than 1,000 web sites featuring links to other sites, signed up 50,000 registrants in a "Win Up To $4,000" game. Another sweepstakes program secured 126,000 registrants. EBags' "Million-Air" sweepstakes, offering 1 million air miles to the winner, generated over 60,000 names in 90 days, almost all of whom were new to the site.

The big issue for any of these sites is—do these promotions and schemes draw attractive customers, who can then be cultivated over time through the various marketing tools available today? And once these customers are on board, are companies doing enough of the right things to keep them, experience by experience?

Or is this another extrapolation of the Casanova Complex? As one site marketing executive said: "This is a great low-cost way for us to acquire new names. The jury's still out on how many of those new people will come back." Companies involved in developing or using promotional tools like sweepstakes, unsolicited email, or wireless spam seem inclined, at least for the moment, to believe that these possibilities generally don't apply to them.

For traditional offline companies, the Internet may be "commoditizing" their industry or undermining customer relationships. Many brick-and-mortar CEOs say that a key corporate goal is to transition more of their offline customers to online usage. Why? Because an online transaction costs dramatically less than a brick-and-mortar transaction, there is less risk for service error, and the company can more effectively capture and leverage information from an online transaction, to cite a few advantages. Certainly, the transactional advantages of e-commerce are very appealing. But what about the effects on loyalty, especially for new customers?

One of the important ways both online and offline companies can discipline themselves to avoid the Casanova Complex is to apply personalization in all contact with customers, both new and established. This, at least, gives companies a better chance of establishing a viral relationship with these customers.

While it's been estimated that over 80 percent of e-commerce sites have customer and visitor email personalization capabilities, only 4 percent of the sites used personalization in follow-on marketing campaigns. For web sites favoring incentive devices like sweepstakes and frontal assault email programs to attract potential customers, personalized communication is perhaps the best opportunity to demonstrate ongoing interest in customers, especially new ones.

Emerging Data Privacy Issues

Data privacy has become a key and critical factor in planning personalized customer marketing and communication campaigns, and even in providing one-to-one support services. Consumers have always been concerned about how organizations use, and potentially abuse, information about their individual preferences and lifestyle details. As corporate data collection and application have increased in sophistication over the past 20 years or so, this has become a central issue.

For many years, U.S. companies have relied totally on self-policing, without the need for direct governmental control or regulation of data collection and management. In Europe, however, there has been much more concern and scrutiny regarding personal information availability. In 1995, the European Union, through its Parliament, enacted rules on the collection of personal data. Movement of this information is now closely monitored and regulated.

What about movement of personal consumer information between continents? The Direct Marketing Association, in conjunction with the European Union, set up a "safe harbor" framework that allows U.S. companies to export personal consumer data from Europe. The program requires these companies to subscribe to outside, third-party dispute resolution to handle European data privacy complaints. In fact, the European Union set up a directive in 1998 that prohibits any non-EU country from receiving consumer data without a sufficient, effective level of privacy protection.

Data Privacy Comes to a Head

In 2000, consumer data compiler and Web advertising agency DoubleClick created a public backlash regarding data privacy when it announced plans to combine individual names it had gathered through Internet site usage monitoring, without permission, with offline data on these same consumers. This occurred when DoubleClick merged with Abacus Direct, an organization that records online catalog company transactions, and said it would combine Web surfing habits—obtained from the 5 billion ads DoubleClick served per week at that time—with personal information from the billions of transactions recorded by Abacus. DoubleClick said it would link its database of consumer profiles with data generated from electronic markets, known as "cookies." Cookies are small text files that are used to track users' movement between web sites and individual pages on those sites.

The U.S. Federal Trade Commission (FTC), through its Bureau of Consumer Protection, investigated DoubleClick and concluded that the company had not engaged in unfair or deceptive acts. Nonetheless, later that year DoubleClick announced that they would not collect information on individuals' Internet surfing habits until, and unless, government and industry reached a consensus on privacy rules.

By 2002, DoubleClick had enhanced and deepened its policies regarding consumer data privacy to include nonuse of personal information to deliver Internet ads, consumer-controlled (i.e., permission-based) email reception, and consumer-controlled use of technologies to collect browsing information. DoubleClick also informed consumers that they were members of NAI, the Network Advertising Initiative. NAI was set up in 2000 by several Internet advertising companies as a self-regulatory compliance program, whose principles are enforceable under FTC authority.

NAI assures consumers that network advertisers will not use personally identifiable data, such as medical or financial information, nor will they merge personal data (PII) with anonymous data (non-PII), recognizing that this merging, though intended for more effective marketing, could potentially compromise the anonymity of a user's browsing history. One of the features offered by NAI is giving consumers the ability to opt-out, that is, to have their anonymous data removed from the database of any network advertiser. However, the NAI also believes it is important that consumers understand how advertisers' and marketers' use of their individual data can benefit their online experiences; and they have set up the Online Preference Marketing program so that consumers can get this information.

Personal Data Privacy and the USA Patriot Act

Intense concerns over terrorism following the September 11, 2001 attacks prompted Congress to adopt the USA Patriot Act just six weeks later. This act gave the executive branch of the government, including the FBI, broad, discretionary access to personal and business data. Without any built-in checks and balances, many consumers, executives, and legislators feel that this is an overreaction, at minimum. For example, the Patriot Act gives the FBI almost unlimited power to obtain individuals' personal and business records, such as medical, library, and bookstore purchases, through access to entire databases. The act also extended to Web activity the already broad authority to monitor every individual phone call made and every email received, thus covering all transactional (non-content) information about communications. In an era when everyday terrorism risk is considered high, the debate about what level of personal information access is appropriate will go on. At this writing, key elements of the Patriot Act will come before Congress for renewal or elimination, and there are strong sentiments for both.

It Could Happen . . . Couldn't It?

Cendant Corporation, the huge multinational conglomerate, is reported to be compiling a customer database with more than 200 pieces of information per customer. The database would integrate profile information from Cendant's 20+ companies, including car rental, mortgage lending, hotels, and travel services, with an overlay of data purchased from public sources. In addition to purchase history data, the database will include credit card numbers, driver's license information, and email addresses. While Cendant has been quoted as saying that the database will be applied only to improving customer value delivery, it's not difficult to understand that this amount of information, in the wrong hands, would be a tremendous threat to data privacy.

The following fictional dialogue was sent around as a nonattributed message on the Internet. While it's meant as a joke, and reads like a two-person comedy routine, the dialogue nevertheless represents how marketers might soon be able to use, and abuse, individual customer data on a *divisible* basis:

Operator: "Thank you for calling Pizza World. May I have your . . ."

Customer: "Hi, I'd like to order."

Operator: "May I have your NIDN first, sir?"

Customer: "My National ID Number, yeah, hold on, eh, it's 6102049998-45-54610."

Operator: "Thank you, Mr. Sheehan. I see you live at 1742 Meadowland Drive, and the phone number's 494-2366. Your office number over at Lincoln Insurance is 745-2302 and your cell number's 266-2566. Which number are you calling from, sir?"

Customer: "Huh? I'm at home. Where d'ya get all this information?"

Operator: "We're wired into the system per the Patriot Act, sir."

Customer: (Sighs) "Oh, well, I'd like to order a couple of your All-Meat Special pizzas . . ."

Operator: "I don't think that's a good idea, sir."

Customer: "Whaddya mean?"

Operator: "Sir, your medical records indicate that you've got very high blood pressure and extremely high cholesterol. Your National Health Care provider won't allow such an unhealthy choice."

Customer: "Geez. What do you recommend, then?"

Operator: "You might try our low-fat Soybean Yogurt Pizza. I'm sure you'll like it."

Customer: "What makes you think I'd like something like that?"

Operator: "Well, you checked out 'Gourmet Soybean Recipes' from your local library last week, sir. That's why I made the suggestion."

Customer: "All right, all right. Give me two family-sized ones, then. What's the damage?"

Operator: "That should be plenty for you, your wife and your four kids, sir. The 'damage,' as you put it, heh, heh, comes to $49.99."

Customer: "Lemme give you my credit card number."

Operator: "I'm sorry sir, but I'm afraid you'll have to pay in cash. Your credit card balance is over its limit."

Customer: "I'll run over to the ATM and get some cash before your driver gets here."

Operator: "That won't work either, sir. Your checking account's overdrawn."

Customer: "Never mind. Just send the pizzas. I'll have the cash ready. How long will it take?"

Operator: "We're running a little behind, sir. It'll be about 45 minutes, sir. If you're in a hurry you might want to pick 'em up while you're out getting the cash, but carrying pizzas on a motorcycle can be a little awkward."

Customer: "How the hell do you know I'm riding a bike?"

Operator: "It says here you're in arrears on your car payments, so your car got repo'ed. But your motorcycle's paid up, so I just assumed that you'd be using it."

Customer: "@#%/$@&?#!"

Operator: "I'd advise watching your language, sir. You've already got a July 2006 conviction for cussing out a cop."

Customer: (Speechless)

Operator: "Will there be anything else, sir?"

Customer: "No, nothing. Oh, yeah, don't forget the two free liters of soda your ad says I get with the pizzas."

Operator: "I'm sorry sir, but our ad's exclusionary clause prevents us from offering free soda to diabetics."

Customer: "How did you . . . ? Never mind."

This is becoming a huge issue for marketers, growing even as the ability to address customers on a divisible basis increases as a result of advanced software techniques. A study by Harris Interactive showed that close to two-thirds of online consumers refuse to purchase from a site based on their lack of surety about how their individual, personal data is being used. The Annenberg Public Policy Center of the University of Pennsylvania concluded that online privacy policies are overly confusing and complex for consumers to comprehend.

While there has been no generalized data privacy legislation in the United States, the Federal Trade Commission has set up four basic consumer information collection standards. These include notice, such as opt-out notification to consumers; consumer choice regarding how data, once collected, can be used; accessibility, so consumers can correct and update their personal information; and security of the data repository, or warehouse itself, so that private data storage cannot be breached. Unfortunately, according to the FTC, only 20 percent of the most active web sites complied with these standards. The NAI, for example, uses a third-party enforcement program, through a company called TRUSTe, to independently receive and investigate consumer privacy complaints.

There is some more formalized movement to assure consumers about data privacy. One such example is P3P, or the Platform for Privacy Preferences, developed by the World Wide Web Consortium (W2C). It enables consumers to have more direct control over how web sites they visit use their data, through a series of questions covering all aspects of the site's data privacy policies. However, it is still in an embryonic state of availability. An evaluation of the privacy policies of 450 sites by the Customer Respect Group, a consulting organization that helps clients improve customers' online experiences, found that only about 5 percent actually have the P3P capability.

Theoretically, It Could Get Worse

Science fiction writer David Brin has argued that the death of privacy is inevitable.[2] In his view, the choice societies face is privacy or freedom. Two centuries ago, Thomas Jefferson wrote passionately about assuring the rights of the individual, in the interest of preserving personal liberty, insofar as keeping private information inviolate so long as it does not threaten institutions such as government. In this age of international terrorism, however, many see us edging closer to Orwell's view of data mining and information management so graphically described in *1984*.

One example of this is a system called Matrix, a powerful interactive database developed by Seisint, a company that has already created a commercial database service for helping locate people based on past and present addresses. Their service, known as Accurint, has the world's largest base of consumer location data; and it can search more than 20 billion records covering relocation and addresses going back more than 30 years. It can also provide previous addresses for relatives, neighbors,

---

[2] Randall Parker, "Surveillance Society," *Future Pundit*, August 14, 2003.

and associates, making it the most detailed source of consumer contact information available anywhere in the world.

Matrix was developed by the state of Florida, with the intent of helping law enforcement officials track criminals and terrorists. While this use of such extensive personal data resources receives little argument, it is also recognized that many companies, such as WalMart, have huge databases of customer transaction records, which could be used for investigation purposes. (Note: WalMart is a customer data mining pioneer that collects point-of-sale transactions from close to 3,000 stores in six countries, and continually transmits these data to its 7.5 terabyte data warehouse). WalMart, for example, allows more than 3,500 suppliers to access sales data on their products and perform data analysis. There is concern, especially for those who monitor search technologies and applications for the public good, that such databases might become available to governmental agencies through minimally regulated access.

Data Privacy Is a Trust Thing: Most Companies "Get It," But Much Needs to Be Done

Provision of personal data is just one element of the trust most companies understand must be inherent in building value and strength in the relationship being created with customers. Customers, after all, are also stakeholders in the brand, and provision of data raises the bar on the "transparency," or openness, in the bond between customer and supplier; so data privacy is part of the unofficial contract that one has with the other. It also covers preferred communication frequency and media.

One recent study by International Data Corporation showed that four out of five U.S. consumers left web sites multiple times over a six month period due to privacy concerns.[3] In a 2003 presentation, Harriet Pearson, IBM's chief privacy officer, quoted other key findings of the study. For instance, 43 percent of consumers feel businesses have no incentive to protect consumer privacy, while 39 percent said that businesses handle personal information properly and confidentially. About one-third of all consumers, according to Pearson, are "privacy fundamentalists," who want limited or no sharing of private information.

About 60 percent of consumers are "privacy pragmatists," those Pearson identifies as seeing data collection and sharing as a necessary, and possibly even beneficial, part of doing business.

A good example of the importance of this trust is Tesco's Clubcard customer charter. About a year after its loyalty program was officially launched, Tesco sent

---

[3] Richard H. Levey, "Building Consumer Trust on Data Privacy," *Direct*, April 1, 2003.

the program's millions of members copies of the "Clubcard Customer Charter," outlining how member privacy would be protected. Among the commitments made in the charter, three directly involved data privacy:

- "Your personal details will not be disclosed to any other company unless it is necessary for the operation of the Clubcard scheme."
- "We comply strictly with the terms of the Data Protection Act 1984" (a UK law, now superseded by Data Protection Act 1998, that governs personal data, the purposes for which data are generated, and the ways in which recipients may use such data).
- "If at any time you would like all your details taken off the database, we will do so immediately."[4]

In addition, in the charter Tesco committed to refrain from conducting research and/or sending any services or offers to members making this request.

There's little doubt that trust is the dominant color in the changing marketing landscape. Customers are becoming very clear in their preferences for how, when, and how often they want to receive communication. Similar to the results of the International Data Corporation study, a 2002 Harris Interactive study showed that consumers have little trust in how companies will manage their personal information.[5] Close to three-quarters of consumers surveyed felt that companies would provide their information to other organizations without permission, that their online transactions may not be secure, or that hackers could steal their individual profile data.

A late 2003 Accenture study that examined consumer and business views regarding privacy, trust, and access to personal data added another layer to this issue, namely the different perspectives each group has about what creates and undercuts trust.[6] Consumers generally trust their employers, banks, and health-care insurance providers with personal information, but have little trust in online retailers or supermarkets. While consumers felt that companies had too much information about them, businesses admitted collecting some consumer data to which they are not entitled.

Just as we often find divergent perspectives between suppliers and customers on what contributes to perceived value, so Accenture found that there was a gap

---

[4] Clive Humby and Terry Hunt, *Scoring Points* (London: Kogan Page, 2003), p. 22.

[5] Humphrey Taylor, "Most People Are 'Privacy Pragmatists,'" The Harris Poll no. 17/Harris Interactive, March 19, 2003.

[6] "U.S. Consumers Not Buying Due to Trust Issues," www.thewisemarketer.com, February 18, 2004.

between what consumers and businesses consider to be undermining trust. As an example, 74 percent of businesses identified online security concerns for compromising trust, while 67 percent of consumers felt that overly aggressive sales and marketing activity was the principal trust negative regarding businesses. Also, businesses most often (43 percent) felt that customer service was the key positive lever of trust, while almost two-thirds of consumers (62 percent) said that trust came from a company's reputation and image, as well as the individual's length of relationship with the company. Obviously, this is a major disconnect.

The study also identified another critical disconnect, this one regarding the importance of data privacy. Most businesses felt that their data privacy policies would be unlikely to influence consumer perceptions of them, while more than half of the consumers interviewed said they would be unlikely to deal with a company whose data privacy policies were unclear or made them uncomfortable.

The study also revealed some inconsistencies between consumer beliefs and intended actions where data privacy was concerned. While 63 percent said they were worried that providing personal information could result in unsolicited emails and telemarketing calls, 69 percent said they would be willing to provide personal information in exchange for rewards—cash, greater convenience, loyalty program bonus points, etc. Such inconsistencies between subconscious thought and action are not particularly surprising, and will be explored in detail in Chapter Six.

An Ongoing Viral Marketing Challenge: The Preoccupation with Pre-Customers

The acquisition mindset of marketers and senior management isn't likely to change anytime soon. We can preach and preach about the advantages of a balanced, or profit maximization, approach to customers and optimizing value over life cycle, striving to "change the basis of their thinking"; but we had also better be prepared to help acquisition-obsessed companies in the real world.

This drive to acquire customers often leads to the twin challenges associated with bringing new purchasers into the fold. These challenges are the superficial approaches to customer targeting and qualifying, and also to understanding the factors impacting perceived value and behavior for the prospect, who has yet to make an initial purchase.

Let's deal with the second challenge first, namely gaining insight on what represents value for prospective customers. Surprisingly, with all the attention given to learning what leverages customer retention, customer loyalty, positive customer relationships, and even customer risk and loss, there is much less research or information collection around what causes a prospect to become, or not become, a customer.

There are, however, some leading-edge approaches for doing this, and they will be discussed later in the book.

One of the three main applications of customer management systems (in addition to the other two: marketing and customer service) is selling and sales force automation, often through integration of multiple sales and communication channels. For prospective customers, however, much of the emphasis is on outbound contact and streamlined lead management. While an enterprise view of customer management is focused on helping sales groups generate customers, and providing seamless support and service once customers are on board, companies infrequently attempt to identify 1) what prospective customers want or need, or 2) how well companies themselves are positioned to address and meet those wants and needs.

As a result, customer management systems tend to be less effective at the front end of a customer's life cycle. Companies that are process-oriented and focused on creating benefit when it comes to keeping customers and optimizing their purchases over time, and even stemming rates of defection or recovering lost customers, rarely give enough attention to prepurchase processes or value creation.

Everyone can repeat stories, for instance, of being ignored, treated poorly, or given insufficient information or service by badly trained, indifferent sales and service staff, thus preventing them from making an initial purchase. And what about unreturned phone calls, nonresponse to email messages, or trying to navigate poorly designed web sites? These are just some of the pre-customer process breakdowns that customer management systems could address, in both b-to-b and b-to-c worlds, but so rarely do.

The other prospect challenge is that of customer suitability. Stating that all customers are not created equal is hardly an oversimplification. But like the pigs in Orwell's *Animal Farm,* some customers are more equal than others. No company has unlimited resources to equally service or support all their customers. Repeat buying power, one key element of customer loyalty, is everything when prospecting for potential customers. Some customers are worth a great deal, some may become more valuable over time, some may be valuable for a brief period but may be easily lured away, some are only seeking a price that would be disadvantageous for the supplier, and some are never likely to become valuable.

At minimum, companies need to segment their customers so they can determine how much longer a particular customer will remain with them; how much revenue and profitability each one will contribute; how much and what kind of services the customer should receive; and what efforts will be needed to keep them whether they are new, at risk, or even already lost. Also, if a company is changing product or service focus—such as beginning a new frequency marketing program—decisions will have to be made about which customers they want to retain.

Just as companies are becoming smarter about keeping the customers they want, or "firing" less attractive customers through stepped-down services, they have to invest more up-front in learning which potential customers will be the most valuable over time. This goes beyond segmentation. It is almost pre-segmentation.

The business of gaming in Las Vegas, Atlantic City, numerous riverboats, Indian reservations, and offshore is built not on a house of cards but a house of numbers. Take the Rio Hotel and Casino in Las Vegas, a Harrah's property. It has 100,000 square feet of casino floor, 2,375 slot machines, a buffet that feeds 10,000 people, and four pools. The Rio serves 50,000 cocktails a day. The 5,200 electricians, slot technicians, laundry haulers, blackjack dealers, show performers, and custodians, toiling in three shifts, make the Rio run like a plush yet high-tech gaming factory.

The Rio's purple and teal colors are everywhere, and the round-the-clock carnival atmosphere has all the feeling of a tropical party. Almost 7 million customers per year play poker, slots, craps, pai gow, baccarat, keno, roulette, and blackjack; but the real game at Rio is how they use data to keep, and attract, the customers they want.

New customers, called players, answer questions about what they like—auto racing, books, wine, types of entertainment, etc.—and then the Rio puts all of the information into a database. Within a minute after submitting the information, the player receives a plastic card encoded with his personal information. Every time the player inserts the card into a gambling machine or presents it for betting credit at a gaming table, his profile is updated with the type of machine or game played, the location on the floor, the length of play, and whether he is up or down on winnings. This information helps the Rio refine its communication, customer by customer, beginning to create a relationship that the casino hopes will be long-term.

Those players who gamble $1,000 a day with the Rio, whether they win or not, receive the designation "hosted guests." These are the kinds of customers the Rio works hard to acquire. Their level of play accords them VIP status, with more "comps" (free dinners, show passes, and other gifts). Each hosted guest has an individual staff host assigned to check on them and provided any needed services. The host is actually a highly paid, personal customer service representative. It's an important position that casino operations like the Rio consider pivotal to their success. The hosts cultivate relationships with the players; and VIP players are encouraged to call their hosts before arriving at the casino, so the host can have show tickets, restaurant reservations, and suites set up per the player's profile.

There's even a higher echelon of gaming customers—those players who have a million dollar line of credit. They get the best suites, and virtually everything the casino has to offer. They're nicknamed "whales," and with good reason. At the Rio, this means a suite with 7,000 square feet of space, and bathroom sinks with gold-plated faucets. These players are relied upon to bet in the Rio's secluded back room, called the Salon, where they may play baccarat and roulette with $100,000 chips.

In an industry like gaming, where the level of customer migration is very high, it is imperative that casinos not only keep the players they want but also target the right customers in the first place. They do this in a number of ways, including geodemographic profiling, for their acquisition. For the high rollers they've lost, many of the casinos make an extra effort to get them back as well.

Other industries are beginning to learn how to profile and focus on the best prospects. In the retail automotive industry, for example, potentially loyal new customers take less time making their purchase decisions, consider fewer dealerships, are less price-driven, and rely less on magazine articles and other media and more on previous experience and personal recommendation. Dealers would be well advised to learn prospective customers' decision dynamics at an early point in the sales process.

Advanced companies have begun applying "conversion" models, to be discussed in depth in Chapter Six, seeking customers who:

- Need less direct motivation (incentive) or indirect motivation (promise of support and committed resources) to purchase.
- Have demonstrated more resistance to claims and attempts to lure them away.
- Are less price-sensitive.
- Are more accepting of occasional value delivery lapses and are less likely to accept alternatives if their brand/service is unavailable.
- Demonstrate more positive attitudes about "their" brand.

Similar attention should be paid to undesirable prospects. Just as attractive customers should be sought, companies should make an effort to identify potential customers who may be an inappropriate match. They may need too much service, have a history of being transitory, require unreasonable price concessions, and the like. Pursuing customers with those kinds of characteristics is simply a waste of resources.

In all the haste to bring in customers, companies can often forget to court the *right* customers, those who represent the best long-term revenue potential, or who won't overtax the company's customer service and support structure and are most likely to stay with the company in the first place. Further, they are less discriminating about the messaging used in acquisition, often going over the line with respect to sending unsolicited messages. This certainly merits at least as much emphasis as the preoccupation with identifying and converting prospects.

How Customer Divisibility, Data Privacy, Buzz, and Viral Marketing Are Likely to Evolve and Converge

Even with the overwhelming volume of advertising and promotional messages to which each consumer is exposed everyday, particularly through electronic media, people's thinking and behaviors can still be greatly leveraged by positive and negative referral and word-of-mouth coming from individuals they trust and respect. This constitutes the essence of buzz creation and viral marketing; and it is unaffected, if used correctly, by data privacy limitations.

Marketers look to certain kinds of people to drive trends and influence opinion on a viral basis. They may be called *Connectors* (people with a large sphere of social acquaintance); *Salespeople* (those with the ability to convert people to their way of thinking); and *Mavens* (essentially, early adopters), as defined by Malcolm Gladwell; *Evangelists,* as Jackie Huba and Ben McConnell call them; or *Influentials,* the 10 percent of the population who lead the thinking of the other 90 percent, as identified by Jon Berry and Ed Keller of NOP World. Whether we're talking about trendsetters or carriers, these are the customers and members of society who stand ready to create "buzz" on behalf of a marketer.

These authors have observed the natural proclivity of people to be viral, or to be impacted by viral messaging. A multitude of studies, such as one conducted several years ago by Jupiter Media Metrix, show that high percentages of customers will choose sites or suppliers based on word-of-mouth recommendation or referral. Still, most viral marketing programs will not succeed. In part, this is because companies tend to define customer loyalty in terms of purchasing frequency in the short term, rather than measuring aspects of advocacy such as the voluntary provision of information to the company, or the passing along of company information to others. This will have to change for future viral marketing programs to be viable.

Viral marketing, so often abused and misapplied in the past, has the ability to get beyond data privacy issues and, at the same time, create value on a divisible customer basis. Marketers are becoming more skilled at tapping into the people power represented by the Internet. Hotmail, in a classic example of online viral marketing, sent each new free email subscriber a note with a recruitment message, asking that they pass along the information with an implied endorsement. This tactic enabled the company to reach 12 million subscribers in just 18 months.

Marketers increasingly understand that there's a great deal to learn about the nuances of peer and community leverage, whether it is called buzz or viral communication. In a joint study by professors from Harvard and Yale on the power of Internet chat room-created buzz, they found that the most successful viral impact comes when it reaches across multiple communities or newsgroups with differing sets of demographics. They also determined that even the most powerful buzz has a relatively short life span. In their study, they looked at the impact of word-of-mouth on ratings for new television shows; and they found that it was effective for no more than six weeks.

One of the principal reasons that word-of-mouth is so strong and effective a medium of conveyance, now influencing over two-thirds of consumer product and service sales according to a 2001 McKinsey study, is the very complexity of media and messages that come at us. Malcolm Gladwell believes that this daily barrage has so isolated and confused people that they are looking for sources with greater believability, simplicity, and personal safety.

This is why, even though the average American sees over 3,000 advertising messages each day, blogs have become so successful as a communication medium. They're simple and easily conveyed, without all of the fancy production values of online advertising and corporate web sites. As will be discussed in Chapter Seven, blogs are beginning to become a fairly standardized and accepted alternative method of corporate communication to customers and others.

Other proven viral techniques will not disappear. Far from it. Permission-based email will continue to be one of the effective methods for viral marketing, so long as marketers are responsible and accountable for maintaining customer anonymity and privacy. Relevancy of message and personal interest for each recipient remain at the core of getting customers to spread the word without being asked, and if marketers maintain a level of honesty and verifiability in the information they communicate, these will also be successful at creating desired actions.

Devices as simple as buttons that allow email message recipients to recommend a web site to others, giving something—even information, in the form of articles and newsletters, or prizes—for free will bring customers to a site. Affiliate programs, offering free samples and items, or free trial periods, will also generate new visitors and help to create a volunteer marketing corps. Related to free samples are other incentives, such as percentage off next purchase for referral to a certain number of acquaintances.

An example of a successful viral program was the incentive offered by a woman's athletic clothing multichannel retailer. The program offer was a free T-shirt and money donation to a national cancer fund when a recipient forwarded the email promotional message to five friends, and three of those friends subsequently opted in to the retailer's email list, newsletter, and catalog. The retailer achieved a newsletter sign-up rate in excess of 30 percent, a catalog subscription rate of almost 70 percent, meanwhile driving down cost per sale by almost 90 percent.

Viral approaches needn't, and probably shouldn't, be considered one-time marketing tactics. Like other programs, they do have long-term financial consequences, and should be tracked accordingly over time for performance on key metrics such as click-throughs, pass-alongs, and conversion rates, as mentioned above. As important, however, are the negative, and long-lasting, effects of pulling or shutting down a standing campaign without replacement or proper notice to participants. Customers and prospects take such things quite personally and have little tolerance for outright removal, which several retailers have learned to their regret.

And though online buzz creation, principally through blogs, is still embryonic (it's estimated that weblog readers comprise only 4 percent of Internet users), companies like Jupiter Research have estimated that almost two-thirds of "bloggers" have annual household incomes in excess of $60,000. This demographic is extremely attractive to marketers. For instance, there's a community blog for the close to 600 people who love Wawa, the highly successful mid-Atlantic chain of 500+ convenience stores. While there's no evidence that the company has used the blog site yet as a marketing device, with a core of devoted fans to generate buzz and interest in new concepts or products, for Wawa it's just a matter of time. If the company can manage to get its messages out to enthusiasts in a noncorporate manner, the way that Dr. Pepper/Seven Up, Inc. did in a four-month program introducing its new flavored milk product, Raging Cow, to a target audience of 18- to 24-year-olds via blog, there's a world of upside communication opportunity.

The bottom line on viral marketing methods is that they facilitate scalable, highly targeted, personalized, even event-based communication of marketing messages. This can be done at any point in the customer life cycle and for any individual or community of customers; and, if done effectively, it can positively leverage trust in the customer- supplier relationships. As noted by Gladwell, Huba, McConnell, Berry and Keller, viral techniques enable querying about, and noting, individual customer preferences by which suppliers can both continue existing demand and build new demand. They rely on extending already positive customer value perceptions by building brands and sharing honest, open, high-quality experiences through the customers' own communication networks.

3

SIMPLER IS OFTEN BETTER: ACQUIRING, MANAGING, AND APPLYING DIVISIBLE CUSTOMER DATA

First, a Few Customer Data Ground Rules

Before a company can even begin to think about using customer information for marketing, service, or sales, they need to think in broad-stroke terms about data sources, data management (storage, warehousing, and mining), and data analytics. The attraction of *doing* things with the data is so incredibly strong that insufficient planning too often takes place in systems and processes with, and around, the data.

To start, companies have to determine who their best customers are and what information to gather about them. It's not about assembling massive amounts of customer data. It's about being logical and converting the information into insight. If knowledge about who good customers are is principally anecdotal, there's some serious research and analytical work to do. If there's only primitive, loose assumption about revenue, profitability, and cross-sell or upsell opportunities, that's an additional challenge. This is where discipline begins, but there's much more.

For example, how trustworthy are the data sources? Without a reliable source or sources of in-depth customer data, most companies would be unable to provide the right products or services, to the right customers, at the right time. As basic and fundamental as such a concept seems to be, many data systems fail right here, depending on "technology" and "software" to make up for absences in other areas. When we speak about customer strategies, customer loyalty and advocacy, and marketing ROI, however, terms like technology or software are not, or should not be, meaningful parts of the discussion.

What's the quality of data being prepared for storage? As introduced in Chapter One, this is a critical issue. Accuracy is often a huge obstacle, getting in the way of many customer data warehousing and application programs. META Group has determined that between 10 and 20 percent of the raw information in a data warehouse is either corrupt or incomplete, and discovering that up to half the customer records in a database require correction is not unusual. There are several steps needed to overcome these problems and confirm data accuracy.

Data first have to be parsed—that is, broken into critical components or elements within each customer's file. For those not familiar with the term, this just means having such customer details as first and last name, title, address, city, state,

ZIP code, telephone number, email address, company name, and so forth confirmed as accurate for input. Then the data have to be corrected. If data are known to come from a variety of sources, they may have such variations as abbreviations, misspellings, out-of-date elements, and keying errors.

Finally, customer data must be standardized, arranged into a consistent, user-friendly format. The same kinds of challenges that exist at the correction stage also exist here, and many companies utilize software specifically designed to create desired, consistent views of each customer.

In many instances, customer data can and should be enhanced to provide any missing, valuable information. As covered in the Detica report mentioned in Chapter One, this may include any combination of demographic (age, marital status, etc. for consumers; sales volume, number of employees, SIC code for businesses), geographic (telephone numbers, county and state, etc.), behavior (credit level, purchase activity, preferred communication channels, etc.), lifestyle/psychographic (political affiliation, hobbies, etc.), event-related (marriage or divorce, childbirth, new address, etc.), and computed (credit ratings, lifestyle clustering models, etc.) data.

Data also need to be matched. In the world of direct response, this is known as de-duplication or de-duping; however, at its core, matching is the elimination of multiple records for the same customer or household. As discussed in Chapter One, in the case of Lutheran Brotherhood, this allows for greater efficiencies in communicating with prospects and customers.

It's not sufficient to address clean data quality and accuracy at time of entry. Equally important is that data be accurate when it's being transformed into customer behavior modeling components, which is a product of matching, or what is known as "consolidation," i.e., when relationships with, and between, customers can be most accurately identified and evaluated. Consolidation is what enables companies to relate with customers in every message and at every point of contact, anticipating their needs situation by situation, whether for sales, marketing, or service purposes. In other words, consolidation is what facilitates customer divisibility.

How Do We Get Useful Customer Data . . . And How Do We Make Sense of It?

There's a world of customer data available to companies, for sure. But with limited resources to gather, manage, share, and apply it, which data will be most versatile and actionable? With the arrival of concepts such as "Knowledge Management," companies are better able to make decisions about customer data; however, even with advanced computer technology, choices have to be made about what information to collect, sort, classify, and interpret to optimize value provision at the individual customer and individual experience levels. Often, however, companies first have to address more fundamental data gathering challenges.

One issue a company may have to confront is its own fears. If a company is proactive, seeking to create strong loyalty and advocacy among its customers, it will generally take a similarly proactive approach to feedback and other customer input. The opposite can also be true. Several years ago, a local cable company in central Pennsylvania became so paranoid about getting the negative feedback associated with its poor performance, it placed its small customer service office on top of a mountain in an attempt to foil subscribers used to making in-person complaints. To its customers, that move represented a rejection of their needs as having any importance.

While it's true, according to organizations like TARP, that for every customer who complains about poor product or service performance many more will not, this only means that companies need to change the basis of their thinking about problems. Indeed, the most progressive companies regard complaints as a golden opportunity to improve their operations.

As defined by customer loyalty experts Ben McConnell and Jackie Huba, generating complaints is just one of what they've defined as "10 Golden Rules of Customer Plus—Delta" for collecting information from customers.

1. *Believe that customers possess good ideas.* If products and services are built around expressed customer needs and wants, instead of executive assumptions and the conventional wisdom that leads to "push" strategies of a priori development, customers are far more likely to find value in them.
2. *Gather customer feedback at every opportunity.* Similar to USAA's approach to gathering customer insight, known as E.C.H.O. (Every Contact Has Opportunity), where each interaction becomes an open window to let in the breeze of customer input, if such situations don't exist on a regular basis, suppliers should create them.
3. *Focus on continual improvement.* Like the Japanese total quality concept of Kaizen, or gradual, ever-increasing improvement, suppliers should regularly engage customers to help in the effort. A wonderful example of this is the Dorothy Lane Markets, a small supermarket chain in Ohio, where good customers are recruited to serve stints as advisory panel members. The purpose of these panels is to identify products and store processes that will enhance value delivery.

4. *Actively solicit good and bad feedback.* As mentioned, complaint solicitation can be a powerful way to not only obtain negative reactions to individual and collective experience; but the very act of requesting hidden complaints and then positively acting on the results can enhance bonds with these customers.

5. *Don't spend vast sums of money doing it.* It's essential to develop in-depth customer insight, but that doesn't mean that every customer survey must be lengthy and strategic. Companies can and should have tactical research vehicles as well. These targeted questionnaires, with as few as three to five key questions, can be used as follow-ups to individual purchase and service experiences. As an example, leading-edge auto dealerships are using simple but directional five- to seven-element questionnaires to assess the future behavioral impact of each sales and service experience of its owners. These take no more than five minutes to complete, and can even be administered by dealership customer service staff.

6. *Seek real-time feedback.* Time can be the mortal enemy of relationships, especially if a customer has had a negative experience. The longer it takes a supplier to identify (and resolve) an issue or problem, the more it undermines customer trust and the perception of honesty on the part of the supplier. Then, being able to translate and apply the feedback, as quickly as possible, demonstrates consideration to the customer. Organizations like USAA, for example, pride themselves on being able to resolve customer concerns within 24 hours of identification.

7. *Make it easy for customers to provide feedback.* The more suppliers can convey the desire for, and receptivity to, input, and the more channels they can offer to make that happen, the more customers will respond. While customers tend to favor a single channel for communication, multichannel feedback increases the likelihood that customers will voluntarily provide valuable information.

8. *Leverage technology to aid your efforts.* Gathering feedback by Internet survey, where data can be prepared for analysis almost as quickly as it is collected, is among the latest in an ever-expanding set of methods to debrief customers. Quick response can be delivered as well, through such methods as IVR telephone text messaging and VoIP.

9. *Share customer feedback across the organization.* If companies are successful in most of their data gathering efforts, they will still fail to capitalize on the input customers provide if the information is siloed in selected parts of the enterprise or if the information travels up the hierarchical chimney but not down. Everyone in the company, from the president to the file

clerk and janitor, should be made aware of what customers value and how they make product and service decisions.

10. *Use feedback to make changes quickly.* Maybe Rome wasn't built in a day, nor did the Roman Empire decline and vanish in a month; but, to reinforce an earlier point, customer relationships can be chipped away or melted down very quickly after a negative experience. Making fundamental process changes, such as customer service problem resolution protocols, may take somewhat longer; however, ongoing and minor process change should be seen as a fact of life for the customer-centric company.

Information *from* each customer, then, can be an incredible strategic asset. While it's an essential learning tool that requires the investment of attention and resources, data generation doesn't have to become top-heavy and burdensome. Companies at the start of this process often feel the pressure of gathering as much information about customers as quickly as they can. Often, they invest heavily in software and data management systems more complex and sophisticated than they need; or they conclude that the data development task is just too daunting and fail to move at all. Usually, as Detica concluded, some customer information is developed, but not enough to effectively manage messaging and experiences at the individual customer and scenario level.

The reality is that there are some essentials of customer learning that companies must have, or develop. These boil down to answering a few basic questions:

- What motivates prospects to become customers?
- What about the company's products and services have enough value leverage to keep customers buying?
- What behavioral patterns can lead to similar purchase or usage actions, again and again?
- What are the characteristics of "first triers," the influential customers who are often the early users of a product or service?
- What are the characteristics of the "typical" customer?
- What causes customers to stop buying?
- If customers defect, can they be won back?

To understand what customers need—the right product or service, at the right price, in the right place, and at the right time to optimize spending—and insights into when and why they are most likely to buy, the typical company often conducts qualitative research. This may include focus groups, mini-groups, depth interviews, and observed shopping behavior. Such techniques are helpful in offering general guidance and direction, and their results can even be incorporated into customer databases; however, they must always be considered as only anecdotal at best.

Quantitative research techniques, on the other hand, extend and enhance customer insight. The research tools available to every company can cover customers selectively, down to the microsegment or individual, or be applied across the entire base. They can offer up detailed, dimensional data on a statistically reliable, projectable base.

Results can now be generated on a daily, even real-time, basis. Among the many learning opportunities, companies can assess patterns of customer purchasing behaviors, and identify where unique sales and communication potential might exist. When predictive modeling techniques are applied, companies can identify product and service associations, forecast and anticipate activities by customer life stage. Divisibility is attainable because these predictions can be executed down to the specific individual's requirement, such as type and method of messaging to use for a product or service offer, and how the customer might respond to that offer.

At the back end of the customer life cycle are risk, loss, and possible recovery among those who have defected. Identifying and interpreting factors contributing to attrition, the point at which trust and advocacy begin to disassemble, may be the ultimate test and value of analytics that predict customers' withdrawal behavior.

Knowing when and why customers may leave is very close to predicting the future. With such models, organizations can become both more stable and more proactive. They give companies deep insights into customers, insights that can be leveraged into management of customer expectations. Endeavoring to anticipate customer actions and identifying customer expectations are where most analytics software has focused.

In predictive models, data go through an "analytical sieve" to help understand what creates perceived customer value, their loyalty, and hence their profitability. Without the added insight that comes from advanced analytics, resource allocation and perhaps even the whole approach to customer relationships become subject to intuition and guesswork. Fortunately, today's software makes such analyses more readily available, without the teams of data mining specialists and analysts that used to be required.

How is the success of marketing, service, and sales efforts measured and evaluated at the individual customer level? It comes down to a process of microsegmentation, analysis, modeling, prediction, and planning. The software will first help determine the most effective metrics for analysis (customer performance ratings, number of complaints, time to resolve issues, customer attrition and loss rates, length of relationship, growth of customer lifetime value, revenue per sale, cost per sale, per customer profitability, cross-sell and referral rate, cost to service, etc.).

From this guidance, baselines and messaging/experience tests can be developed to address and prioritize the biggest problems—i.e., those contributing most to risk and loss—and biggest opportunities, the so-called low-hanging fruit or Holy Grail marketers so often seek. The baselines should actually be established for each initiative, incorporating the metrics listed above as needed.

At least as much emphasis needs to be placed on generating data *about* customers, individual by individual, with the objective of applying it at each contact point and experience.

From the array of detailed purchase profile, demographic, qualitative and quantitative customer research insight, geographically based lifestyle data, unstructured information from sales and customer service interactions, plus online and offline customer correspondence, companies next have to make wise choices about what is relevant or not. This requires capabilities and specific, practical guidance on how to source and intake the right information at the right time.

Companies will need to develop both classification and reduction skills in assessing incoming information, making decisions about what to accept, reject, and store. As discussed in the Chapter One, they will certainly have to make sure that the data are as high quality and error free as possible. They will need to determine how well different types and streams of data from multiple sources can be interwoven— sometimes referred to as "bricolage"—to determine if conceptual models can be developed, suggesting customer patterns and behavioral likelihoods.

Customer data experts David Smith and Jonathan Fletcher have identified two key dimensions for determining what customer data to collect and when: *Relevance* and *timing.*

The first consideration of relevance is saliency. Does the information have an impact on the organization, either direct, indirect, or remote? If direct, it will be used immediately. If indirect, it will most likely be "banked" for later use. If remote, it might be held for historical purposes or discarded.

Another aspect of relevance is contribution to existing customer knowledge and insight. This will include new facts about customers and markets; however, it can also include information that has potential value, such as application to a new product or service. Of course, this depends at least somewhat on who, i.e., what groups within the organization, are using the data.

Generalizability also has to be considered. Each customer observation, transaction, or incident has inherent data value for its prospective added worth of dealing with customers on a divisible basis. That said, however, data should not be so very specific that they also can't be rolled up to create value on a microsegment or more macrosegment basis. In other words, it may be both useful and timely for a company to know that a customer is interested in having a favorite clothing store offer Western clothes because he likes to line dance. If enough customers feel that way, the store might begin to offer Western garb on a selective basis; however, if this is such a super-singular and remote issue, the company may elect to do nothing with the information.

Companies also have to determine how applicable data are to campaign, development, and communication planning. For example, if the company is looking to upgrade the usefulness and page click-throughs of its web site, does it have enough focused, directional information from customers to do that? If not, then customer input on alternate web page redesign scenarios should be sought.

Finally, when all the customer data sources are brought together, can relevant themes, trends, and models be developed? Are there enough of the right colors and shades to paint a landscape? Does the new piece of customer data, when combined with what is already known, offer fresh insights and evidence?

The other key consideration is timing. Are data current enough to help make sales, marketing, and customer service decisions? Some information, to be sure, may quickly go out of date, while others have long-term value.

Will the data generated have strategic or tactical value? Will the piece of customer information collected have application to the scripting used by customer reps, or will it have longer-term applicability for helping design a new product or service?

Smith and Fletcher urge companies to go through a form of audit, a customer data "robustness" check to help determine whether a piece of information is worth gathering, storing, and applying to decisions. First, is the information believable? Is it consistent with other learnings, or is it way outside the parameters of what has already been proven as accurate? How precise and professional is the piece of data? If there is a lack of attention to detail in how the information has been harvested, it may have little applicability to management and marketing issues.

Last, is the piece of information in any way ambiguous, biased in favor of a certain perspective, or potentially unreliable? Can it be corroborated or confirmed against similar findings from other sources? Can it be related to norms and benchmarks, such as customer survey data and purchase histories?

For customer information to be converted into a strategic asset, companies need an effective process for applying the analytics and models. As in developing the data for analytics in the first place, this will require *having all customer information in one place.*

In this multichannel customer contact and transaction age, if call center reps are getting customer interaction data via only a single channel, they cannot give the customer either the speed or caliber of response that is considered high value. All data about a customer—across channels, business and service lines, etc.—and pulling together disparate data sources for cross-enterprise sharing and application is the first step. We'll look at this in detail in the next section.

Next comes *data mining,* the process of discovery and conveyance of insight to key user groups within the organization. Here is where segmentation, around purchase and other behavioral characteristics, and demographics, lifestyle, and other attributes come into play; and companies can construct target profiles to generate the most value from current customers and identify the best potential customers. We'll also cover data mining and warehousing.

Finally come *action* and *refinement,* the application of customer insight to improved, more effective customer messaging, processes, and experiences. Within this stage of using customer information as a strategic asset, all of the insight and analytics are leveraged to identify the ideal message components and communication channels for each customer, resulting in the optimal interaction experience for both parties. Individual customer predictions, or scores, coming out of the models help maximize the desired direct and indirect behaviors, such as increased spending or referral. For example, a select group of customers, or even an individual customer, may wish to exchange products by telephone service contact and mail, versus use of Web-based service, if this is the company's norm. If, after looking at the costs and customer-perceived benefits, this makes economic sense in terms of optimizing the customer's long-term loyalty, this combination of service channels would be made available.

Addressing Universal Truths About Integrating Data Sources

For many companies, the amount, types, and sources of customer data seem overwhelming. Merging, or fusing, data requires proficiency in CDI, or customer data integration. CDI isn't just another set of letters consultants dredge up to confuse everybody. This is where information from the data sources—all available and relevant streams of insight—are brought together to create a single, integrated view of the customer. As discussed elsewhere in the book, study upon study into enterprise-wide focused customer awareness has eluded most companies.

One problem is that even with faster computers and better processing methods, CDI technology hasn't really evolved much in the past 15–30 years. Most companies, large and small, are still using traditional merge/purge technology for customer segmentation. Related problems are data quality and completeness, the accuracy of both content and grouping (customers and activities), and the speed of data access. After all, if a company makes the effort to obtain high-quality customer data, but it takes weeks or months to pull it out of the system for program formulation or refinement decision making, how effective can the efforts be?

Some companies, however, have solved—or at least are solving—the complexities of managing CDI. They are utilizing what is known as "linking technology," a technological improvement that, among other advantages, dramatically enhances—i.e., by a factor of ten times—more traditional forms of data de-duplication. Linking technology draws on knowledge bases, huge data warehouses of consumer and business names and addresses, available from outside suppliers, that is continually maintained and updated. Creating the links between these bases and internal customer warehouses requires close interface between inside data professionals and their consulting counterparts. This is where much of the challenge comes into play.

In my household, we do our share of direct response shopping. A wrought iron floor lamp from Morocco and a wall clock from France for the kitchen, a cast brass walking stick holder from New Zealand for the foyer . . . you get the idea. As a result, our family, especially my wife, gets a ton of catalogs and other promotional mail. Not a week goes by that she doesn't get two of the same catalog. Clearly, companies sending these duplicate catalogs have an inaccurate and incomplete picture of my wife as a customer. They're using both her single and married name in the address, when her married name is the rightful, legal one. It's a data completeness and accuracy issue, to be sure; however, it's really a reflection of their inability to paint a comprehensive customer portrait. The lack of clean, integrated data impacts the entire customer relationship with her because, on the occasions where she has ordered something from one of these particular catalogs, they typically record the transaction under the wrong name. If there are returns issues, the problems become compounded. It can be very frustrating.

This type of individual customer recognition "blind spot" situation is precisely what advanced forms of CDI have been designed to minimize, even avoid altogether. Customer data integration is what enables store sales clerks, customer service reps, and tech support staff to have all available customer data at each contact point. And, as essential as CDI has become in the consumer products and services world, it is even more important in business-to-business sales, marketing, and customer service, especially where multiple or independent operations are in contact with the same customer, possible for multiple products and services.

A (Passing) Note Regarding Data Marts, Warehousing, and Mining

There have been entire books devoted to data marts, warehousing and mining and the complex alchemy of sequential patterns, neural networks, genetic algorithms, data visualization, and decision trees and laddering; so we're going to, hopefully, simplify and cover these subjects specifically as they pertain to customer divisibility.

Customer information, to begin, covers any set of facts, numbers, or nondimensional text that can be stored or processed on a computer. Taking this information and creating patterns, associations, and relationships from it—such as using computer site sales information to identify what products are selling, when, and to whom—is the start of customer knowledge discovery, aka data mining. *Knowledge,* the conversion of information through morphing historical customer behavior patterns into future trends, is the next step. If a supermarket chain wishes to analyze individual customer purchase activity by department, product group, or promotional program, knowledge is the learning phase where this happens.

Data warehousing is basically the centralization of data capture, transmission, and storage of various databases into a single repository or resource for ready retrieval, analysis, and application. In essence, this is the customer data integration just discussed, necessary to optimize user access and analysis, and customer understanding, across the enterprise.

What's the value of data mining, especially when endeavoring to deliver customer value on a divisible basis? Essentially, it's the ability to create relationships between what can be called "internal" customer factors—i.e., pricing, product and service array, employee skills required at the point of interaction—and "external" factors, such as competitive product and service set and customer demographics.

Mega retailer WalMart, which has perhaps the world's largest data warehouse, with point-of-sale transactions from close to 3,000 stores, uses its database to help its more than 3,500 suppliers perform analyses on customer buying patterns. This information, in turn, helps WalMart manage product-by-product inventory on a local store level and also to identify new merchandising and promotional opportunities.

One of the chief benefits of data mining is that applications are available for virtually any size business, whether the customer (or member) database is managed on a mainframe, client/server, or PC. Complete systems can range in price from several thousand dollars for small customer databases to $1 million or more for the largest. It's a high-return investment. In retail information technology studies by consulting organizations like Ernst & Young, close to two-thirds of companies with active data mining programs report increased gross margin, development of new strategies and markets, increased sales, and improved return on investment.

The *data mart* is a single database, or several databases, that can be applied to help managers make tactical and strategic decisions. For those who don't use these terms every day, the difference between a data mart and a data warehouse is that the former will focus on a key activity, subject, or department—such as optimizing customer divisibility—while the latter looks to combine, or integrate, databases across the entire enterprise. Both are important and have enormous value;

however, for our purposes, the data mart is where much of the customer-related action takes place.

Data marts, occasionally also called data stores, tend to store data that most users require on a real-time or "near-real-time" basis. Principally, this is transactional (purchase, inventory, accounts receivable) type information that is updated daily, even hourly. For users such as marketing, customer service, and sales, this doesn't require the formality of a data warehouse architecture; yet they still need a single source of information that is easy to use, has reporting flexibility, and is as current as possible. For the kinds of divisible applications we're addressing, data marts are increasingly the storage method of choice.

The supermarket chain mentioned above can look at each customer's point-of-sale purchases over time to send targeted, highly individualized purchases based on that customer's buying history. Blockbuster Entertainment, for instance, can look at individual customers' video and DVD rental history to recommend rentals. Amazon mines its customers' purchasing history to recommend CDs, DVDs, and books for purchase. American Express can send targeted promotions to individual customers based on an analysis of their purchase expenditures, over any period desired.

High-end supermarket Green Hills Farms uses data mining for customer-specific marketing down to the occasion level. When they ran a free Thanksgiving turkey promotion, one of the most venerable programs in the supermarket industry, they used their wealth of customer information to drive significantly more value from it. Before data mining, the store gave a turkey to each customer who spent $500 in the ten weeks prior to Thanksgiving. Though this is still the basic reward, Green Hills Farms also put in a $300 minimum for senior citizens, separately identified in the database. Additionally, there were two upgraded components: a turkey and a decorated Christmas wreath for spending $750 over that same period, and a turkey and a Christmas tree for customers spending $1,000. Data mining enables the company to reward customers for maintaining their spending levels, but also gives them the opportunity to move into a higher tier.

Applying Data for Customer Advocacy: The View from Ground Level

One of the cornerstone concepts of this book is that companies are most likely to be successful, or not, in terms that success is understood, based on how well they use individual customer data on an individual customer basis. Brokerage firm Morgan Stanley has expressed this succinctly and well: ". . . the value of a company will be directly tied to its knowledge, retention, and monetization of its customer base."

In Chapter One, we presented an overview, and offered several examples, of companies effectively applying customer data for both advocacy and divisibility. There are, increasingly, companies putting customer divisibility and advocacy together. Franklin Covey, for instance, provides organizational and personal effectiveness and related training for more than 750,000 participants each year. The company does business with three-quarters of the *Fortune* 500, and has offices in 32 countries. Their products and services are available in 32 languages and in 75 countries around the world. Franklin Covey sales channels include 150 retail stores, training seminars, catalogs, and multiple Internet sites.

This array of data collection points produced a huge amount of customer information stored in a number of databases, with many duplicate records. Further, customer data were entered inconsistently between these databases, and staff from different lines of business weren't able to draw out the data in a manner that would enable them to compare results and profiles. In order to better package its array of products to match the needs of individual customers, the challenge was to create a single, comprehensive information source that would allow staff who managed the lines of business to interact.

Franklin Covey created a single database that would achieve its four requirements of accuracy, timeliness, relevance, and consistency. They were able to link existing legacy-type data with real-time customer contact data, generated across multiple touch points around the company. The principal benefit of this integrated database is that any Franklin Covey employee, whether at a retail store, customer service, training center, or elsewhere, can recognize individual customers, irrespective of any record variations. Employees can, as well, execute cross-sell and upsell opportunities, on a situation-by-situation, divisible customer basis. Franklin Covey's goal, using the database as a fulcrum, is to integrate all business and marketing channels within the enterprise.

E*TRADE was able to directly translate an integrated, single view of the customer into greater profit. As they analyzed their customer base, they uncovered a classic Pareto Principle situation, namely that a small proportion of customers represented most of the profit. Overlaying individual customer profitability data onto customer service center processes, E*TRADE made certain that their best, most profitable customers were serviced first and most personally. Unprofitable customers were placed at the back of call queues, or handled on automated IVR systems.

Commerce Bank, known as "America's Most Convenient Bank," is well known in its Mid-Atlantic marketing area for extended banking hours and extraordinary customer service. Several years ago, as the bank was rapidly increasing its geographic coverage and opening new branches, Commerce was experiencing challenges in sharing the increased volume of individual customer information being collected and stored, and this was influencing response time for such functions as wire transfers and new loans.

Applying data integration and information sharing software technologies, Commerce was able to become far more efficient in handling and applying customer knowledge for decision making. One very evident change was in wire transfer processing time. Before the customer data software was installed, wire transfer approvals typically took from four to six hours, in part because the right staff members had to be available at the right time for authorization. This was reduced to three minutes, and these impressive results led to further efficiencies. One of these was the "The Wow Answer Guide," an indexed knowledge base that enabled customers to answer virtually any bank-related customer question. If a customer wanted to know, for example, how and where to buy Euros for a trip, or fees for certain transactions, the database could provide it in a heartbeat. And, with individual customers' information in hand, the requesting Commerce Bank employee can offer divisible response. Employees thought so highly of the concept that it was extended to become a self-service feature for customers on Commerce's web site, adding to the bank's "wow" service factor.

Another bank, Royal Bank of Scotland, was challenged to revamp its database, covering over 7 million customers, so that information was more readily available for the marketing department to execute highly targeted, event-driven messaging programs. Before making the conversion (which also migrated database management responsibilities from the IT department to the marketing department), endeavoring to market on an individual customer basis involved labor-intensive manual processes. As a result of the integration and related technologies, much of Royal Bank's marketing development processes can be automated, enabling the creation of more precise and frequent messaging for customers.

Proving that these technologies can help companies of any size get closer to their customers is the Union Bank of Norway. Several years ago, customer information was stored in six separate databases, inhibiting their ability to understand individual customer needs. Further, customer communication was in disarray, with customers having the same requirements, but living in different areas, receiving different messaging. By integrating its several databases into one warehouse, individual customer profiles could be developed, along with predictive models. Now, Union Bank has a single file for each customer, concentrating especially on Most Valuable Customers (MVC's) for a VIP loyalty program. They are able to use the data warehouse for an array of applications aimed at improving the messaging and experience for each customer: process improvements, program development, customer channel prioritization, and communications frequency management. The executive responsible for making this conversion noted that the reduced marketing costs and improved effectiveness of their programs, in the first year alone, covered the entire database integration investment.

The gaming business probably makes more active use of multisource customer information—from socioeconomic databases, loyalty programs, credit card data cross matching, etc.—than any other business. Harrah's approaches to leveraging customer data for divisibility will be discussed later in the book, but, almost a decade ago, they were the first company to identify the potential of integrating and sharing customer data.

Other casinos have followed this lead. Foxwoods Resort Casino, for example, is able to parse and match its customer database against publicly available demographic profiles to identify family characteristics, such as household size, age of children, and total income. The casino compares these data to customer spending patterns to create customized messaging and experience opportunities. Similar to the other gaming companies, much of this customization is built around customers' use of loyalty cards.

4

TARGETING MESSAGES AND MANAGING EXPERIENCES

PART I: WHAT CLICKS WITH CUSTOMERS, AND WHAT DOESN'T

The "Brand": A Chemical Composition of Messaging and Experience

How does a supplier develop, and sustain, customer advocacy? It's the age-old question of whether the chicken or the egg comes first. Ultimately, creating true advocates out of first-time, and even seemingly loyal, customers, requires top-notch, value-based, individualized experiences accompanied by the before-and-after impact and continuity of top-notch, value-based, individualized messaging.

When customers are considering alternative suppliers or making final purchase decisions, it is becoming increasingly well understood that they do so according to personal, individualized formulae comprised of tangible (cognitive) and intangible (affective, or emotional) anticipated benefits. This absolutely requires that the meld between messaging and experiences be as seamless as possible.

Well-managed relationships include both the messaging and experience. These elements, combined, represent a discipline of monitoring customer contact across multiple channels of interaction, leveraging in-depth customer information to optimize customer service, and the delivery of a positive result whenever and however the supplier and customer come in contact. The "brand" is delivered through a combination of processes, culture, organization and technology at every point of the customer's life cycle.

Businesses have long tended to undercategorize customers, based almost entirely on purchase history, plus basic demographics. This results in relationships that are both narrow and reactive, with little leverage to build advocacy. With the maturation of online commerce and customers' growing desire, even demand, to deal with suppliers on a multichannel basis, the focus on both messaging and experience must increase.

The Experience Begins with Messaging

The Greenfield Consulting Group, a Connecticut-based qualitative research firm, has expressed the following perspective about messaging: "More than ever, products and related marketing messages suffer from the doubts of increasingly skeptical consumers."[1] That's a polite way of saying that suppliers are having to deal with customers who are increasingly sophisticated regarding what is promised and provided. If a company cannot communicate value in pre- and post-encounter messaging, and then over-deliver in the encounter itself, intelligent and cynical customers will quickly depart.

Companies tend to believe that customers experience their business through people, products, and services. True enough, but they often don't realize that what is said to customers, and how it is said, through communications media has an equal, if not greater, impact. Communication is about *relevance*, which has critical impact on the value prism customers use to express their regard, and their trust, for suppliers.

Many decisions must be made about communications. For customers to respond in the ways planned and intended by suppliers, the value proposition must have a sound communication and messaging strategy. Messaging is about getting the right information to the right audiences at the right time, and having that information create the desired action. It has the responsibility of generating awareness, expressing the supplier's position, and creating sufficient credibility (confirmation of claims and qualifications) in the customer's mind.

One of the principal reasons for supplier switching is that companies often look at their involvement with customers as individual, discrete encounters or events, while the customers experience their suppliers in a far more longitudinal manner. Messaging should emphasize the desire for long-term relationships rather than transactions. It should address the customer at his or her appropriate life stage (prospect, new customer, active/loyal customer, at risk customer, former customer, recovered customer, etc.). As a result, the tone, frequency, and content of the message should be appropriate to that customer's needs and desires.

Customer contact strategies, and the messages conveyed to the right customer, through the right medium, at the right time, and with the right frequencies are all important here. Significant messaging questions must be addressed and re-addressed. For instance, the number of "touches," depending on each customer's priorities, preferences, and demographics, have to be determined. The tone of the message, as well as the content, has to be tested and refined. When companies like Royal Bank of Scotland and Tesco can custom-design promotional communication programs so that there are in excess of 250,000 variations in content, it's clear that messaging is a key consideration in building and sustaining customer relationships.

---

[1] Paul Jacobson, "Usability—V2.0," *Something to Think About,* October 2001.

Messaging can take place at any point in the customer life cycle and for almost any purpose. In fact, the more purposes—so long as the message delivers value to the customer—the better. This can be in the form of newsletters, account and order status updates, time-based reminders, promotions, responses to inquiries, general or customized information provision, and even simple informational letters. Messaging can even come through less traditional methods, such as in-person or Web seminars. Relevant content, as well as timing, is key to helping create and sustain commitment. It is more important than the format followed.

One approach marketers have applied to build commitment and trust is to provide messaging, in the form of information, targeted at specific customer groups. As mentioned, this can be concise letters, such as to customers or inquirers. A company sending out detailed informational letters to frequent travelers, who are also customers, on what to do if their purse or wallet is stolen, for example, would find a welcome response and high interest.

A frequently utilized messaging method of getting a customer to invest time, in between actual transactions or experiences, is a newsletter. Newsletters help suppliers keep prospects and customers informed of noteworthy events. The aim is not to convey massive amounts of information, but rather to be anticipated and read; so, if a supplier can make reading newsletters a habit, that habit can be translated into commitment. Ultimately, habit is much more important than content. The challenge, of course, is that an increasingly large number of marketers have discovered the effectiveness of newsletters. They realize that readers will carefully pick and choose what they want to see, and what they prefer not to receive.

Where possible, the messaging should be two way, enabling both the customer and supplier to accumulate knowledge. Companies need to understand how the messaging is received and how this influences the experience. This, in turn, can be used to refine customer profiles down to microsegments, individual customer, and scenarios. At the point of contact between the supplier and customer, whether personal, written, or electronic, the messaging can be completely customized.

There are no "rules" per se for sales, marketing, services, and others regarding how messages should be composed; however, there are some general, universal guidelines that can be followed. First, messages should be simple and straightforward. Nothing is as off-putting to customers and prospects as complexity, or the use of "insider" language (such as we hear each week as used by doctors on *ER*).

Next, messages should be as crisp and concise as possible. Direct marketers, for years, have been encouraged to create copy that tells a story and creates a value proposition. This is sound advice, but suppliers also have to deal with customers' "need for speed" in getting quickly to the heart of communication.

Messages also have to be clear and consistent. There should be extra care taken that messages aren't confusing in any way. Also, message content—especially in multiple messages over time, such as for a campaign—must not be conflictive or contradictory. There should be continuity in message theme development.

Finally, suppliers must recognize that the emotional leverage created by messaging is every bit as strong as the emotional messages of the customer-supplier experience. Messages thus should focus or at least concentrate more on benefits and solutions rather than on tangible features.

The media used for communication—direct response, digital contact, telemarketing, email, etc. on a micro level, and radio, TV, press, posters, etc. on a macro level—should be planned with great care. These are the select "routes" for reaching customers. Communicating the proposition through the most appropriate combination of approaches, i.e., the communication mix, is as important as the amount of segmentation, microsegmentation, and customization in the messaging itself. Suppliers are now applying more and more science to optimize communication "reach" (the number of people, or customers, to whom the messaging is sent) and "richness" (the effectiveness of the communication in achieving specific goals).

It's important to note, however, that indirect electronic channels—chiefly the Internet—will not become a full-time replacement for more direct, person-to-person contact. A Price Waterhouse Coopers study[2] found that only 13 percent of consumers considered the Internet their preferred form of contact, while 70 percent preferred the telephone. This puts tremendous pressure on companies looking to find the lowest-cost form of customer messaging and communication, because that same study found that 60 percent of consumers say they are less likely to do business with a company that doesn't use their preferred communication channel.

Personalization and Permissioning: The Case For and Against

When every customer gets the same message content, with the same media, the same frequency, and at the same time, there's little opportunity for the supplier to learn what clicks and what doesn't. Microsegmentation and micromessaging are now possible through advanced database and software techniques. Companies can look at purchase and billing profiles, appended demographics, and even layer on

---

[2] "Loyalty: Companies Must Understand What Customers Want," www.thewisemarketer.com, December 29, 2001.

real-time customer insight to tailor messages down to the customer and purchase scenario level. Communication, and reward, strategies can be designed to customize messaging to keep the most loyal customers through service, problem detection and intervention, and setting up the most positive next experience.

The more microsegmentation and micromessaging companies apply, the greater the opportunity, or potential, for effectiveness because it enables them to use variations in the value proposition for each target group, and ultimately for each customer and each purchase situation. That said, however, these propositions must be consistent and noncontradictory, as discussed above with messaging. For instance, if wireless telecoms are making offers of free or low-cost cell phones with advanced bells and whistles as an incentive to new customers, they can't assume that current customers won't learn of this and be extremely upset. The best advice is to develop values and benefits that are consistent across the different audiences.

One of the hotter topics in micromessaging continues to be personalization, especially via email. Since Seth Godin's book *Permission Marketing* addressed the opt-in/opt-out issue of email communication several years ago, the jury has been out on how effective this form of personalized messaging truly is.[3] It's clear, however, that trying to send personalized email messages, or any messages, without permission is a negative. Quris, Inc., an agency that specializes in customer-centric, personalized email marketing, has found that 45 percent of consumers will cut off relations with any company engaging in poor email practices.[4]

For several years, Internet penetration has remained at about 65 percent of the population, and users have become increasingly wary and sophisticated about messages they will accept. As a result, even "nominal" permission seeking, situations where there was once passing interest in a product or service that has long since expired, can be a problem. Quris learned that almost all consumers (93 percent) simply delete permission messages that no longer interest them; and on average, 43 percent delete, unread, all the permission email they once requested.

Having recently passed the tenth anniversary of the birth of spam (at a Phoenix law firm sending unsolicited messages hoping to drum up business over the Internet, on April 12, 1994, with one angry recipient responding that the sender should be cursed with shipments of damaged cans of Spam, hence the term), approximately half to three-quarters of the email messages received are classified

---

[3] Seth Godin, *Permission Marketing* (New York: Simon and Schuster, 1999).
[4] "How Email Practices Can Win or Lose Long-Term Business," *A View from the Inbox,* October, 2003, p. 3.

as junk; and one e-mail management provider, Postini, determined that spam now makes up over 77 percent of the 5 billion emails sent each month.

Basex, an analysis firm, has estimated that the cost of wasted time and purloined network resources is $20 billion a year.[5] Many companies support a law (Can-Spam) passed in 2002, but it has done almost nothing to slow the pace or the growth of spam. Quris, through one of its studies, determined that the average consumer receives 12 permission emails per day but receives 30 spam messages daily.

Some Internet companies, fearful that a prospect or customer will consider them spammers, have gone to what's called a double opt-in option. How does this work? When a customer sends a request for information, the supplier response will ask for confirmation of the initial communication. If the customer does not confirm by a "click and send," his or her email address will not be added to the messaging database. While this approach reduces the number of those agreeable to receiving communication, at the same time it assures that there will be stronger relationships that are freer of criticism.

Another recently developed approach for spam control is Bonded Sender. Developed by IronPort, of San Bruno, California, and managed through Microsoft's email platforms, Bonded Sender doesn't attempt to directly control spam email. Instead, it requires that mass emailers post a bond assuring the legitimacy of their messaging. They are then provided with lists of eligible mail accounts. To prevent spammers from securing a bond, they must pass a security check by TRUSTe, the independent privacy firm. Early indications of Bonded Sender's effectiveness are encouraging: Microsoft claims that Bonded Sender reduced the amount of spam on Hotmail by 60 percent during a six-month test.

It should be noted, as well, that email is not the exclusive method for annoying customers or violating their privacy. Although the national DNC list has dramatically reduced the amount of unsolicited telephone contact, there is still a great deal of activity by nonprofit organizations. Also, home and office fax machines remain glutted with unwelcome faxes, the cost of which is borne by recipients, not senders.

With all of this as a backdrop, there is still general consensus, and a great deal of supportive evidence, that getting permission and personalizing content, in all communications and messaging, can dramatically improve their effectiveness in setting up both the value proposition and the customer experience to come. Quris has learned that one-third of the customers who were subscribed to permission

---

[5] Paul Festa and Evan Hansen, "Happy Spamiversary," CNET News.Com, April 12, 2004.

messaging programs had remained in them for at least three years; and, of those long-term messaging recipients, two-thirds said they had purchased something directly as a result of the email. Further, half of this group said they would rather purchase from a company that sent personalized, permission-based email than with a competitor.

Suppliers, at an early stage of customer contact, must first determine the degree of personalization they want to achieve (and also what the customer desires or will be responsive to). Degree of personalization? Yes, while messages can be specific and unique to individuals or groups, they can also be further segmented according to the promotion or the purchasing circumstances, which is where divisibility comes in.

Delivering personalized, permission-based messages—through written, electronic, or personal media—is very much a "push" tactic, helping to familiarize customers, or potential customers, with value propositions, potential purchase experiences, or participation on promotional activities. Depending on the database tapped for messaging—i.e., whether it contains customer-by-customer transactional information, whether it can be updated in real-time on a continual basis (via email survey or periodically appended with other information)—a supplier can apply the degree of personalization desired.

Why personalize, especially through email, even given all of the challenges associated with it? Personalization helps to develop and enhance a relationship, to interact with the customer or prospect on an individual level, demonstrating a deeper level of interest and commitment. It helps to differentiate otherwise comparably perceived companies.

In the prospect stage, personalization aids in conversion, helps upsell or cross-sell, even at the initial purchase, and communicate special offers. For instance, Quris has found that 57 percent of customers they surveyed said they bought something online in the past year as a result of personalized, permission-based email messages.[6]

Once a prospect becomes a customer, of course, personalization can communicate specific product information, remind the customer of upcoming events (which should be of interest given their profile), offer upgrades, provide updates on product delivery status when orders have been placed, and revitalize a relationship if the customer hasn't purchased in some time.

Personalization builds dialogue between the supplier and customer, communicating the most relevant information to each customer, when and as needed. The

---

[6] "How Email Practices Can Win or Lose Long-Term Business," *A View from the Inbox,* October, 2003, p. 2.

dialogue, in turn, helps to update the customer's profile and provides input on recent transactions. If troubleshooting is needed as a result of a recent neutral or negative experience, personalized communication in the form of email customer service helps both increase the level of loyalty and reduce the service costs per customer.

Finally, at the macro level, personalization helps build the supplier's equity with customers. Newsletters, customized ad and promotional content, and highly targeted news can be communicated on a customer, and scenario, basis.

The bottom line is that personalization is the most effective method of setting up a divisible experience, through divisible messaging.

Companies like RightNow Technologies, through electronic customer management approaches they've developed (RightNow Outbound), can send such messages to highly targeted groups of customers and prospects, enabling them to send, and simultaneously test, alternative messages, manage responses (if response is called for), and gauge their effectiveness at the same time. This level of personalization facilitates optimum messaging customization, certainly down to the individual customer and prospect level, but also with the ability to vary message by customer based on the specific sales or promotional situation. At the same time, this service conforms to NAI data privacy and email filtering guidelines, as explained in Chapter Two.

The ultimate in personalization is achieved through what is known as an ongoing integrated system. It blends, or integrates, all aspects of a supplier's organization, online and offline, Web, phone, and mail. Email messages, for example, can be personalized based on each customer's navigation and purchase patterns on a supplier's web site. As a set of tools, it is somewhat more cost prohibitive than other forms of personalization; however, it has the advantage of utilizing the most current available online profile, purchase and navigation data, plus the offline data, such as telephone contact.

Why Fuzzy Value Proposition Messaging Doesn't Work

When customers are mentally sorting through value propositions presented in the blasts of messages coming at them and trying to determine where they will place or continue their patronage, they determine "Hey, it's all about *me*, isn't it?" The decade of the '90s has been referred to as the "Me Generation"; but, for customers, every decade, every year, and every day is about them as individuals, and individual need represented in specific service and purchase situations.

Long-distance telephone companies, for example, are actively competing for that very scarce commodity, the high-volume caller. They make telephone contacts with prospective customers ad nauseam (usually around dinnertime), and their offer usually has some oddball, complex plan of pricing that includes in-state and out-of-state, daytime and nighttime, weekdays and weekends, etc. There are often loopholes and hitches in even the simplest of these plans, such as charges based on the nearest five seconds or when there is no answer to a call. Einstein and John Maynard Keynes would be hard pressed to figure out where the real value propositions are. The U.S. government has even stepped in to try and regulate what is told to consumers.

The net result in this confusion and tactical marketing, of course, is that there is very little loyalty, and a great deal of switching, in the long-distance industry.

Worse, however, is the fuzzy value messaging created by bank marketers and their affiliates in the mad scramble to lure consumers to their credit cards. There's a great deal of money to be made through the extension of credit to qualified card users, so it's no surprise that there's so much competition to obtain them, or steal them away from the cards they already have. It has been estimated that the average American household receives at least three credit card offers a week. That's over 150 a year! One online credit card search engine carries close to 350 different credit card offers.

Most of the sales approaches are disappointingly (and annoyingly) similar. That's part of what makes the value proposition for these cards so indistinct for the customer. There's usually a low introductory APR (annual percentage rate) for new purchases or balance transfers from other credit cards. Then they layer on services like high credit lines, 24/7 "relationship managers" available by phone, email, or online chat, email account reminders, travel insurance, and on and on.

That's just the beginning. There are credit cards that provide a 1 percent or 2 percent yearly cash rebate on purchases. There are sports/theme credit cards (university alumni, *National Geographic Magazine,* Bass Pro, Six Flags Entertainment, National Hockey League, U.S. Ski Team, Universal Studios, World Championship Wrestling). There are frequent flyer credit cards where a cardholder can earn miles on any airline, plus other assorted benefits. Also, of course, are credit cards the airlines themselves issue. Alaska Airlines, America West, Delta, Continental, United, TWA, USAir, Northwest, and British Airways have credit cards. Most of these travel-related credit cards come with an annual fee, but they have a fistful of "benefits" like anniversary bonuses, low-cost companion tickets, class upgrades, bonus miles at sign-up, bonus miles at first usage, and free subscriptions, adding to the confusion.

There are automobile company and buying service credit cards, such as GM's, where cardholders can earn points on usage that apply to the purchase or lease of a new car or truck. Gasoline companies like Phillips 66, Citgo, Texaco, Exxon, and BP; specialty retailers like Barnes & Noble, Eddie Bauer, Home Shopping Network, L. L. Bean, Kmart, and Toys 'R' Us; other specialty issuers like *Reader's Digest,* Sony, and even *Star Trek* (!); and many grocery/supermarket chains also have their own Visa and MasterCard programs. Most of these offer points or per-centage rebates on purchases from these companies plus lower percentage rebates from other merchants.

The big question is: With this blinding array of so-called benefits, which have cus-tomers identified as having value—i.e., enough benefit to attract them and keep them? Where's the customer data that support these programs? By what process, divine or otherwise, have the card issuers decided which combination of benefits to offer? One credit card issuer, Juniper, is not at all bashful to say they use their own staff, called Product Innovators, to help design benefits. Their advertising says: "We're all customers, too. So we designed products we'd want to use ourselves." At least they've made an effort to gather and use "valid" anecdotal customer information.

As in any market space, there is a small percentage of companies that are both innovative and customer-centric, gathering customer data intelligently and apply-ing it well. In bank cards, MBNA has maintained one of the highest rates of card-holder retention, despite higher APRs, by a focus on proactive benefits, such as quick and easy credit limit increases, and building relationships through their call center. Customer loyalty is also tightly interwoven into MBNA's culture.

Some other credit card issuers have now begun utilizing data mining and person-alization techniques to give them an edge. HSBC, having seen its base of 2.5 million card customers remain unchanged for the past three years, has eliminated their reward points program. Instead, the company is introducing a variety of retail discounts, com-petitions, and special offers tailored to their spending patterns. The key is, of course, whether current and potential customers will see value in the revamped program. In other words, is this move intuitive on HSBC's part, motivated by a desire to save mar-keting dollars, or is it based on customer insight and designed to increase value?

Customer service expert T. Scott Gross has said: "Satisfaction is easy. Quality is a notch up the ladder. Value is where it's at."[7] Only clear value propositions devel-oped from the right data and executed well, in any industry, can take the confu-sion out of product and service marketing.

A Failure in Messaging Exercise: Airline Industry Loyalty Program Solicitations

Since 1981, when American Airlines inaugurated the industry's first frequent flier program to reward its best customers for their loyalty, there are now close to 50 airlines with such programs, having a combined, though overlapping, mem-bership of close to 300 million.

---

[7] Michael Lowenstein, "Fuzzy Value Propositions = Confusion Marketing," www.searchcrm.com, September 26, 2001.

The *Official Airline Guide* reports that the most active of business travelers will average more than 20 flights per year, so their loyalty has definite value for the airlines. While Accenture reports that 80 percent of business travelers say membership in these programs has an influence on their travel decisions, more than 60 percent of those holding memberships belong to three or more programs. A McKinsey study has found that, paralleling the Pareto Principle, 20 percent of frequent flier program members account for 80 percent of an airline's profit, and under 5 percent represent one-third of an airline's profit.[8]

Obviously, the airline industry is not targeting program members very well at all. When only one-quarter of any airline's program members actually fly in any given year, and when the annual membership base churns by at least 20 percent, something is wrong with the value proposition and the messaging. What's the problem? The poor performance of these programs is multifaceted, but it boils down to sameness of message structure and content, usage of media that cannot target and recruit the right members, and non-differentiation of value proposition.

If the airlines can't isolate the most valuable customers, and customize program invitation messages and components specifically to these travelers' individual needs, this will only continue. The technologies to make such improvements exist; however, the will to invest in them apparently does not.

Messaging, and Selling, By Cell By Gosh!

Targeted electronic messaging has gone super high tech. We have entered the era of the text message. Though most people in the United States know about text messaging through *American Idol,* despite the fact that an estimated 90 percent of American cell phones are set up to accept them, under 30 million people actually use the short message service (SMS) technology.

Though only 160 characters are available for a single text message, it has become a huge means of targeting customized messages outside the U.S. About 20 million text messages are sent in Europe every month through cell phones and PDAs, of which 10 percent are marketing or customer service related. Like personalized email messaging, the same capabilities, on a Lilliputian scale, are available on cell phones. Banks in Finland, for example, can send account information to individual customers to offer them new or related services. Typically, perhaps because of their newness, personalized text messaging has shown dramatic response, much higher than the typical email message program. In Japan, snack

---

[8] Philip Charlton, "Targeting—the Achilles Heel of Frequent Flyer Programs," www.thewisemarketer.com, February 2004.

and beverage companies, travel agencies, and others are using SMS for viral marketing programs, such as promotions and contests, with some message personalization. In the U.S., companies like Ford, Coca-Cola, and Adidas have used SMS as an advertising device, but not for personalized messaging.

While the attraction of SMS for marketers is that they can target specific customers with the right message at the right time, and also use the same technology for customer insight collection (following a purchase experience, for instance), there is also credible research evidence that consumers will not respond to a cell phone message unless it is personally relevant. Thus, although Burger King might like to offer Whopper coupons to its customers when they are in the vicinity of one of their restaurants (using GPS location software to assure that the customer is in the right place), the likelihood is that they'll have to be much more creative and more personally focused to succeed.

Just as spam has created deep negative inroads in personalized email messages, it has already infected the SMS world. The European Parliament has enacted legislation to limit unsolicited text messaging. If U.S. companies are to avoid the kinds of fines and penalties being levied on offenders in Europe, they will have to move quickly. Otherwise the same challenges that marketers have with email messaging will be visited on the well-intentioned users of SMS. Most of the major text message marketing companies have already entered into anti-spam agreements with the principal cell phone carriers.

The New Value Agenda: Morphing Transactions into Experiences

Steve O'Keefe, an expert in Internet publicity and online marketing, has nicely defined the (hopefully) irreplaceable value that right-thinking suppliers endeavor to build and defend in the minds of customers with each engagement: "What is a brand? I've heard it described as a promise to the consumer, but I think that's putting it too strongly. A brand is more probability than promise—a consumer calculus that is built-up, torn down, or left unchanged by each encounter."[9]

Most companies, to their discredit, don't understand the concept of long-term customer value creation. There is surprisingly little strategy applied to building a sufficiently customer-centric organization such that customers will perceive optimum value in supplier experiences with sales, marketing, and customer services. While suppliers should be gathering information about what customers want in the relationship, converting it to knowledge, distilling it to insight, and putting this

---

[9] Kelly O'Keefe, "Intrinsic Branding" (presentation, AMA Regional Spring Conference, Pittsburgh, PA, April 30, 2004).

insight in the hands of employees at the point of customer contact, few companies have done this in a consistent manner. The majority approach customer engagements as "one size fits all."

Instead of enhancing the customer's experience at each touch point, many carry the misconception that ever greater technological advances are what is needed to manage customer relationships. In the meantime, customers have very different, and highly individualistic, ideas about value. They want consideration, attention, proaction—and sometimes personalization, and the choice and efficiency of self-service—when so often they are met with complex web site menus, phone IVR systems, and excruciating wait times. Customers have an increasing desire, as well, for multichannel pre- and post-engagement communication, such as online communities and forums, interactive messaging, and wireless phones.

In a Bearing Point financial services market study among senior executives, under a quarter believed that their customers were committed and enthusiastic about their financial institutions (credit unions, banks, brokerages, and mortgage lenders).[10] As with most industries, they found that financial services companies were more focused on applying advanced technologies to manage customer relationships than on optimizing the experience itself.

The Bearing Point study concluded that financial institutions, like so many other businesses, have a fundamental lack of insight as to the kind of experience customers want from their suppliers. While 85 percent of the executives felt that the customer experience was essential to the institution achieving its strategic goals, 91 percent admitted that customers would be more loyal with a higher-quality experience; and fully one-third felt that they could attain a dramatic increase in the level of customer loyalty by working to improve experiences.

The "long-term" aspect of value provision in communication and experience management, especially, appears too infrequently on the radar screens of most companies. Companies are challenged to do a better job of managing customer experience and engagement. Bearing Point advises building company-wide commitment to customer engagement and experience around three simple concepts:

- *Adapting the customer's perspective.* Deep understanding of customers' needs, throughout the life cycle.
- *Creating mutual value.* Benefit must be established at each point of customer contact.

---

[10] "Wake-Up Call: To Fix CRM, Fix the Customer Experience Now," *Bearing Point White Paper,* 2004.

- *Encouraging transparency and trust.* Building a "partnership picture" of customers, and organizing processes and technologies to match.

As will be discussed in much greater detail in Chapter Nine, customer service has a critical, and exponentially growing, impact on customer engagements. The objective, as stated by Bearing Point, is to "reward customers for the totality of their relationships, provide a consistent and integrated experience across multiple points of contact, and infuse much-needed transparency into relationships that many customers currently suspect are one-sided."[11]

While many companies acknowledge that service is important, the majority still view these functions and departments as cost centers. As a result, they are frequently measured and managed around metrics that have everything to do with supposed efficiency and little to do with the delivery of value on an individual customer basis. A Genesys survey found that 85 percent of customers would stop doing business with a supplier after a negative customer service experience. This is similar to a study by Modalis Research Techologies among 1,000 online consumers, where 72 percent would no longer purchase from a supplier if they experienced poor customer service.[12] Many industries have found that high percentages of customers, often two out of three, or more, will defect if they have received poor service.

When suppliers use multiple channels for service—telephone, emails, and Web service—customers anticipate a benefit. It's supposed to reduce the "hassle factor" for customers as they try to navigate their way through the service maze. For suppliers that can effectively integrate these channels, the customer benefit (along with reduced cost for the supplier) is realized. For those that don't, it's often a further contributor to customer disaffection.

Essential to individualized service is in-depth data availability for each customer. The Genesys survey confirmed the frustration caused when service agents have incorrect or incomplete customer information. Getting passed from representative to representative before finding one that has the right data is a major cause of customer unhappiness with service experiences. Often, the insufficiency of customer information at the point of purchase and service experience, due to poor data integration, business intelligence, and customer analytics, is the principal cause of customer risk and loss.

---

[11] "Wake-Up Call: To Fix CRM, Fix the Customer Experience Now," *Bearing Point White Paper,* 2004.
[12] Bob Thompson, "Multi-Channel Service," *CRM Guru,* August 2003, pp. 4, 6.

No customer technology, irrespective of how advanced, can overcome a negative purchase or service experience. As customers are the first to tell suppliers: It's about benefits, not innovation. For companies to deliver differentiated, beneficial treatment, these processes must be both smooth and transparent to the customer.

The Experience Pantheon

There's a reason companies like Walt Disney, Ritz-Carlton, Nordstrom's, Land's End, Baptist Health Care, Enterprise Rent-a-Car, Chick Fil A, and Southwest Airlines are so frequently mentioned as leading the way in optimizing customer experience creation. It's because they focus on efficient delivery of tangible and intangible benefits, and making each encounter as positive as possible.

Southwest Airlines, particularly, stands out in an industry noted for commoditized experiences. For over thirty straight years, Southwest has attained earnings growth. For those unaware of the distinctive Southwest model, they fly short routes, attain scheduling and flight turnaround efficiencies by flying only one kind of plane—the Boeing 737—and offer no assigned seating, no first class, and no on-board meals. Their fares are among the lowest in the industry, with few restrictions; and they don't charge for making reservation changes. In other words, in comparison to other airlines, flying Southwest is uncomplicated and inexpensive.

Their "secret" is not just the low fares, reliable service, and on-time departure and arrival record. Staff make the real difference. They're cheerful, productive, and friendly. Why? Beyond just sharing the fruits of its profits with employees, the Southwest employee "attitude" is a combination of customer outreach and a light-handed company culture. Southwest hires for positive employee attitude and interpersonal skills, especially among service counter and on-board staff where it impacts individual customers, because they've long since determined what a difference it can make.

Customers absolutely require that the basics—on-time departure and arrival, as well as safety—be consistently delivered. That's where most airlines (try to) begin and end. Southwest does much more. Their positive experience differentiation, for example, might be a flight attendant leading all the passengers in a hearty rendition of "I've Been Working on the Railroad," telling jokes, conducting a raffle, or playing trivia games along with seatbelt fastening instruction. For the truly lucky passenger, there's even the opportunity to win a free drink for having the largest hole in his or her sock.

On the ground, the experience for passengers is just as unique. Southwest has been known to celebrate events by doing fun things for passengers while they are in the gate area. One such example was when, to recognize a milestone, neck massages were given to weary Southwest travelers by roving masseurs in Houston's Hobby Airport. When Southwest entered the Philadelphia market, they put up a row of ten seats taken from the recently demolished Veteran's Stadium at their gates; and they arranged with Krispy Kreme to build a franchise store just opposite the Southwest gates. This kind of customer-focused innovation demonstrates that the airline is passenger friendly.

The company accepts only about three percent of employment applicants, irrespective of position, and frequent passengers are often recruited to serve as employee selection panelists along with company HR professionals. Southwest has so perennially been selected to *Fortune* magazine's list of "100 Best Companies To Work For In America" that it no longer submits its name for consideration. Making the emotional connection between customers and employees, and intertwining it with no-frills effectiveness and efficiency, make all the difference.

T. Scott Gross, the customer service expert responsible for many of Southwest's approaches to staff training, calls the experience the airline delivers "random acts of delight." Passengers get, as much as possible, all the positive elements of a supplier relationship and none of the negatives associated with other airlines.

Enhancing the Online Experience

The online communication and commerce channel has become critical to the success of companies in many industries, including financial services, entertainment, insurance, airlines, automotive, hospitality, and health care. Interestingly and importantly, Forrester Research sees the proportion of all customer retail transactions initiated on the Internet doubling to one-fifth by 2005.[13] When this is coupled with the Jupiter finding that customers who are comfortable with multiple purchase channels (stores, Internet sites, television shopping, and print catalogs) will spend up to 30 percent more than customers who prefer to use only one channel, improving the experiences through all channels takes on great significance.[14]

Online customer experience management is particularly challenging. Despite the speed associated with high-speed DSL and cable Internet access, site and purchase abandonment rates continue to increase. This is due to multiple factors: number of customers on a site at any given time (web traffic); difficulty of navigation page to

---

[13] Cliff Conneighton, "It's All About the Customer Experience," www.destinationcrm.com, May 3, 2004.

[14] Michael Pastore, "Customer Behavior Continues to Mystify Some Businesses," *Cyber Atlas,* July 16, 2001.

page; number of graphics and fancy, slow-loading features (server processing); request for personal customer information; and multipage purchasing/checkout transaction requirements. Customers, in sum, have become frustrated with the lack of online presentation relevance of products and services, the inability of search features to provide desired answers and resources, and the failure of many businesses to deliver effective online customer service.

In a study conducted by Zona Research for Keynote, an online experience consulting organization, they saw the rate of user delay continuing to increase over time, with the projected loss in revenue at more than $25 billion through abandoned orders.[15] With the rate of e-commerce site abandonment rate so high, improving the online experience is clearly a priority.

Anything that inhibits a customer or prospect's ability to navigate from page to page is perceived as delay. And Internet customers have shown themselves to have very little patience. In interpreting the impact of transmission errors and navigation errors on abandonment rate, some web site performance analysts have quoted the "eight second rule." In other words, researchers have determined that most online consumers will give the site, once a link is clicked, an average maximum time of eight seconds before abandonment.

Specialty consulting organizations like the Customer Respect Group (CRG) have identified the factors that contribute to a relevant, rewarding online experience. In a recent survey they grouped these as *simplicity, attitude, transparency, responsiveness, principles,* and *privacy.*[16]

1. *Simplicity* is really about ease of navigation. Site visitors have to absorb a great deal of information and then make choices. Because the online shopper's attention span is notoriously short, suppliers have to make it as easy as possible for customers to locate key pieces of information, get product or service information, and move from page to page.
2. *Attitude* is about how customer focused the site is. Is the site loaded with unneeded material, or are the messages—particularly those in which customers will find relevance and value—and content presented in a crisp, concise, and attention-retaining manner?
3. *Transparency* refers to the openness and honesty of the supplier's policies. For instance, CRG learned that up to two-thirds of online customers could potentially abandon a site if they don't trust how the supplier plans to use their personal data. This should be made very clear to

---

[15] "The Need for Speed II," *Zona Market Bulletin,* April 2001.
[16] "About Us—What Is Customer Respect?" www.customerrespect.com, 2005.

customers so, if the supplier wants to continue personalized messaging, customers should have the flexibility to "opt-out" of receiving this kind of communication, and be assured that the supplier will respect that decision. This also covers the site's privacy policy, so the site should make clear how information is being collected and used.

4. *Responsiveness* is the speed and thoroughness of follow-up to customer online inquiries. Too often, companies either discourage communication or make a contact point difficult to locate on the site. In fact, CRG found that an average of 30 percent of all sites do not respond at all to questions posed on their sites! Customers should be encouraged to communicate with the company's service staff, to have questions answered and problems resolved. In an increasing number of retail and service sites, most prominently organizations such as eBay and Amazon, responsiveness also includes the ability of customers and other visitors to communicate with each other. Often, this capability is very positively perceived by customers and has the added benefit of relieving some service costs by providing a forum for question and problem resolution, without having Customer Service directly involved.

5. *Principles,* for these purposes, are the way a site values and respects the customer data it collects. As the well-publicized case of data sharing by DoubleClick a few years ago certainly affirmed, providing customer data to others without their consent is completely unacceptable. Although there are companies still doing this, they do so at peril of their very existence. Data sharing practices should be clearly explained to customers.

6. *Privacy* is very straightforward. If customers are reticent and conservative about providing suppliers with personal information offline, online provision of personal data borders on the paranoid. CRG has determined that 82 percent of Internet users decline to provide personal information, principally because little explanation is given about why such individual details are requested.

Once online customers pass these areas of proactive treatment and individual respect, CRG strongly advises that sites make certain all messaging and confirmatory communication is as personalized as possible. This helps to establish the overall tone, and equity, represented by the site. CRG encourages, for instance, the use of autoresponders. Autoresponders, still used by a minority of Internet sites, are an inexpensive way of bouncing back to a request for a report, further information, specifications, etc. with an automated e-mail. It definitely represents responsiveness to both prospects and customers.

One of the emerging factors companies need to be aware of when looking at multiple customer support and response channels is integration. Specifically, as a result of Voice Over Internet Protocol (VoIP), the lines between a phone customer and an Internet customer have increasingly begun to blur and merge. One estimate, determined by Miercom, a network communication consultancy, projects that telephone calls placed over IP networks will increase to 30 percent of all calls within just a few years. Whether customers are using regular telephone, VoIP telephone, or a VoIP connection on their computer, all connects would be integrated to the Internet. As a result, customer service will be able to apply the same database for all inbound and outbound channels. This will have dramatic impact on customers' service experience, it is felt, in that suppliers will be able to focus resources, and provide higher quality service, around a single platform.

A Concluding Note

Strategic differentiation and customer-perceived value are the cornerstones of customer divisibility and creation of advocacy. Customer experiences are critical; however, they cannot be executed without the right messages. As observed by pharmaceutical executive Michael Lam: "The competition for mindshare—customers' time and attention—is ferocious. Merely locating them won't do. Message must match target and immediately connect. If content, tone, timing, and form are not attuned to customers' emotions and habits of mind, they are unlikely to notice, much less respond."[17]

---

[17] Michael D. Lam, "Psychographic Demonstration: Segmentation Studies Prepare to Prove Their Worth," *Pharmaceutical Executive,* January 1, 2004.

5

TARGETING MESSAGES AND MANAGING EXPERIENCES

PART II: BE MINDFUL OF THE CUSTOMER LIFE CYCLE

What Is the Customer Life Cycle?

Most companies don't look at the complete spectrum of a customer's life as a part of having a single, integrated view of customers across the organization. Just as relatively few companies have developed algorithms and processes for estimating lifetime customer revenue value, so also few companies look at how processes and programs, and especially messaging, have to be modified depending on the customer's life stage. They recognize its importance, such as in a recent Forrester Research study showing that senior executives at 92 percent of companies studied saw it as critical or very important; but they just don't do it. In that same study, only 2 percent of executives felt that their companies had achieved a single, enterprise-wide, customer perspective.

Organizations in industries like banking, telecom, and automotive, for instance, are still rather notorious for devoting large proportions of their marketing budgets to new customer conquest, and then treating customers pretty passively once in the fold. Professor Adrian Payne of Cranfield Institute in the U.K. has noted, for instance, that 80 percent of companies overspend on customer acquisition at the expense of customer retention; and, of course, very few consider the profitability associated with winback.[1]

More recently, we've witnessed the furious and expensive prospecting for new customers among e-commerce companies, only to lose them, through poor follow-up and service, at an almost equally rapid pace. Research companies like Jupiter and Forrester have noted how attraction activity contrasts with the low-level service and nondifferentiated messaging these customers tend to receive after coming on-board. Chartered Institute of Marketing, the UK's version of the American Marketing Association, conducted a study in which it was noted that under 20 percent of Internet customers in their study felt that messaging personalization was important to them, a technique that some marketers believe is "the

---

[1] Adrian Payne, *The Handbook of CRM* (Amsterdam: Elsevier, 2005), p. 147.

answer" in relationship marketing.[2] These are clear communication breakdowns, and missed opportunities for targeted messaging, as customers move through their life stages.

We view customer management as a never-ending process that embraces mutually beneficial and value-producing relationships for all customers—i.e., past, present and potential, and internal, intermediate and external—creating not only enticements to become customers, but also barriers to exit or churn. Most particularly, it makes perfect sense that companies have either sub programs or elements in their overall customer management activity plan that address each customer's life stage. As we see them, there are three fundamental phases of a complete customer life cycle: 1) *Targeting/Acquisition,* 2) *Retention/Loyalty,* 3) and *Loss/WinBack*. Obviously, there will be different messaging imperatives at each phase. In *Acquisition*, the goal is to target and attract high-value prospects and turn them into first-time customers, so the messaging will center around identifying superior value and benefit, especially relative to suppliers currently used. In *Retention*, and the leveraging of loyalty behavior, messaging is aimed at strengthening the relationship by increasing value; and, if good customers are identified as being at risk, stabilizing the relationship. If customers are lost, *WinBack* messages are focused on redefining value and rebuilding trust in the relationship. Of course, reasons for defection must first be determined here so that contra-messaging can be built around this insight This translates to seven stages of a customer's life with a supplier:

- *Suspect,* or early stage supplier consideration; get attention/create awareness
- *Prospect (Active/Developmental),* or defined customer interest and opportunity, bring suspect into sphere of influence
- *First-Purchase Customer (New/Recovered),* the initial opportunity to demonstrate value and establish the basis for a relationship
- *Retained/Loyal Customer,* or one who has demonstrated interest in being cross-sold, upsold, providing information when asked, and referring others
- *At-Risk Customer (Attrition),* where there is some breakdown in perceived value and loyalty behavior
- *Defected/Lost Customer,* or the stage where purchase and relationship has ceased
- *Recovered/Won-Back Customer,* or situation where value and trust have been re-established, at least to the extent of resumed purchase

---

[2] Yvonne Bailey and Hank Stroll, "SWOT Team: The Hope, Glory, and Folly of CRM," www.marketingprofs.com, January 27, 2004.

Customers have unique needs at each stage, so the messaging must be unique as well. For example, first-time buyers will often have questions or issues related to their start-up or installation that longer-term customers wouldn't. Initial purchases are an important, impression-forming time for customers. Promises made during the prospect stage will be seen as kept, or not; and proper messaging helps reinforce the impressions suppliers hope to create. If the first interactions with a supplier are disappointing because a marketing brochure created expectations that were not met, or because a sales representative "oversold" a product or service, the likelihood of that customer's continuing business may be compromised. At the very least, the messaging misalignment with transactional reality may require additional service or support resources to retain that customer.

Information gathered from customers at each stage, either through secondary sources or directly through qualitative and quantitative research, will also help to develop messaging strategies. Service and sales records, complaints, purchase histories—all of these are key data resources in understanding customer needs. To be successful customer life cycle managers, though, companies have to go beyond discernment of customer needs. They must be sensitive to signals and triggers that indicate when a new stage is likely to occur. In addition to getting feedback on brand perceptions—image, quality, relationships, competitive strengths and weaknesses, etc.—at the prospect stage, companies should also take pains to determine why prospects may be lost. In other words, identification of real reasons for prospects declining to make an initial purchase can be converted to a learning opportunity that will make future prospect messaging more effective.

Once a new customer has begun to have transactional experiences, companies may reduce the level of relationship and involvement, going on "cruise control" and allowing customers to revert to a mindset of again viewing the supplier relative to competition. Failure to dialogue and target messaging at this stage often results in the supplier not understanding that the criteria for repurchase are, typically, different than prospect and initial purchase motivation.

As with prospects, if a supplier can discern when a first-time customer shows signs of again becoming a "shopper," messaging and services can be targeted to stabilize the relationship. Many executives, especially in high-churn industries like cable and cellular, believe that the principal reasons for shopping behavior can be ascribed to poor service, product/service quality issues, or price; however, these are often smoke screen issues, masking the real causes of turnover. Because long-term value in these industries typically isn't emphasized, and viral marketing approaches—super-attractive introductory rates, and even free services and products such as high-tech phones—may be effective at luring new customers, but not at keeping them (and even supportive of postpurchase shopping behavior), it becomes imperative that companies identify the patterns of attrition leading to loss. Organizations like T-Mobile—which, with 50 million customers worldwide, is the second largest international mobile operator—have learned from customers that supplier choice or switching doesn't occur because of products, as customers assume that all competitors have similar products. So the company focuses on customer-centricity, brand image, service, and communication.

T-Mobile keys on managing both acquisition and retention. They've determined that their expected customer lifetime is between 30 and 50 months, and they segment customers based on need, usage, and often contract life stage as well; and they frequently contact customers according to where they are in the contract period. T-Mobile doesn't, however, appear to expend much energy or budget on creating focused messaging for former customers, and this is a missed opportunity.

For the telecom industry, targeted messaging for former customers would appear to be an extremely attractive opportunity. On an overall customer segment basis, for example, the prepaid customer base, which was once a niche market but has become a core business, is both growing faster, and is larger than, postpaid (Chorleywood, a U.K. consulting company, predicts that prepaid market share will reach 60 percent in 2005). It's been determined that, though prepaid and postpaid customers appear to have the same overall service needs and requirements, the average annual prepaid churn rate is 40 percent higher than postpaid (42 percent vs. 30 percent).[3]

Prepaid user characteristics are many and varied (SME/Large Businesses, Students, Children and Youths, Elderly, Ethnic Groups, Cultural Groups, Business Travelers, Professionals, Seasonal Usage, etc.), so there's a great deal of divisibility at play. These users, further, tend to be more transient, more anonymous, more price sensitive, and less willing to be desirous of a relationship with their supplier, so there are multiple challenges to retaining them.

The life cycle experiences of prepaid customers, as they see them, tend to be those of second-class citizens. There are a perceived lack of service and more restricted roaming. As this group of customers matures, telecom will need their input to develop targeted messaging, services, and features (multiple recharge methods, international roaming, GPRS, self-care tools to check balances and obtain services, offer advanced information capabilities, etc.). In other words, messaging must convey a positive differentiation in service and performance, as well as create a form of relationship between customer and operator. This begins with understanding why these customers have churned at such high rates.

---

[3] "Global Mobile Prepaid Strategies," *Chorleywood Industry Report*, June 1, 2001.

To design messaging for helping to recover lost customers, these customers must be debriefed. Company records may indicate that a customer has not purchased for weeks, months, or even years; however, time of last purchase may have little to do with how former customers see themselves. For some, the period may be very short. For others, they may see their cessation of purchase as a hiatus rather than a defection. This latter situation showed up in research among formerly very active purchasers from a major TV shopping channel. The channel identified multipurchase customers who hadn't bought from them in a year or more as defectors; however, the majority of these customers saw themselves as merely taking a respite from active buying. At the same time, they provided direction for targeted future messaging for their own reactivation.

One of the fundamental premises of this book is that companies are only as successful as their level, and application, of customer insight. This premise certainly applies to customer management at each life stage. Again, this is especially important in understanding the reasons for diminished purchases and depends as much on good profiling and record-keeping as learning obtainable from customers. If companies can identify the point at which shopping begins among active customers, and discern the reasons for this attrition behavior, proactive and prescriptive communication can quickly and effectively take place. The following model of customer life stage management will graphically demonstrate how companies can think of cycles and can also point the way for the types of information required for strategic message development:

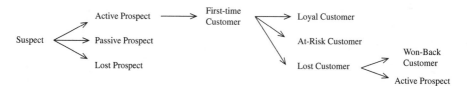

Figure 5.1 Customer Life Cycle Management

A Real-World Fable of Customer Life Cycle

Here's how the life stages work. Taking, as an example, a town with two bakeries, the Suspect stage would begin when a potential customer first desires baked goods. That desire may come on its own, or it may have been encouraged or stimulated by one or both of the bakeries advertising/promoting their wares. The potential customer then becomes a Prospect, going through a screening process, sorting through perceptions of each bakery's image and reputation, array and quality of desired products and services, awareness of prices, and other information, such as referrals, advertising, or promotional materials. The Prospect is considered either Active or Developmental, depending on how strong the purchase desire for baked goods is at this stage.

Then the final bakery selection is made, and the Prospect becomes a New Customer. The bakery's complete value proposition—personalized service and communication, product quality and range, and price, to cite a few of the key elements—creates a level of emotional commitment within the customer. If that commitment is strong enough, the New Customer will make repeat purchases over time and become a Retained/Loyal Customer. Frequency and volume of purchase will mark the customer's long-term value to the bakery.

If any negative perception develops regarding an important aspect of value—product quality, price, communication, or service—the New Customer or the Retained/Loyal Customer will enter an attrition mode and become an At-Risk Customer. This is where the bakery should be most aware of customer perceptions, because the undermining of perceived value is the strongest contributor to exit or churn. It is also where targeted messaging may be the most critical, because communication of sufficient benefit to stay as a customer, what we sometimes call "barriers to exit," is particularly important at this stage.

Should the customer's problems or complaints with the chosen baker not be resolved, or if the problems or complaints become stronger than the benefits provided, then the customer is Lost, or Defected, most likely to the other bakery in town, if the desire for baked goods is still strong.

Assuming the bakery is like most companies, once the customer has been Lost, rather minimal resources or effort will be devoted to either understanding the reasons for the customer's exit or winning the customer back. Let's be positive, though. Let's say the bakery *does* know the customer on a one-to-one basis, *does* make an effort to know why the customer left, *does* have a process to win the customer back, and *does* succeed in getting the customer to return. Then the customer could be considered Recovered or Won-Back. During this win-back process, the customer might be viewed as a Prospect again, especially if the value proposition needs to be completely re-expressed. Once again, messaging takes center stage, as the bakery shores up the value proposition, reassuring the customer that the trust, again invested, will not be misplaced. Most bakeries, again like most companies, typically set their customer management goals around increased spending and purchase frequency, and to increased profitability and market share. They do this by offering something of presumed positive value so that the customer will have a stronger emotional relationship and identification with the products and the bakery itself. But that's where the majority of these programs begin and end. They tend to be rather one-dimensional.

Customer management programs should also function as referral vehicles to attract new customers. This can happen in two ways. The New Customer or the Retained/Loyal Customer will offer positive word-of-mouth to Suspects and Prospects, i.e., friends, colleagues, and relatives. The other way is that the bakery's products or services are so strong and attractive that noncustomers learn of it and are drawn in. Their experiences, assuming they're positive, then serve to repeat this process.

How does the bakery's program respond when the customer becomes At-Risk? If it's an organic program, the bakery will have collected and interpreted insights during its customers' earlier life stages. If service or product problems surface, the bakery should be able to have intensified contact and communication with these customers to stabilize the bond and commitment. The bakery may also offer some type of value incentive to the At-Risk customer to help re-establish the relationship.

Relationship dynamics, especially when the customer has been Lost or Defected, are quite different than when the customer is active. At the point of exit, the customer has become emotionally detached from the bakery. There is no longer sufficient value in product or service for the customer to remain. Especially if the customer has had high volume and/or frequent purchase activity, once the customer has been identified as Lost, the bakery has to do two things: 1) find out why the customer has left, and 2) have techniques and processes in place to recover the customer. If the root cause of departure has been a product or service issue, restating the value proposition and offering some "please come back" incentives may be enough to re-establish the relationship. If the customer has moved, had a lifestyle change (such as going on a diet), or been lured away by lower prices, any recovery effort will probably not be worthwhile or successful. If won back, the customer is Recovered. Companies' customer management programs tend to focus principally on attracting new customers or rewarding customers who are either new or who spend a lot or spend frequently, mostly in the short term. That's fine and completely appropriate, but it makes secondary many customer groups and life stages that may offer attractive revenue and profit opportunity. It may, as well, completely bypass some customer groups—notably those who are At-Risk or Defected.

Several centuries ago, Takeda Shingen, a samurai general in medieval Japan, wrote: "A person with deep far-sightedness will survey both the beginning and the end of a situation, and continually consider its every facet as important." The same kind of thinking should be applied to messaging and customer life stages. Every life stage represents attractive potential revenue and profit, as well as learning that affects the other stages. Smart companies should not miss the opportunity to build (or rebuild) customer relationships, irrespective of stage.

What Is the Role of Customer Life Cycle and Messaging in Customer Divisibility?

Hewlett-Packard is definitely a company that addresses customers on both a divisible and life cycle basis, so their approaches will help us understand how life cycle, media, and targeted messaging work in conjunction within a divisibility framework.

HP, of course, markets many products, about 100 in all, each supported by product group teams. The company's customer communication, whether by direct mail or email, was conducted without any centralized understanding of messaging product/service needs. What HP wanted was a consolidated email marketing program, based on individual customer requirements. Further, the marketing program had to gather and interpret customer data based on life cycle stage, product by product.

Since research indicated that most customers wanted support communication rather than marketing information, HP worked with an outside specialist software company to help develop a newsletter that would contain microsegmented, even personalized, messages based on each customer's product ownership and Internet browsing behavior. The objectives were several: conserve marketing, promotional, and advertising budget; reduce customer service expenses; increase customer loyalty behavior across HP product line.

When customers register for the newsletter after purchasing an HP product, they identify which HP product(s) they have, and how long each has been owned. Products identified are linked to specific HP web site content pages through the newsletter. Over time—usually about six months or so—their browsing activity can be matched to the products owned and length of ownership, enabling divisible messaging to be custom- prepared. Divisibility comes into play because, of the array of products offered by HP, a customer may only have a PC, or a printer, notebook, handheld device, digital camera, monitor, or projector; and it might be new or an older model, simple or with more features; or a customer might have more than one HP product, each with a different age and array of features. Further, their applications can vary according to business size and type. About two-thirds are SMEs and the rest are companies with larger staffs. The personalization "engine" draws this information from HP's content and customer profiles, and this facilitates the sending of 50,000 to 100,000 different content combinations every month to more than a half million companies. At least half of the messaging is specific to customer and product life cycle at the time the newsletter is sent, and sequenced according to the date of product purchase. Customers receive messages that are tailored to them, including usage tips (varying with product age and sophistication), assistance with specific business challenges, detail on new HP products, and encouragement to continue purchasing from HP—all of which is accomplished with no overlap from other product groups. So one customer, say a purchasing manager from a large company, will learn about a reduced-price program on a product category. The CFO for a small company would receive information on how to improve networking capabilities. An architect might receive specialized links to information on what others in his field are doing with HP equipment. And, further, the messaging will be even more precisely targeted according to the business specifics and HP products owned, and other customer profile details.

Since 2002, when HP began divisible and life cycle targeted messaging through its email newsletter, they have saved close to $4 million in annual marketing costs. Another $4 million was saved in customer support, because the newsletter encouraged customers to make online inquiries rather than telephone. (Note: HP found that they needed to spend only 3 to 8 cents per online inquiry, rather than $15 for a telephone service call.)

HP has also achieved some impressive revenue results since making the move to target messaging on a divisible customer basis. They've generated more than $20 million per month from their email customer contact lists as a result of this program.

How Are Customer Life Cycle, Divisibility, and Messaging Applied to Specific "Touch" Processes?

It's fair to say that taking a life cycle approach to customer management, addressing customers on a divisible basis, and looking at successful process outcomes can be both highly correlated and highly effective. Companies want practical solutions and applications for these concepts. Fortunately, they're available, economical, and user-friendly. Let's look at how various touch points, and the messaging inherent in each, will help to optimize loyalty behavior at all of the customer life stages. Beginning at the Prospect to New Customer stages of a product or service—we'll use an ISP as the example here—companies can use inbound sales and service to handle order requests and answer questions from prospective customers. Questions might include billing, service features, software installation, and other start-up inquiries. Often, the objective here is to make the Q&A and ordering process as seamless and painless as possible; and customized messaging, perhaps through direct mail or follow-up phone calls, can reinforce positive brand equity created during the critical transition from Prospect to New Customer. Also, if there were situations where Prospects had received information, and even start-up ISP software, but had not yet enrolled in the service, customer service could personally follow up with them, asking if they had questions and educating the prospective customer.

If considered appropriate and helpful in moving the prospect to new customer status, targeted informational materials could also be sent.

Once the prospect had become a customer, customer service could conduct outbound "welcome" calls, conveying information based on any issues/questions raised at the prospect stage. Such calls, and support materials and messaging sent in print form, would reinforce the new customer's purchase decision and help leverage continued usage, build brand equity, increase service usage by explaining benefits, upsell/cross-sell to related services, and obtain early experience insight.

Inbound customer support, as the months of usage continues, answers technical and billing questions, as or if they arise. Continuity communication is done on an outbound personal call and direct response basis. Here again, the messaging can be customized based on information in the customer's profile, which covers services purchased, service contact records, and specific questions, etc.

If ISP customers contact the company wishing to cancel their service, a not infrequent situation for many Web, cable, and wireless companies, they may be routed to special customer "save" groups. These groups are charged with the goal of minimizing cancellation, and are often electronically supported with immediate access to each customer's entire purchase profile and contact record, perhaps even showing results to research questions, and response to specific promotions. Customer service representatives in these units frequently receive special training in save and stabilization techniques, asking probing questions to identify building or "trigger" issues that may have prompted the desire to cancel; and they are also schooled in personalized scripting, pointing customers to positive service features and benefits. Finally, if necessary, representatives may be empowered to offer billing adjustments or other continued purchase incentives.

When customers churn, customer service is often the first line of targeted messaging and inquiry, calling former customers to identify their reasons for leaving, re-establishing the relationship, and encouraging them to come back. Based on individual customers' profiles and service contact history, representatives customize dialogue around specific features, benefits, and program elements. Based on an initial contact, customer service staff can also help identify messaging frequency and content most likely to recover that specific customer. This information can also be aggregated for overall marketing communication planning.

While the results of such personalized efforts cannot be accurately forecast, and will vary considerably industry to industry, it isn't at all unusual to see prospect conversion to new customer lift rates of 20 to 40 percent, over control groups; cancellation reduction rates (during the first year as a customer) of 15 to 25 percent;

save/stabilization rates of 30 to 80 percent; and recovery/re-enrollment rates of 20 to 80 percent. Certainly, targeted messaging, at each life stage, has proven its economic worth as a loyalty-leveraging tool.

Right Customer, Right Process, Right Messaging—Optimum Life Cycle Management in an Unlikely Place

One of the most obvious examples of likely continued shopping behavior after having become a customer is in the automotive industry, where even the companies most adept at creating repeat brand purchase can only manage rates of 50 to 60 percent. The average U.S. owner buys a new car every two to three years; and there's a strong tendency among dealerships, once a prospect becomes an owner, to more or less forget about them, intermittently sending them nonpersonalized marketing literature or making generic missionary calls.

For those dealerships that truly understand the value of the customer experience, and the value of managing the relationship, including message targeting and continuity, the results are often quite different. Price Auto Group, comprised of several auto dealerships located in two states, and headquartered in New Castle, Delaware, is not only an innovator in prospecting and sales to new customers but in retaining existing customers and leveraging referrals from them as well.

At the prospect stage, they proactively work to understand each dealership's market, looking on a household basis at the presence and number of children, income, and lifestyle of current customers in the area. This enables them to customize the marketing program, targeting to the most desirable customers. Price is looking for households with similar profiles to their customers, first marketing to create awareness, closely tracking prospects who visit the dealerships in terms of readiness to buy, response to messaging, etc. They also actively follow up on lost sales.

Price has become a proponent of the leveraging power of consistent, well-managed processes at each customer life stage, and this begins with the sales experience. New customer research has taught them, for example, that customers want streamlined sales processes and that they dislike the uncomfortable back-and-forth of negotiating. So their messaging at the time of sale is aimed at creating an emotional bond with the sales rep and the dealership. They've found, for instance, that when the best price is offered up front, when communication is customized to the needs of each customer, when the purchase transaction time can be held at two hours or less, when the financing portion of the transaction can be held to under 25 minutes, the loyalty effects are staggering. Of the 75 percent of their customers who purchase in under two hours, 100 percent plan to repurchase from them, 97 percent plan to service with them, and 67 percent have already referred other prospective customers.

After the sale, tight customer management continues. Price understands that postpurchase value can be sustained throughout the ownership experience, so they have created an individualized customer follow-up and messaging program. This includes personal contact; postcards announcing customized, special offers; and material sent through their Business Development Center (BDC). Distinctive benefits that have come from debriefing service customers include overnight loaner cars; mobile service for light repairs; extended service hours; a service menu option that allows for fast write-up, quick problem or complaint resolution; and ongoing personal, customized follow-up and reinforcement through the BDC.

When this approach to combined benefit provision and customized messaging went into effect, Price experienced a 77 percent increase in service visits. They also learned that, through the contact and value created in the acts of service, and by increasing the frequency of service visits, they could leverage a repurchase mindset. If they do experience service visit declines or churn, Price's reconnection approach is to first send out a "Talking Wrenches" direct mail piece restating their service value proposition, and offering a free diagnostic check-up and oil change (as an initial incentive, which expires 30 days from mail receipt) as well as a free wheel balance and tire rotation, and another oil change (as a second incentive, to be used after the first incentive, and up to 90 days after receiving the mailing). This mailing is then followed up with a personal call to reopen the lines of communication, invite these customers back, and even turn them into referral sources.

Retail Customer Life Cycle Management

The leading-edge customer divisibility approaches of Gary Hawkins, CEO of specialty supermarket Green Hills Farms, will be more fully explored in Chapter Eight; however, his opinions on customer life cycle are introduced here to demonstrate that this concept can be applied to companies of any size. Customer life cycle, Hawkins has found, is a critical differentiator for successful companies, because it enables them to understand the ebbs and flows of customers into, through, and out of (and potentially back to) the base.[4] For instance, using this understanding of customer movement, they found that nearly half of their new customers did not make a second purchase and that, after a year, only one-quarter of these new buyers—i.e., people new to their loyalty program—were still active customers. While Green Hills worked to provide immediate value to these new

---

[4] Gary E. Hawkins, "The Best Little Grocery Store in America: Competing Through Customer Knowledge," *Retailing Issues Letter,* Spring 2003, p. 5.

customers such as savings certificates and coupons for free samples, this only increased the retention levels by another 10 percent.

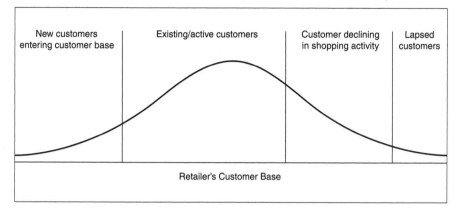

Figure 5.2 The Customer Life Cycle
Source: Gary E. Hawkins, "The Best Little Grocery Store in America: Competing Through Customer Knowledge," *Retailing Issues Letter* (Center for Retailing Studies, Texas A&M University) vol. 15, no. 2 (Spring 2003), p. 4.

Continuing competitive pressure, and a weak economy in their market, prompted their move to a more upscale repositioning. This was supported by a deeper understanding of their customer base, principally a thorough assessment of customer lifetime value. For instance, over a five-year period, Green Hills discovered that the top 10 percent of spenders represented almost two-thirds of their sales during that same period. Over the course of their purchasing lifetime, Green Hills' best customers may spend several hundred thousand dollars with the supermarket. New customers are those identified as joining their loyalty program for the first time. Hawkins makes certain that these customers are engaged immediately, providing them with an attractive brochure explaining the products and services of the store, hours of operation, etc. They are given a savings certificate allowing them to benefit from the first shopping experience onward, and a special, time-sensitive new customer offer that gives them a $30 gift certificate if they spend $300 in the first six weeks. This is accompanied by direct mail messaging, welcoming them to Green Hills Farms, describing the store's unique products, and providing them with a coupon for free samples of selected products. With this approach to new customers, as Hawkins explains, Green Hills has been able to retain 10 percent more new customers after a year than before they went to a customer life cycle approach.

Customer life cycle, as a result, is at the center of Green Hills Farms' successful methods of applying customer divisibility concepts, something any company, of any size or industry, can emulate.

6

Targeting Messages and Managing Experiences

Part III: How Committed and Engaged Are Each of Your Customers? Better Find Out—Fast!

Question: What Is True "Customer Commitment" . . . and How Can It Be Attained?

Many companies have recognized a need to be committed to their customers. Banks, airlines, wireless telecoms, retailers, insurance companies, realtors, utilities, business-to-business companies, and even government agencies feel compelled to express the strength of their commitment and allegiance, particularly in areas of service. Some companies even build commitment into their organizational vision and values statements. Such articulations have become pretty standard fare. US Airways, for example, carries the following explanation and set of customer commitments on its web site:

> This document, entitled Our Customer Commitment, outlines our Commitments to you when traveling with us. At the same time, it provides us with a set of focused principles that guide our business, shape our policies, and influence our decisions that directly affect you and your fellow travelers. Additionally, through monitoring, internal audits and customer surveys, we are constantly measuring ourselves to ensure that we are living up to these Commitments every time you fly.
>
> As a result of these Commitments, we now have programs in place to:
>
> 1. Offer you the lowest fare for which you are eligible
> 2. Give you accurate, timely information on flight delays or cancellations
> 3. Provide on-time baggage delivery
> 4. Increase the baggage liability limit
> 5. Permit you to cancel a purchased ticket within 24 hours without penalty
> 6. Make prompt refunds
> 7. Clearly disclose policies for customers with special needs
> 8. Make you as comfortable as possible during long on-board delays
> 9. Supply basic information and policies about "oversold" flights
> 10. Furnish details about our frequent flyer program

11. Require the same quality of service from our US Airways Express partners

12. Respond promptly to your complaints or requests for information[1]

These 12 statements are then followed-up with detailed explanations. Is this, however, what makes customers committed to US Airways? Are statements of commitment true differentiators of perceived benefit and value, generating customer loyalty and engagement, or are they just expected basics of performance?

Results of study after study have shown that loyalty will not be earned by promising what suppliers *believe* customers want but rather by understanding what they absolutely value in the relationship and experience. A 2003 Walker Information research project found that, for retailers, despite the high incidence of loyalty programs—cards, coupons, credit points, etc.—and whether customers were rewarded on when, what, how much, and the channel from which they purchased, only 45 percent of customers were truly loyal, meaning that over half were not.[2]

Another large segment of customers report themselves as "trapped," or reluctant, using that retailer more out of habit than convenience or specific intent. If a competitor enters the scene and offers a more attractive alternative, many of these trapped customers become high risk; and the Walker study found that 12 percent, or one in eight shoppers, is at strong risk and may defect.

Additionally, Walker found that 83 percent of customers thought their retailer was easy to do business with. Isn't that what companies like US Airways are trying to achieve with their statements of customer commitment? But how about what customers think of how well the company cares for them as a customer? Only 68 percent rate the company as customer focused in this way.

One of the reasons that some advanced companies, including retailers, have been successful at creating and sustaining high levels of customer loyalty and advocacy is that they center their information gathering and application in areas of need that are important to customers. In retail purchase situations, these are transactional components such as ease of locating products and check out time. The Walker study found that, while high percentages of customers were pleased with the capabilities of sales and service representatives and the assortment of

---

[1] US Airways Customer Commitment.
[2] Jeffrey Marr, "Retail Service, Consumer Loyalty, and Market Share," *Stakeholder Power*, October 2003 (special ed.).

products offered in retail settings, only 59 percent were positive about the ease of locating products. A bigger concern is check-out time, because only 55 percent were positive about it.

In a study by the Food Marketing Institute, it was found that 20 percent of food shopping trips involve stores other than supermarkets. Commenting on these results, Bill McEwan, president and CEO of Sobeys, Inc., a Canadian supermarket chain, said: "Consumers have their own agendas. More and more, those agendas don't align with ours."[3]

Preliminary results of the study indicate that retailers don't know enough about their shoppers to provide what they want and need. For example, shoppers don't give high priority to convenient locations or extended hours of operation anymore, yet grocers still emphasize those features in marketing campaigns. "We have to be in the business of building stores that connect with the real needs of the people who can choose to, or choose not to, shop with us," said McEwan. Many retailers look to loyalty programs as a surrogate, or agent, for creating perceived value; and it's absolutely true that they have some effect. These programs are specifically designed to attract new customers and retain and reward existing, high-spending customers. The retail portion of a recent Maritz study (gauging attitudes and behaviors of retail, hotel, airline, credit card, and restaurant loyalty program members) found that, while close to half of the rewards program participants interviewed said that the programs have some influence on where they spend their retail dollars, and many belonged to multiple programs, almost 40 percent have never redeemed rewards earned from the programs they had been enrolled in the longest.[4] Further, the study found that members were not feeling engaged at all points of contact, what Maritz saw as the programs lacking "continuity of outreach." In other words, there was an insufficiency of connection that results in less than optimal customer loyalty behavior. Call it laziness, call it the effect of competition, call it a perceived sameness in program components. The results are the same. Clearly, these kinds of disconnects between customer requirement and supplier response erode trust and commitment.

---

[3] "FMI Study Shows Shoppers Depend Less and Less on Supermarkets," www.colloquy.com, February 6, 2004.
[4] Maritz Loyalty Marketing, "Retail Rewards Programs Lack Consumer Outreach" (news release, March 2, 2004).

Answer: Commitment Is About Attitude, Perceived Performance and Value, Emotional Attachment and Engagement, and Resultant Motivations of Behavior

In their 1994 white paper "Customer Loyalty: Toward an Integrated Conceptual Framework," academics Alan S. Dick and Kunal Basu examined how attachment was a prerequisite for loyalty and that the attachment a customer feels toward a supplier, product, or service is driven by 1) the level, or degree, of preference and desirability (the extent of the customer's conviction about the product or service) and 2) the amount of strategic, positive perceived differentiation offered (how significantly the customer distinguishes the product or service from alternatives).[5]

Dick and Basu went on to demonstrate how, after attachment, the second factor that determines a customer's loyalty toward a product or service is repeat, largely voluntary transactional activity. They concluded that four distinct types of loyalty emerge when low and high attachments are cross-classified with high and low repeat purchase patterns: *Premium Loyalty* (high attachment, high repeat purchase), *Inertia Loyalty* (low relative attachment and high repeat purchase), *Latent Loyalty* (high relative attachment and low repeat purchase), and *No Loyalty* (low relative attachment and low repeat purchase).

We can conclude that "true loyalty," i.e., high attachment and commitment, must have both perceived value and an emotional component. While the emotional, or intangible, components of value are often far more important in terms of driving shareholder value, the tangible, or principally physical, elements cannot be forgotten or moved aside. For example, when purchasing a new car, the sales and financing transactions may have gone smoothly, with respect for the owner's time and investment. However, no matter how much the owner trusts dealership management, the sales rep, and the service manager, if the car has physical or operating problems when delivered, the attachment and commitment are at least somewhat impaired, maybe even undermined. The Dick and Basu model is a convenient, basic, and easily understood way to interpret how customers assess their degree of commitment. Walker Information has converted the model into a "Loyalty Matrix." composed of four elements: *Truly Loyal, Accessible, Trapped,* and *High Risk* (Figure 6.1).

---

[5] Alan S. Dick and Kunal Basu, "Customer Loyalty: Toward an Integrated Conceptual Framework," *Journal of Marketing Science* 22 (1994): 99–113.

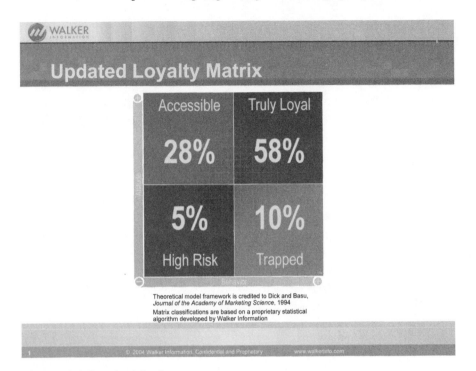

Figure 6.1 Loyalty Matrix
Source: © Walker Information, 2005.

Essentially, Walker Information has defined loyalty as the sum of emotional, perceptual, and attitudinal commitment and behavior, as seen in the results of customer studies. Those whom Walker classifies as *Truly Loyal* have both strong positive perceptions and attitudes toward the supplier and positive likelihood to continue purchasing. As long as the supplier has identified what elements of delivery are positively leveraging both perceptions and purchase intent, and can minimize the negatives in both areas, this should continue.

Accessible customers have positive perceptions but weak behavioral proclivities. A competitor may have created attitudinal and perceptual impressions that are just as positive, and these customers are now available to other suppliers. This is a situation which we frequently see occurring in the automotive business, where many manufacturers can receive high attitudinal ratings, but correspondingly low customer loyalty.

High Risk customers, if they haven't already defected, are readily available to competitors because both perception and purchase intent received low research scores. In industries that tend toward commoditization and difficulty in communicating strategically differentiated value, such as banking, newspaper subscriptions, and wireless telecom, high percentages of customers are, at any point in time, at high risk. Premium package cable television, in part because of dramatic price increases over the past few years, has fallen into this category. Through small satellite television alternatives, the cable companies' traditional customers have become vulnerable. Some multimedia cable companies, as a result, have taken to offering bundling opportunities such as Voice Over Internet Protocol (VoIP) solutions, essentially Internet-based voice communication and data transmission. Such new telephony voice and data products offer consumers, businesses, and telecommunications service providers a lower-cost, more feature-rich alternative to traditional telecom services.

Finally, those customers whom Walker classifies as *Trapped* are somehow forced to continue using their current supplier, even though there is a low level of connectedness. For example, there has been a great deal of discussion among companies that have made large investments in CRM software suites and support packages, only to see little or no positive financial return from these expenditures. Decision makers who selected these CRM suppliers give them low performance ratings, often citing high levels of complaint as well. At the same time, they are reluctant to abandon these suppliers because of the high rate of financial exposure.

Should Companies Be More Focused on Customer Satisfaction, Customer Loyalty, or Customer Commitment?

Commitment and advocacy are the highest level of customer involvement with a supplier, representing not only high dollar share of purchases and basic lifetime value but also the other elements of a truly loyal customer: They can be more appropriately defined as those who purchase regularly and across product lines over time, refer others, provide information proactively or when asked, are immune (or are at least quite resistant) to the pull of competition, are somewhat less price sensitive, and can withstand occasional lapses in support. They may also communicate, informally and positively, about the supplier. So we believe that understanding commitment requires a more in-depth investigation and interpretation of customer perceptions, motivations, and methods of making decisions.

Unfortunately, the vast majority of companies still include aspects, or elements, of satisfaction in trying to interpret how customers perceive value. Satisfaction, as we will see when getting into an in-depth discussion of commitment, has some directional benefit. Principally, satisfaction reflects attitudes and perceptions, largely with recent transactions. Perceived value, without question, must include some representation of attitude; however, building satisfaction or value indices primarily around attitudinal questions or key metrics will typically have little relationship to actual customer behavior in the marketplace, either on a lead or lag basis. Companies historically using such indices often find, to their regret, that they are challenged to understand why their indices go up or down. The cold reality is that they aren't measuring the right things. If, further, these companies have been giving incentive compensation to staff based on index score improvement, or withholding it based on index declines, either way it's an inappropriate apple-on-a-stick. As Forrest Gump might have expressed it, that's really all there is to say about satisfaction and value indices.

At the same time, some research and consulting organizations have suggested applying more intermediate steps between satisfaction, retention, loyalty, and commitment. McKinsey, for example, conducted a study of more than 1,200 consumers in 16 industry groups to better understand the state of customer loyalty.[6] Their conclusion: Companies should focus on *migration* rather than satisfaction or retention. Migration is directly tied to economic value, looking at rates of defection and switching and what they describe as the "loyalty profile" of the customer base. Some customers can be described as "loyalists," with varying levels of engagement and frequency of re-evaluating their purchasing decisions. Others are "migrators," likely to switch and frequently re-evaluating their purchasing decisions based on specific negative events, desire for variety, or change in individual need.

As concluded by McKinsey, companies can change customer behavior by identifying the right "loyalty levers" to use at the right time. This may include redesigning the product or service, enhancing the channels of delivery, and developing new communication or marketing programs, such as rewards, relationship building, or offering online channels.

Another intermediate approach has been developed by Phoenix Marketing. In bank customer studies, they learned that even high levels of customer satisfaction may hide future retention issues.[7] In other words, banks endeavoring to learn how loyal their customers are based on satisfaction surveys are likely to find little correlation between the two, since satisfaction and loyalty measure different things.

Their affluent bank customer studies examined both bank satisfaction and bank loyalty. Key satisfaction drivers were service, relationship with the bank advisor, and ease of doing business with the bank. However, the principal drivers of these same customers were very different, and quite specific. They included quality and frequency of communication, percentage of customer

---

[6] Stephanie Coyles and Timothy C. Gokey, *McKinsey Quarterly,* 2002 (no. 2).
[7] "Banking Satisfaction Is Not Loyalty, Says Study," www.thewisemarketer.com, March 1, 2004.

assets that reside with the bank, and whether the bank advisor has prepared a financial plan for the customer. Clearly, then, there was a gap between what optimizing satisfaction would yield and what could be realized by focusing on desired behaviors.

Phoenix defines customer loyalty as "willingness to take action on behalf of a brand," and they see this as the depth of a customer's involvement with the supplier or brand. The research device they've created to help assess this is what they call a barometer, essentially an additive score based on willingness to recommend the brand, giving the brand first priority when a new product is needed, resistance to switching, and the level of overall perceived value represented by the brand.

The McKinsey and Phoenix approaches are kind of halfway between the Dick and Basu model and where we see the journey's destination: *Customer advocacy.*

It's beginning to be understood that there is much more than a subtle difference between customer loyalty and customer advocacy. Mere repurchasing over time is what a lot of marketers and corporate executives are used to thinking defines loyalty, and this is one of the reasons that most "loyalty programs" tend to have few of the true value components that would make customers committed to that supplier. It has also been the definition by which some academics have argued that what they see as customer loyalty isn't a profitable corporate objective. The reality is that if customers are committed to a supplier, product, or service, they will tend to pay more for it, tell others about it, and be less likely to defect, all of which have direct bottom-line benefits.

Commitment requires both attitudinal, or perceptual, loyalty and behavioral loyalty. Behavioral loyalty is essentially the likelihood that the same customer will purchase a product again and again, be up-sold or cross-sold, provide information, and refer the product or service to others. Perceptual loyalty, the process of opinion development, consideration, evaluation, and decision making that leads to continued purchase, tends to be influenced by recent transactions.

When compared to traditional definitions of loyalty, commitment is far more psychological in nature. It goes beyond what people do, essentially their loyalty, to how people feel about the supplier and perceive value in what the supplier delivers. In other words, commitment is what is in their mind and what then motivates their behavior. It helps to clarify, for example, why customers who complain to a company, and are positive about the interaction experience between them and the supplier in the resolution process, are more likely to purchase at an accelerated rate following the complaint resolution. It also explains, at least in part, why customer satisfaction scores tend to be poor predictors of switching, or defection, behavior.

Hofmeyr and Rice's Conversion Model™: The Role of Commitment in Why People Buy What They Buy

In 1989, Butch Rice was running a highly successful marketing research company in South Africa, and Jan Hofmeyr was an instructor and researcher at the University of Cape Town. Hofmeyr's particular areas of interest were religious and political commitment, looking at the psychological underpinnings of how people make choices; and Rice recognized that the conceptual analytical framework Hofmeyr had developed could have commercial applications. The approach they refined has come to be known as the Conversion Model™.[8]

The model, which is now used in close to 100 countries, has been applied in over 3,500 individual brand and supplier projects. (Note: A newer, more powerful customer behavior model is presented in the Afterword.)

At its core, the Conversion Model™ goes further than the Dick and Basu concept of understanding customers. It first divides the supplier's reservoir of current and prospective customers into two groups, Users and Non-Users. Simple enough. It then further segments Users into four levels, or degrees, of commitment:

- *Entrenched*—Spend most of their "wallet share" on brand; high purchase and recommendation likelihood
- *Average*—Spending likelihood lower than *Entrenched*; spend less with supplier
- *Shallow*—In attrition/at risk mode, and may already be spending more with other supplier
- *Convertible*—Strongly at risk, with low likelihood of repurchase or recommendation

The first two groups of Users can be identified as Committed. The second two are identified as Uncommitted.

Non-Users also have four levels, these based on degree of availability:

- *Available*—Prefer competitive supplier to their current supplier; most likely to switch
- *Ambivalent*—Indecisive about whether to switch or not
- *Weakly Unavailable*—Some affinity with supplier other than theirs, but not strong
- *Strongly Unavailable*—Very little affinity for other supplier(s), and unlikely to switch

---

[8] Butch Rice, "Conversion Model™: Understanding Commitment, the Key to Relationship Management" (presentation, Pan-Pacific Direct Marketing Conference, Sydney, Australia, and Auckland, New Zealand, June 1999).

The first two groups of Non-Users are segmented into Open customers. The second two are Unavailable.

As, increasingly, companies are willing and able to address customer needs on an individual, and even venue or scenario, basis, the concept behind this model takes on singularly important meaning. It enables management, marketing, sales, and customer service to assess the relationship between the supplier and customer in a unique manner. Suppliers can identify what elements of process, communication, campaign, product, or service must be modified to increase perceived value. Marketers, for instance, can test components of programs designed to increase the number of customers committed to the supplier, honing the message and content down to the purchase scenario level. They can look at switching patterns across all suppliers in the market to identify where there are opportunities and vulnerabilities.

On a microsegment and individual customer basis, the model can help determine levels of commitment to each supplier in a market, the likelihood of churn for each supplier, availability of customers for conversion, and what would cause them to convert. Since we are principally concerned with what each customer feels and perceives as value, this measure will help clarify how they think and how they are impacted by each transaction or experience.

From a marketing research perspective, which is where much of the model learning takes place, commitment as an incremental metric may be at least as important as other measures. Because satisfied customers sometimes (even often) defect, and even some loyal customers churn and are at varying levels of risk, commitment measures are more accurate determinants of the degree of individual customer behavior. In tracking studies, where the "health" of the brand, service, or overall supplier equity is paramount, a commitment measure can open dialogue that helps to clarify how all messages are received.

Some (Unsettling) Thoughts About the Model, Commitment, and Advertising Strategy

When formulating advertising and other communication strategies, the impact of media, creative, copy point, and frequency variables can best be understood in the context of how committed the customer really is. One of the unique facets of the Conversion Model^{TM} is that it recognizes efficiencies and effectiveness according to supplier customer share, and dollar share, within the marketplace. In other words, the model recognizes that larger suppliers produce higher advertising effectiveness scores than smaller suppliers. This is a major flaw in most advertising testing, especially when normative performance scores are applied, principally because these norms don't take usage or levels of commitment into account.

Hofmeyr and Rice's studies have shown that active brand or supplier users are approximately 50 percent more likely to be aware of that brand or supplier's advertising or other communication efforts. Further, fully committed customers, the Entrenched, are more likely to be aware of advertising when compared to Average, Shallow, or Convertible customers.

Hofmeyr and Rice have concluded that brand or supplier advertising will be most effective among those customers already strongly committed, providing reassurance about their choice, and giving them information about future purchase opportunities or scenarios. It's ineffective, however, as a conversion vehicle, having little leverage on usage among those who are mildly or strongly committed to other brands or suppliers. So advertising should not be considered as a mass communication device because its effectiveness will vary so much from customer to customer, based on the pre-existing relationship with the brand or supplier. This is a precept that absolutely confounds some advertising and marketing traditionalists.

Advertising to the individual is a critical part of experience management. If, as strategies and executions are being formulated, a company can understand how each customer feels about the brand or supplier, planning becomes much more straightforward, and it is easier to obtain both financial and communication efficiencies. Among Entrenched customers, those most committed, the criterion for success will be to maintain the current relationship. Hofmeyr and Rice consider it unrealistic, for instance, to expect that advertising to Entrenched customers will increase sales to this group; nevertheless, suppliers should focus their advertising on showing appreciation for these customers and making sure that the level of commitment remains intact.

Unfortunately, many companies devote considerably more energy and resources to winning or capturing customers than they do to keeping them. "Conquest" is a frequently used term for new customers, especially among automotive retailers. Consultant and author Robert Tucker has stated, "Companies are often so concerned about attracting new customers that they denigrate their unique value proposition to loyal customers."[9] They focus instead on chasing down the next sale, competing on price, and compensating employees more for winning new accounts than for keeping existing customers happy and loyal. Parenthetically, as commitment increases among existing customers, price evolves to being less important as a brand or supplier choice element.

When customers are uncommitted to a brand or supplier, this becomes a huge challenge in planning advertising and communication. Why? To begin,

---

[9] Robert B. Tucker, *Win the Value Revolution* (Franklin Lakes, NJ: Career Press, 1995), p. 121.

uncommitted customers' reasons and motivations have to be thoroughly researched because they can vary so significantly; and, frequently, this kind of analysis is either superficially done or entirely avoided. Depending on the industry, customers with the highest potential for spending are among the least likely to be committed to any single supplier. One result of this is that their profile within a database may identify them as light or modest purchasers, so they do not receive the attention or investment necessary to build their interest, advocacy, and profitability.

A multi-industry continental Europe study by Professor Adrian Payne of Cranfield University in the UK showed that 80 percent of companies spend too much of their marketing budget on customer acquisition.[10] He calls these companies "Acquirers." Unavailable customers typically represent, to Hofmeyr and Rice, a "money pit" for advertising, or generally a wasted investment. If a company can identify those non-users whose perceptions and feelings toward the supplier make them *available*, creation of awareness is often more effective when it is direct, such as through sales reps or at point of purchase in retail situations.

Conversion Model™ Interpretations, Applications, and Successes

The model, uniquely, facilitates interpretation and understanding of almost all the components involved in decision making (except word-of-mouth), customer-by-customer and situation-by-situation, making it an excellent approach for creating true divisibility. It enables suppliers to link perceptual and attitudinal insights and behavior likelihood with each customer's profile from the database.

We've often identified customer-perceived value as the sum, or product, of the tangible elements of delivery (availability, speed, accuracy, completeness, cost, physical appearance, etc.) and the intangibles, such as service, brand equity and image, and various forms of communication. The model goes beyond traditional thinking about satisfaction and loyalty in understanding value to focus on commitment, i.e., customers' deeply held reasons for making choices.

Supplier, brand, and service choice are about the tangibles and intangibles, and they're also about factors that, in the past, may have been considered somewhat elusive and esoteric: accessibility, share of voice, and geographic presence and strength. All of these factors evoke strong, relevant associations in customers' minds; so, in moving toward a more holistic awareness of why and what customers choose, these factors must be incorporated into planning.

---

[10] Adrian Payne, *The Handbook of CRM* (Amsterdam: Elsevier, 2005), p. 147.

Satisfaction, which often correlates poorly with loyalty, does have importance and relevance in customer commitment. It's a building block element. Satisfaction is principally attitudinal in nature; and, in building customer commitment, it helps suppliers determine the extent to which their products or services meet individual needs, across the tangible and intangible elements of value. If this seems too abstract a definition, just think of it as a first step in identifying the customer's strength of relationship with a supplier, which may range from Entrenched commitment to Strong unavailable.

One of the problems with satisfaction measurement is that most suppliers don't go beyond this basic step. There is, as stated, a weak relationship between needs and value, as defined by the customer, and how it connects to decisions and resultant behavior. What the Conversion Model™ considers is the level of involvement, the extent to which the relationship has personal importance.

"Involvement" is far more psychological in nature than other decision factors. The degree of individual engagement, and investment in supplier values alignment, tells suppliers a great deal about how secure current customers are; and, among noncustomers in the marketplace, how available or likely to switch they may be.

The Conversion Model™ establishes both value and commitment by asking just four simple questions:

1. How happy are you with the product or service?
2. Is the product or service something you care about, i.e., want to be involved, or have a relationship, with?
3. How do you rate the alternatives?
4. If the alternatives have high ratings, how (strategically) differentiated are they from each other?

One of the attractions of this model is that its interpretation is simplicity itself. If a customer is "perfectly committed," for example, the questions will identify that this customer is happy with the choice he or she has made; the choice is something they care about; and none of the alternatives appeal to them, either because they don't rate high enough or are differentiated.

This helps to explain the cardholder retention success of MBNA and the customer appeal of a bank such as Commerce Bank. In a business where there is a great deal of perceived sameness between credit card offers, MBNA has in-depth information about its customers. They offer personalized service and high perceived value, such as rapid credit limit increases when requests are made. When a customer wishes to cancel his or her card, MBNA representatives can present an encyclopedia of value offers to keep that customer in the fold. As a result, MBNA loses under

2 percent of its customers annually in an industry where 10 percent, or more, annual loss is the norm.

Commerce Bank's hundreds of branches in the Mid-Atlantic area each have a strong local presence. They operate more like nimble local retailers than bankers, with extraordinarily well-trained and customer-focused employees, extended daily hours, weekend hours, holiday hours, and a broad array of financial and investment services. Even though Commerce's CD rates are lower and its loan interest rates are higher than other banks, their positive value delivery, in tangible and intangible ways that are meaningful to customers, have created high advocacy levels for them.

At the other end of the commitment spectrum, uncommitted consumers may be dissatisfied, as marketers and market researchers understand dissatisfaction; however, since satisfaction scores and loyalty, or disloyalty, behavior don't match up very well, the dissatisfied customer may, and often will, keep buying. As Hofmeyr and Rice point out in explaining the model, if increasing dissatisfaction is coupled with increasing involvement, commitment can increase.[11] Commitment only decreases when involvement decreases. When that occurs, the proclivity of a customer to purchase from that supplier will also decrease. The model can also identify uncommitted customers as those who cannot make a selection from an array of alternatives.

The model also helps to explain the essential difference between customer loyalty and customer commitment. At its core, customer loyalty will, principally, be about behavior, with some elements of attitude and perception included. Commitment is principally about converting attitudes and perceptions to more deeply held beliefs. These beliefs then translate into commitment, and the behavior that derives from it. When commitment drives loyalty behavior, supplier shifts in the marketplace have little effect on customers.

As we've discussed, it's entirely possible to have loyalty without commitment. When customers exhibit loyalty behavior, with shallow or no commitment, this often reflects situations where brands or suppliers have extraordinary strength. Companies, like Microsoft and Siebel, that are dominant brands or suppliers in their marketplaces, engender loyalty, but customers may come to them grudgingly, feeling "trapped" by Dick and Basu's definition. This has also occurred in certain areas of customer management software, where there has been high financial investment and lengthy, or minimal, return on that investment. Other brands, like Coca-Cola, Intel, or Butterball Turkeys, have such strong market presence that even uncommitted customers can be swayed.

From a U.S. soft drink study conducted in the early '90s, now one of the thousands of research programs conducted using the Conversion Model™, comes a

---

[11] Jan Hofmeyr and Butch Rice, *Commitment-Led Marketing* (Chichester, UK: John Wiley & Sons, 2000), pp. 21–52.

representative example of its application.[12] At the time of the study, the model showed that Pepsi users represented 34 percent of the customers in the market-place, and that 11 percent of them were Shallow or Convertible (Figure 6.2).

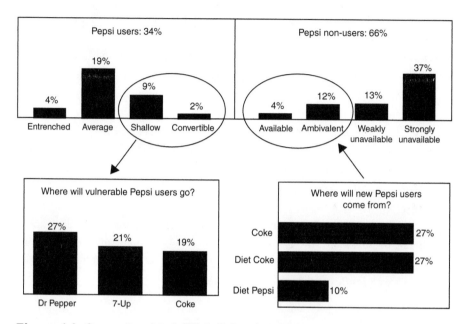

Figure 6.2 Conversion Model™ Soft Drink Market Study Results
Source: Jan Hofmeyr and Butch Rice, *Commitment-Led Marketing* (Chichester, UK: John Wiley & Sons, 2001), p. 48.

Under the marketplace conditions that existed in 1991, the model indicated that 27 percent of the vulnerable Pepsi users were likely to migrate to Dr. Pepper, 21 percent to 7-Up, and 19 percent to Coke. The model also indicated that 16 percent of the Pepsi non-users were open to change, and that 27 percent of new Pepsi users would come from Coke, 27 percent from Diet Coke, and 10 percent from Diet Pepsi.

The model applies equally well to B2B or B2C services. Here's a very interesting set of findings for a major bank. Through the mid-1990s, Lloyds TSB, one of the largest retail banks in the UK, conducted traditional customer satisfaction studies. This type of research, however, gave them little insight into which customers were truly loyal and which were likely to defect. Lloyds' first use of customer commitment research was aimed at understanding the extent to which

---

[12] Jan Hofmeyr and Butch Rice, *Commitment-Led Marketing* (Chichester, UK: John Wiley & Sons, 2001), pp. 217–21.

1) profitability could be optimized among loyal customers and 2) profitability could be increased among the remaining customers; and they needed to profile customers as well as establish a working, reliable model for identifying the likelihood and proclivity of customers to do added business with the bank.

Fortunately, Lloyds had a fairly advanced database. They could segment checking account customers according to profitability. Clearly, customers with only a checking account, and who maintained a low balance, were borderline profitable or unprofitable. Those who carried large balances and used multiple services were more profitable. The intention of the commitment study was one that every marketer can understand: Provide the most effective messages and offers to the most receptive customers, at the right time and through the best media.

As can be seen in Figure 6.3, the initial study showed that, among customers identified as unprofitable, only 8 percent were Entrenched; and even these customers showed little inclination to use more Lloyds services. Convertible customers were interested in increasing their banking business on an overall basis, but not with Lloyds. The next 35 percent of Average Committed unprofitable Lloyds customers, those whom loyalty expert Martha Rogers would refer to as BZs, or Below Zero in profitability, offered little in the way of potential "growability," principally as a result of age and income levels.[13]

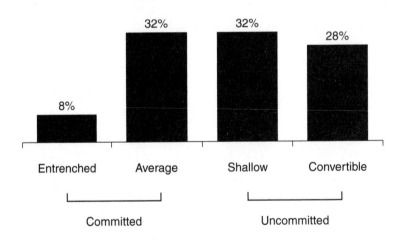

Figure 6.3 Commitment Profile of Lloyd's Unprofitable Customers
Source: Jan Hofmeyr and Butch Rice, *Commitment-Led Marketing* (Chichester, UK: John Wiley & Sons, 2001), p. 193.

---

[13] Jeanette Hansen Slepian, "Finding Profit in Customer Behavior," www.crmtoday.com, September 2003.

Profitable customer commitment results yielded some concerns. While 54 percent of them could be regarded as committed to Lloyds, that also meant that almost half were not committed, with 17 percent being classed as Convertible, potential defectors who were at risk (Figure 6.4).

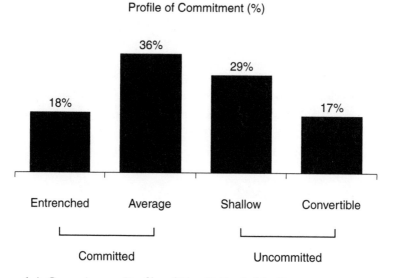

Figure 6.4 Commitment Profile of Lloyd's Profitable Customers
Source: Jan Hofmeyr and Butch Rice, *Commitment-Led Marketing* (Chichester, UK: John Wiley & Sons, 2001), p. 193.

Uncommitted profitable customers, they found, were likely to be affluent and had a high propensity to do business with a bank, just not with Lloyds. So Lloyds saw them as a prime target for cross-selling, if the bank could find a way to increase their level of commitment and involvement. An additional, and not unimportant, finding of the commitment research was that there was a strong relationship between commitment and complaints. Of all the Committed Lloyds customers, only 8 percent had expressed a complaint. Among those who were Convertible, 50 percent had complained; and, of the remaining half who hadn't complained, 40 percent, or 20 percent, indicated that they had complaints but didn't register them. As will be discussed and demonstrated in Chapter Nine, this is a situation that can negatively leverage future purchasing and recommendation behavior.

Upon digesting and collating all of these commitment study results, Lloyds' first order of marketing business was to develop a communication strategy that would be as personalized as possible for each customer. In 1996, they began publishing a magazine for their top-tier, most profitable customers, with a selection of 35 customer variables (including age, education, income, products carried, channel usage, transaction patterns, and complaint record).

The bank included a self-completion commitment questionnaire flyer in the magazine; and, although this generated under 10 percent response (subjecting the results to prospective nonresponse bias), Lloyds still had enough information to develop a predictive commitment model that was more than 80 percent accurate. The model enabled them to update the level of commitment for each of its most profitable customers.

Having in hand the early results and applications of Lloyds' learning using the Conversion Model™ within a year after the model identified customers' level of commitment, it was determined that the profitability of those pegged as least committed to the bank declined by 14 percent. At the same time, those identified as most committed increased their profitability by 9 percent, in part because one-fifth of that group had increased the number of Lloyds products they held.

Lloyds also learned that between 5 and 10 percent of all customers were likely to change their commitment levels on a quarterly basis. This strongly suggests that banking commitment will be in active flux, and should be regularly researched.

The bank made some immediate marketing program changes as a result of learning from the research and the model they developed. For those customers with little or no commitment to the bank, Lloyds segmented out those who were identified as high value. They were further researched to identify channel and product preferences, plus queried on the types of service to enhance their relationship with the bank. Individualized personal reviews were conducted with each customer, followed up with special product offers. Among this group, levels of positive consideration for Lloyds products increased from 24 percent before the reviews and communication to 66 percent afterwards, with a 5 percent actual increase in product holdings.

For customers who were already committed to Lloyds, and also identified as both representing high value and open to having more of its products, the bank created the "Personal Choice" program. Each of these customers was assigned to a "Personal Choice" manager who was available to provide detailed, individualized explanations regarding products and services. A loyalty program was created for these customers, as well as special, differentiated products and service offers. This group of customers, like those who formerly had little commitment to Lloyds, also showed increased sales, greater profitability, and higher account balances.

Let's Go Deeper: Understanding Perceived Value, Supplier Persuasion, and How Customers Make Purchase Decisions

Companies are always looking for an edge in understanding what it takes to persuade, influence, or leverage customers' thinking and behavior. Fundamentally, what any supplier endeavors to do is, ethically, increase the level of their influence with customers. And doing this requires building and sustaining a mutually beneficial relationship and demonstration of value for the customer.

Robert Cialdini, Professor of Psychology at Arizona State University, and president of Influence at Work, a company that helps businesses understand how to successfully persuade customers, has identified six universal principles of influence and persuasion:

1. *Reciprocation*—Receiving something of perceived value, such as service, information, or concessions, unsolicited—what customer service expert T. Scott Gross calls "random acts of delight"—can create a sense of obligation on a customer's part. So, when a waiter provides extraordinary, personalized service, the diner often reciprocates by giving a higher tip.

2. *Scarcity*—When something legitimately has less availability, or has unique features, this can often increase customers' desire for it. Thirty years ago, The Franklin Mint built a business model around "limited edition" collectibles, where only a certain number of products were available or they were only available if ordered during a limited time period.

3. *Authority*—Unique expertise, knowledge, and sources of information can be powerfully persuasive in purchase decisions. In addition to letting prospects know about areas of proficiency, another effective means of doing it is to let current customers carry the bricks—through voluntary referrals or references. Some companies are able to generate incredible revenue levels through active cultivation of influential referral sources.

4. *Consistency*—Another term for consistency is stability. It is related to reliability, and both of these are essential in creating commitment. When companies can demonstrate consistency, especially in responding to product or service features customers consider desirable, customers are more positively inclined toward them than toward suppliers who fail to do this.

5. *Consensus*—Covert or overt peer pressure, which can be seen in so many facets of society, often leverages supplier choice. Advice of colleagues, friends, and relatives regarding products or services is tremendously influential, impacting both perceptions and behaviors. Following a trend represents a form of "social validation," which many find a powerful motivator.

6. *Liking*—Identifying commonalities, a context for aligning the supplier's interest with the customer's, enables successful companies to influence purchasers. By deeply understanding his customers' needs and lifestyle issues, used car super-salesperson Joe Girard became hugely successful, much more so than dealerships focused on selling car features and benefits.

Perceived value is a great deal more than merely meeting, and even exceeding, customer expectations. It is how customers move past being satisfied, to having whatever they feel is beneficial and advantageous in a supplier relationship.

Companies that have become successful at going beyond expectations to build commitment and advocacy have come to understand how customers think, and how they make choice decisions between alternative suppliers. As customers continue to demonstrate lessening loyalty behavior, it's essential that companies, and their sales, marketing, and customer service staff go beyond the words customers use and begin to delve into their thought processes.

Customers use both emotion and reason. They process using both verbal and nonverbal expression, and up to 80 percent of communication—i.e., the exchange of messages and meaning—is nonverbal (touch, vocal intonation, gestures, posture, eye contact, etc.). Though there are some basic, universally shared human values and perceptions such as justice, concern for the young, and consideration for the ill and elderly, Harvard marketing professor Gerald Zaltman has determined that as much as 95 percent of customer thinking occurs within the unconscious mind, using images rather than words.[14]

Consumers, he has found, don't think and process in strictly logical, well-reasoned, linear, hierarchical ways in how they evaluate alternatives and make decisions. Nor, as stated, do consumers necessarily think in words. Thinking, as scientists have determined, precedes the conscious formation of words. How does this play out in a buying situation? For example, as many auto dealership managers have discovered, prospective owners making decisions about automobiles don't look at them feature by feature, but rather by unconscious processes, influenced by needs, desires, and social considerations. If dealerships ask superficial questions, they may learn little about what motivates customers' decisions. If they allow customers to express their needs and desires, they will find that customers prefer this form of engagement.

Often, since much of decision making is below the conscious surface, consumers can't fully explain either their reasoning or resultant behavior. Also,

---

[14] Gerald Zaltman, *How Customers Think* (Boston: Harvard Business School Press, 2003), pp. 50–53.

consumers' memories don't necessarily directly reflect their experiences. They are greatly influenced by time. So, if a company is trying to evaluate the customer's shopping experience a week, a month, or a year after the fact, what the customer plays back is likely to be very divergent depending on the interval. This means that traditional approaches to qualitative research—in-depth interviews and focus groups—may not get to consumers' thoughts and feelings.

In developing products or services, knowing *what* a customer prefers, while useful, may not get at *why* an element may be preferred, for that customer and for a specific purchase scenario. So, as we learned when helping a container company design the shape, size, and color for a new beer can, our in-depth probing into the "why" of feature selection found that female beer drinkers were concerned about cleanliness and disposability of the cans, as well as likelihood to dent (because the beer could be spoiled or possibly "fizz" when opened). Women were also focused on ease of opening. Why? Because opening beer cans can be painful for women, and their nails could get ruined. Men were more concerned about the "different," or aluminum, flavor they said beer from cans had. When it came to new designs, women liked fluting, because it was attractive and easier to grip, and they liked silver colors as opposed to gold, because they thought gold was more masculine. Men liked larger, 24-ounce cans (and didn't care so much about fluting) because they would be better for parties. In addition to gender differences, there were design preference variations according to age, geographic location, income, their favorite brands of beer, frequency of consumption, and the situations or occasions for which the beer would be purchased.

Getting to this depth of understanding means that, when looking at purchase decisions or product/service design, companies have to develop awareness not only of the tangible and intangible aspects of value, but the purely psychological and emotional aspects as well. While beer in an aluminum can creates definite sensory response, it also evokes emotional responses, such as safety and cleanliness (women), color (gold for men, silver for women), and size (men). If a beer company adopts a new can design, both the functional and emotional aspects of that design must be considered.

To fully explore the "customer experience," companies have to listen to customers and prospects in new ways. In other words, they are now tasked with having greater awareness of how mental activity occurs when customers are making decisions. It's not about having lots of data—because much of the demographic, attribute preference, and purchase intent data companies collect from customers and prospects are relatively superficial—it's about having the right data at the right time. It's about carefully interpreting the blending of conscious and logical parts of customers' thinking with the emotional, sometimes illogical aspects of that thinking

The more of this in-depth data companies have about their customers, the more they are able to design situation-based products and services for each customer.

The process Zaltman developed has been "codified" into a patented research tool, the Zaltman Metaphor Elicitation Technique (ZMET), which allows people to understand their individual thoughts and to share this thinking with trained analysts. It enables deeply held constructs and ideas, and the connections between them, to surface. The process is both unique and effective, building on fields as diverse as cognitive neuroscience, neurobiology, sociology, anthropology, semiotics, and psycholinguistics. Blending them together enables researchers to elicit information from consumers in the form of visual images, metaphors, and the meaning behind expressed emotions. These can often be far more powerful than words. Using this tool, companies can learn what truly motivates their customers' decisions, on an individual basis and situation by situation.

Zaltman concludes: "Without a deep understanding of consumers—that is, without knowing consumers' hidden thoughts and feelings and the forces behind them—marketers can't accurately anticipate consumers' responses to product designs, features, and ideas that cannot be tested directly with consumers because of time, budget, or competitive reasons."[15] Zaltman terms this new awareness of how customers make decisions, possibly coming to commitment, "a voyage from the familiar." Most suppliers may be unready, even unwilling, to address these new customer decision-making realities, but all too soon they will have to—before their competitors do.

---

[15] Gerald Zaltman, *How Customers Think* (Boston: Harvard Business School Press, 2003), p. 17.

7

Best of the Best Customer Relationship and Data Tools

Part I—Dealing with the Essentials

(Data) Quality Costs . . . and the Costs of Data Quality

According to the U.S. Census Bureau, more than 43 million Americans, or about 16 percent of the current population, move to a new residence each year. In a typical day, 6,800 people get married, many changing their names. Half that number—about 3,400—divorce, also frequently changing their names. Close to 7,000 people die and over 11,000 are born.

Each year, 550,000 businesses open, and over 38,000 file for bankruptcy. According to The Data Warehousing Institute (TDWI), in any given month 2 percent of the records in a customer file are obsolete.[1] That doesn't even take into consideration records that contain incomplete or inaccurate information.

It's fair, and accurate, to say that data quality is perhaps the most strategically important consideration of any work with customers. And it's the most costly. TDWI conducted a study, "Data Quality and the Bottom Line," that put a $600 billion annual cost on dirty data.[2] Since poor, or defective, data can directly lead to customer complaint, attrition, and defection, there are costs associated with data quality far beyond what is involved in having incorrect and inconsistent customer details, duplicate records, lack of synchronization between multiple databases, or databases located in different departments, and even sub-organizations, around the company. A Gartner Research study estimated that, through 2005, over half of business intelligence and customer management deployments will have limited success, if not fail outright, because of inattention to data quality issues.[3]

Data quality must be looked at in real-world profitability terms to be taken seriously. Duplicate records, for example, is probably the most common type of data quality issue. When variations in spelling, or having multiple addresses for the same customer, occur, customer data, and the analyses and campaigns

---

[1] Carol Ellison, "When Quality Counts," *CRM* 8, no. 4 (2004): 6–10.
[2] Carol Ellison, "When Quality Counts," *CRM* 8, no. 4 (2004): 6–10.
[3] Ted Friedman, "A Strategic Approach to Improving Data Quality," Gartner, June 19, 2002.

performed with them, can easily become corrupted. Not only is the same customer likely to receive multiple communications of the same message, which impairs credibility, but this inflates marketing costs and reduces back-end performance.

Upgraded data quality is an organization-wide investment in people, process, and technological tools. Central to the success of a strategic approach to customer data quality are sets of data-validating process rules for everyone entering and pulling data from a centralized database, and what is known as "data scrubbing." Simply stated, scrubbing is the set of processes used to correct, complete, or de-duplicate individual pieces of data *before* they are sent to the database. It is intended and designed to eliminate the two key viruses that can impair data quality: errors and redundancy. Also, it helps to make the data uniform.

Bottom line: Because data quality have such strong impact on companies trying to optimize return on investment and efficiency, the right combination of technology and procedures has to be a central focus. For companies to achieve the advocacy and profitability promises of customer divisibility, all points of data collection and application must have well-profiled, correct, and fully integrated information.

Leading-Edge Approaches to Customer Support

Traditionally, customer management initiatives have been driven by sales, IT, or marketing departments. Even when they have shown a modicum of success, these efforts have often resulted in customers being treated more like numbers than individuals, at least in part because of the lack of availability and/or the inappropriate application of actionable customer data. As will be discussed more fully in Chapter Nine, customer support is rapidly morphing from a traditional reactive role with customers to that of a proactive partner, internally and externally.

Increasingly, customer-facing employees will have access to better, almost 360 degree customer data. Data are being used to optimize customer service processes, offering the opportunity for more data generated during post-sale contact, and leveraging improved customer retention, loyalty, and advocacy.

Companies are now realizing that to truly be customer-centric, every customer contact point must be recognized, as Jan Carlzon of Scandinavian Airline System dubbed it many years ago, a "moment of truth." Each customer-supplier encounter is an opportunity to create value, encourage interest, conduct business, meet a need, or exhibit commitment to the relationship.

In Chapter Five, the importance of customer life cycle was discussed. One of the cornerstones of customer life cycle is the ability to generate actionable customer data at each stage of the customer's relationship and interaction with the supplier. Information gathered about prospects can be leveraged into sales activity. Presuming that prospects can then be converted into active customers, customer service's role in providing information continuity cannot be overstated. This is especially so in customer service's evolving role as both data harvester and distributor across the organization, and this will be discussed in Chapter Nine.

Finally, if the customer is identified to be at-risk, or does defect, customer service has developed stabilization and recovery skills to bring desirable customers back. It has been amply demonstrated that customers with problems or complaints who have them successfully, and positively, handled by customer service are significantly more likely to demonstrate loyalty and advocacy behavior toward the supplier proactive enough to identify and resolve them.

In Part III of this chapter, the new customer communication channels and their effects on relationships will be presented. Customer service is squarely in the middle of this mix, offering customers the flexibility of using all communication channels, at any time, and at any point in the relationship life cycle. This not only serves the customer's desire for channel choice, it also makes for greater supplier economy by encouraging interactions through the most efficient channels.

Customer Data Fusion

SME retail organizations, in particular, but also companies of any size and in many other fields of business, have been challenged to allocate scarce money, staff, technology, and time resources for scalable software. Its purpose is to help them both obtain intelligence, customer by customer, and aggregate it with detailed profile data to leverage optimized loyalty behavior.

Recognizing this need and opportunity within the SME retail and related service market space, companies like SeaBridge Software have created technology that enables these companies to build more value into customer relationships with fully integrated customer information streams. Retailers are able to reshape product and service life cycles around current and future customer needs, coordinate customer-related processes and support, leverage marketplace opportunities (and overcome vulnerabilities), and build sustainable, profitable advantage with better service and more targeted programs and communication.

SeaBridge Software, as cited, has developed Customer Data Fusion, a scalable, flexible, and economical approach to generating and applying strategic customer intelligence for greater, more cost-effective revenue and profitability. For the first time, this can be done on a microsegment, and even individual customer and purchase experience, basis. It brings together customer profile (recency, frequency, dollar amount, product/service purchase information), appended demographic/lifestyle data, customer service and/or sales rep input, and third-party/self-conducted insight from loyalty and advocacy research.

From this base of easily accessible, user-friendly information, companies have the tools to better upgrade and/or enhance customer-related processes, develop products or services and new business lines, and target customer communication and value enhancement programs through more refined media selection, message development, and experience management.

Data Management Can Also Be a Low-Tech, Team-Based, Cultural Thing: The Rackspace Approach

One of the key objectives of developing detailed, experience-by-experience, customer data is the ability to share this information between and within company groups so that loyalty and advocacy can be optimized. Sometimes, especially if an organization is otherwise good at collecting and applying this insight, all it takes is a little restructuring, with the emphasis on teamwork.

We've seen teams effectively used for all kinds of customer-related activities, from boosting service levels, to increasing security, to winning back at-risk and former customers. Why not build a team structure to use as a mechanism for sharing customer knowledge?

The fact is that this is already being done, and there are excellent examples in a number of industries. One of the most outstanding is Rackspace, a San Antonio-based turnkey Web hosting company. Their clients range from small companies with a single server to larger clients that may have as many as 30 or 40 servers for a single web site. Some of their clients are web site designers, some are e-businesses. All of them need 100 percent uptime, and Rackspace has worked hard to meet that requirement.

Over the past few years, Rackspace has developed a trademarked program, called Fanatical Support^{TM}, for team support of customers, which is offered free of charge. The Fanatical Support program includes immediate forwarding of any breakdown in service to the entire team of technicians, who are available on a 24/7 basis. Depending on the issue, one or more of the team members can troubleshoot client databases.

Though Fanatical Support is deeply embedded in Rackspace's culture and structure (more people at Rackspace are devoted to customer service than any other function), it's driven by available, in-depth customer data.

Employee Empowerment, Built on Shared
Data and Customer Understanding at Rackspace

Every Rackspace employee is empowered, even required, to identify processes that can make customer experiences more positive. Employees utilize their team processes and share customer data to build value. The company has found that some of the best ideas come from customer feedback, gathered on a monthly basis, which becomes a living element of each customer's profile, available to each employee providing services to that customer.

Rackspace believes that its employees are special. Each new hire, as Rackspace expresses it, has "a strong passion and dedication for helping people." Continuing, Rackspace "hires based on values and trains for technical expertise."[4] Then employees are formed into account teams.

Dedicated team support is on a modular basis, with one-to-one, consultative relationships rather than incident by incident through a call center. Teams function like a mini business unit, with specialists in support, technical assistance, security, billing, business development, and account management embedded in each team. This modular approach enables team members to develop a close rapport with individual customers, often on a first-name basis, blending their knowledge and insight regarding that customer's specific environment, plus access to that customer's profile data, for active troubleshooting and recommendations.

What really brings all of the Fanatical Support resources together, however, are systems, the real-time flow of customer data. Teams are able to monitor each client's hosting situations, pinpoint problems at an early stage, root cause the problems, create potential solutions, and institute changes—all while causing minimal or no disruption to the client's business.

Rackspace's web site offers several examples of Fanatical Support "customer stories," and one of the more intriguing is Gattaca, Inc.[5] Gattaca is a specialized service company that brings advertisers and audiences together through a network of Internet businesses, most of which are online community and forum based. This uses a tremendous amount of bandwidth, and requires that its web sites be up and running at all times so they can respond immediately to every customer inquiry. Rackspace, through its team support approach and immediately available and shared customer data, makes certain that Gattaca has both reliable uptime and unparalleled, proactive support.

---

[4] Patrick R. Condon, "We Bring Fanatical Support™ to Managed Hosting," Rackspace Managed Hosting, June 2004.

[5] "Customer Stories: Gattaca, Inc.," www.rackspace.co.uk, July 1, 2004.

Part II—Anticipating and Monitoring Customer Behavior

The Growing Role and Contribution of Predictive Churn Modeling

Churn modeling is very much like the creative alchemy that is cooking. When done well, it has a little bit of art, a lot of science, a dash of finesse, and even a pinch of intuition. With rates of customer defection reaching epidemic levels in industries like retail, travel, health care, and banking, predicting turnover has become significantly more important to business in recent years. Having reviewed material on many churn models, in a multitude of industries, prepared by individual companies and specialized consulting organizations, some basic and some sophisticated, we've concluded that perhaps no industries have more predictive modeling going on than telecom and financial services. This makes sense because of their high degree of customer risk and defection.

Let's begin with simple predictive churn modeling. At Wachovia Bank, headquartered in Charlotte, North Carolina, they look at demographics, especially life events (divorce, losing jobs, opening a business, graduating kids, etc.), declines in account balance levels, and the like as precursors to negative action. They also conduct research among high-value customers who had defected to look for other root causes. These results get factored into how they approach customers who are considered, as a result, to be at high risk for defection. Another bank, PNC in Pittsburgh, depends very heavily on analytics that come from behavioral customer research, especially activity information regarding accounts at other institutions; and, like Wachovia, they also look at account balance levels.

It's always interesting to have the perspectives of experts in any field of endeavor, and this is particularly true in churn prediction. Professor Adrian Payne, of the Cranfield University School of Management in the UK, and perhaps the planet's most knowledgeable academic on the subject of retention and turnover modeling, believes that companies first have to look at cost of acquisition, build in retention spending, and other costs such as up-sell and cross-sell. He's seen segments being built around behavioral-based market research (similar to what the banks are doing), eventually getting down to a microsegment, and even individual customer, level.[6]

He also felt that few companies have sufficient customer information to develop really accurate models. That's where the alchemy, and some intuition, often comes in, because final decisions regarding potential churn may be left up to internal staff. Confused? Well, he added that companies should also look at

---

[6] Adrian Payne, *The Handbook of CRM* (Amsterdam: Elsevier, 2005), p. 147.

competitive intensity, the industry retention average, overperformance and under-performance on service, and the like.

Before we return to reasonable churn prediction approaches, we'll first get really complicated. At a recent wireless telecom customer loyalty conference in London, one European telecom's information systems "expert" presented sets of predictive churn models that had as many as 240 individual qualitative and quantitative variables, and up to seven streams, or sources, of customer data. Model characteristics included:

- Use of local calls
- Frequency of calls to customer service
- Number of successful/failed calls to customer service
- Number of international calls
- Single/multiple line subscription
- Intensity of Internet usage
- Calls to land-based vs. mobile phones
- Use of automatic checking/savings account debit

Principally, the model was set up to predict the level of potential turnover—i.e., the likelihood that customers would migrate to another service or simply abandon their current service. He was using information sources such as customer service data, invoice information, satisfaction surveys, claims data, informal customer feedback, competitive data, socio-demographic information, and, as he stated, "[a]ny data that can increase one-to-one knowledge of the customers."

Although the telecom's representative offered some general results of model application to marketing programs, such as significantly reducing customer contact costs among certain segments, many of his findings were labeled as "confidential." This, to me, was mystical, black-box churn prediction alchemy in its purest sense. He was in effect saying: "Trust me. I'm an excellent chef. The food will taste wonderful." To paraphrase what Jaggers, the lawyer in Dickens' *Great Expectations*, said to Pip, without evidence there is no proof, only guesswork.

Getting back to the real world of predicting churn, there are several professional firms that stand out in their approaches to modeling. SLP Infoware, based in France, has a model called Churn/CPS that tracks multiple end-user defined churn behaviors, so that clients can engage and refine their retention strategies.

Their clients are almost exclusively in the telecom industry. One of them, Cellular One of Puerto Rico, equips customer service agents with predicted at-risk customer behaviors, so they can apply any of several potential scripted marketing approaches to reduce churn.

Using the Churn/CPS model, they've been able to reduce customer turnover by one-third. Since telecom churn averages about 30 percent in the U.S. and Europe, and over 50 percent in the Asia-Pacific region, this is really significant. SLP figures that, with their model, something like 62 percent of churn behavior can be modified if spotted in advance, so this offers clients a fair amount of flexibility in how they approach at-risk customers.

A second noted modeling firm is UK-based Quadstone. Quadstone positions itself as a holistic predictor of customer behavior; and, through their Decisionhouse software, they offer marketers the opportunity to profile and segment customers "both visually and interactively." Like SLP Infoware, they have taken complex statistics and mathematical algorithms and converted them to hands-on application for marketers. Quadstone has clients in retail, telecom, and banking, helping predict churn, determine which products/offers will encourage at-risk customers to stay, and identify what it will take to win-back lost customers.

In the telecom industry, they estimate they've been able to double response rates to add-on service campaigns, reduce customer churn by over 10 percent, and reduce the costs of churn management by half.

The third innovative churn modeling consultant is @RISK, Inc., based in Pennsylvania. @RISK, Inc. uses advanced techniques—neural network protocols, artificial intelligence, and causal inference algorithms—to detect patterns and trends in customers' transactions that could mark them as potential defectors. Their Pathfinder™ program "learns" the stable, causally associated indicators of defection from the transaction data itself, yielding better predictive accuracy and precision. This, in conjunction with systems that can produce unique prediction equations at the microsegment level, has enabled @RISK, Inc. to identify the vast majority of "would-be" defectors months in advance. @RISK Inc.'s clients include fund companies, brokerage firms, and banks, and they have used Pathfinder™ to help identify high-risk customers and alternative positioning approaches. @RISK, Inc.'s techniques have proven both leading-edge and highly effective.

The Modeling Agency, located in Texas, has developed both a customer attrition and a time-until-attrition model. The attrition model forecasts which customers are most likely to churn, irrespective of time. The time-until-attrition model produces a score for each customer based on the probability of churn at a chosen time horizon, say six months from today. Alternatively, the model can be designed to estimate the actual time of churn, although with less accuracy.

One business writer, commenting on the emergence of churn prediction in the fund industry, said: "As this technology advances, the marketing departments of fund companies will start to look decidedly different. You may be hiring segment managers rather than product managers into your marketing group. And sooner than you think." This opinion can apply to any industry and business where excessive defection is a concern, and certainly, the telecommunications industry is one of these.

The average rate of annual customer churn in the telecom industry is 25 to 30 percent, with companies at the higher end of this rate getting no return on new subscribers. Why is that? It typically takes about three years to recover the cost of losing a customer with a newly acquired one ($400 in the United States and $700 in Europe). The challenge for telecom management, and for churn models as well, is to determine which customers are likely to leave, when, and why. While telecoms tend to be among the most active users of IT systems, data warehousing, and data mining techniques, they are principally focused on meeting tactical, operational goals. They still desire, however, to create a list of customers that are likely to cancel service in the near future

Telecoms may offer special incentives designed to reduce churn among targeted customers, but the models they develop seek to identify reasons for potential defection, such as billing problems or connection quality. Models will also begin by looking at usage—i.e., frequency and number of calls—and revenue generated from each customer, to establish regression and decision-tree techniques. This is known as automatic interaction detector, or AID, where customers are split, variable by variable, into ever finer segments and microsegments, each of which will contain a very high or very low proportion of customers who have churned. These models, in essence, create an equation that can match the variables against the likelihood of defection. Finally, the model can assign defection proclivities for each customer based on presence or absence of churn characteristics for that customer.

. . . And Don't Forget About RFID

The incredible array of customer information available in the '90s has now grown many-fold. Much of that information is available in real-time, or almost real-time, form, through what Forrester Research calls the "extended Internet."[7] This includes data generated through RFID tags, smart appliances, sophisticated cell phones, and personal computers, all of which are, or soon will be, connected to the Internet. Advanced as some companies are in handling data, they will soon

---

[7] Lyn Gubser, "Enhancing Online Customer Loyalty—New Tools and New Traps," *Customer Interaction Solutions*, February 2001.

have to learn even more leading-edge techniques, or risk being drowned in a flood of customer information.

RFID (radio frequency identification) has the potential to be the most powerful enabling medium for both collecting data from customers and communicating with them. Essentially, an RFID tag is little more than a microchip with a built-in antenna. It can be placed on a product for tracking sales movement or monitoring processes; or it can be embedded in a card or other reading device and placed in the hands of consumers. The "reader" receives radio frequency signals, and if there are any tags or receivers nearby, they communicate. Although RFID has many applications for product movement monitoring and inventory control—i.e., supply chain management—consumer cards and other reading devices are what we're considering.

As a technology, RFID isn't particularly new. In fact, it has been around since World War II. Over the past few years, however, the use of RFID has increased dramatically. Why? There are now global standards on protocols and frequencies, meaning that the volumes of data collected can be communicated, computer to computer, in an almost effortless manner. The costs of both tags and RFID readers are also rapidly declining. Finally, and perhaps most importantly, Internet information technology investments have changed the landscape for collecting, storing, and applying RFID-generated consumer data. Major companies, like Mobil, through its *SpeedPass,* and Wal-Mart, by insisting that its suppliers fully implement RFID by January 2005, have led the way in making this technology a universal data gathering and sharing device. Other major retailers, such as Target and Tesco, are installing specially designed shelves that can read radio frequency waves emitted by microchips in the packaging of millions of products. So the technology, as both an inventory tracking and customer personalization device, is gaining traction.

In Japan, for example, a shopper browsing the shelves of bookstores can be tracked to identify patterns of book selection. By placing tag readers on shelves, booksellers can identify the range of books a shopper has browsed, how many times a particular title was handled, and even the length of time looking through each book. Then at the check-out, buyers can receive bounce-back coupons based on their current shopping behavior and purchase records.

Companies will need to devise strategies to take advantage of the speed and mode of generating data for analysis through RFID.

Of course, as with any other database application and method of monitoring consumer activities, there is the inevitable concern over customer privacy. RFID, after all, provides the technical capability for marketers to obtain information on a vast array of consumer preferences, from the clothes and books they like to the food they prefer. This issue will undoubtedly grow as the use of RFID technology increases to make customer experiences more relevant and divisible continues to expand. In one test of RFID systems at the retail point-of-sale, for instance, there is experimental software technology that will allow customers to "kill," or erase, information they consider private from RFID tags before leaving the store.

A (Potential) RFID Data Gathering/Application Scenario

A national high-end seafood restaurant chain, let's call it Red Sail, issues contactless smart cards to patrons as part of its loyalty program. Diners use the card to identify themselves at every visit, and the chain can then enter such visit details as number in the party, menu selections, and related item purchase onto their records, enabling them to customize each dining experience. Once identified, the restaurant's manager or maitre d' also receives a small printout of the customer's profile specifics, enabling highly personalized service.

Red Sail also periodically conducts diner purchase behavior and loyalty research, looking at performance ratings, overall metrics, elements of complaint, and perceived changes in performance over time. All of this becomes part of that patron's record. Red Sail is, in addition, in an excellent position to use these data to develop marketing and promotional campaigns, improve patron-related processes, tailor communication programs, and create new products and services on a customized, and even purchase scenario, basis.

That's just the beginning of what this new technology can offer. When a cardholding customer visits any one of Red Sail's restaurants, they can swipe their card past the front of a wall-mountable "kiosk." The kiosk has a color display that, depending on that customer's individual profile, can recommend menu items and wines. It can even suggest, and provide special offers for, post-dinner entertainment, such as shows and movies. Red Sail is in negotiation with noncompeting national retail chains, such as office products and DIY supermarts, to share data, so there will be opportunity for cross-promotion.

And How Do Consumers Feel About RFID? Is It a DVD Player, or Just Another Eight-Track Stereo? Is It a Net Benefit or Net Curse?

It's fair to define RFID as a new technology, at least in terms of customer data gathering and application. So it's important for marketers to understand consumer awareness, mindset, and acceptance of RFID, and in particular their willingness to purchase RFID-enabled products, and their perceptions regarding the benefits and potential concerns about the technology.

In late 2003, consulting firm Cap Gemini Ernst & Young (CGEY) conducted a survey among a demographically representative sample of 1,000 North American consumers, 18 and older, to meet these objectives.[8] What they learned has both positive and negative implications.

Only about one-quarter of the consumers had ever heard of RFID technology; and of those, 42 percent were favorably inclined toward it, 10 percent were negative, and 48 percent had no opinion. Most of those aware of RFID had gotten their information from the media and word-of-mouth. Additionally, although about half of those surveyed either use or have heard of current applications such as Mobil's *SpeedPass* or *E-Z Pass* devices for automatically paying bridge and highway tolls, close to 80 percent didn't know that these devices use RFID.

When asked about potential benefits of RFID in terms of savings and security that the technology might bring, consumers cited faster recovery of stolen items, better car anti-theft protection, and reduced product costs. From a strictly informational perspective, consumers could see that RFID would facilitate recognition of their preferences and better in-store service; and, while many consumers said they would be willing to buy RFID-enabled products for these benefits (such as lower prices, convenience, a better shopping experience, privacy assurances, etc.), fewer said they would pay more for these products.

Reflective of concerns discussed regarding data privacy, study respondents said they had potential issues with third-party data usage, the detailed tracking of their purchase preferences, and a resulting increase in communication, particularly through direct marketing campaigns. Also, while they did not have in-depth understanding of RFID technology, they felt that RFID had the potential to impact personal privacy as much as mobile telephones, credit and debit cards, and customer loyalty card programs.

Part III—The New, New Things

A Blurb About Blogs

What are blogs, and why should every company care about them as an instrument for 1) gathering vital information about customers and 2) communicating with them as well? Simply, blogs, or weblogs as they are alternatively (but far less frequently) called, are in many ways the community embodiment of the Internet.

---

[8] "The Consumer's Genuine Attitude to RFID," www.usingrfid.com, February 2, 2004.

They are individuals' personal expressions of interest, often in stream of consciousness form, made available to others through Web links and automated publishing. There are blogs for IT professionals, authors, redheads, science fiction junkies, people who live in Los Angeles. Name it. If there's a topic that can interest or involve small segments of mankind, chances are there's a blog or blog group that covers it. Blogs have become a pervasive aspect of communication, ways for people to share electronically their opinions and ideas.

Communities and blogs are related, to be sure; however, unlike communities, a sponsoring organization will have rather less control, but perhaps greater opportunity to achieve macro and micro communication goals. How micro? Well, individuals can post their blogs via a series of email addresses, sending photos or portions of their blogs as desired, and they can do it as frequently as they wish.

While most companies are still getting up to speed on the basics of site development for their organizations, some forward-looking companies have discovered blogs as perhaps the "next big thing" for communicating with customers on an individualized basis. *Fast Company* magazine, for example, uses blogs created by its staff writers to convey quick, personal opinions on news stories that might not appear in the magazine itself, generating interest beyond basic editorial content. ESPN and Sega blog ideas on videogames to prospective customers, collecting ideas on how to improve their products. International travel guide Fodor's has a blog called "Right This Way," in which its editors give their perspectives on interesting travel stories from around the world. So, as these examples suggest, blogging is likely to be considered more and more frequently as marketers and advertisers plan their communication media mix.

Companies, though, must address very savvy communicators when using blogs to help meet their messaging goals, both inbound and outbound. First, the blogs must provide new and authentic information, inspiring trust among customers. More than that, they must be a source for the type and relevancy of information unavailable elsewhere. Blogs have many benefits, not the least of which is customer knowledge and insight development. When companies like DaimlerChrysler, Hartford Financial Services, and IBM currently devote an increasing share of customer data gathering resources to blogs, it's clear that they are becoming mainstream.

Profile Management and Flexible Hierarchies

Speaking of the communication mix, no one has to be told how complex it has become, nor how complex it will continue to grow. With telecommunications customers using services such as text messaging and personalized content delivery to receive information on their cell phones, Blackberriers, pagers, PDAs, mini-PCs, and laptops, it's little wonder that growing relationships between suppliers and customers has become more of a challenge.

More than customer data integration (CDI), or advanced techniques like customer data fusion, which brings together real-time research findings with other internally and externally available streams of customer information, is an emerging technology—*profile management.*

Profile management enables each customer to build pictures, or more accurately landscapes, of their preferences and attributes into a single, aggregated set of insights. For example, a telecom customer's profile would include not just account, payment, demographics, and perhaps research information, but also the services used—voice, voicemail, Internet—content preferences (such as sports, entertainment, news, and business), and even settings on the customer's handset (alarm, ring volume, Internet settings, band, etc.). In examples such as this, the customer organizes and manages his or her own account and communication preferences, and is an equal partner in helping the supplier conduct business more easily and flexibly. Service providers do their part by making it easy to do business online, or by land or mobile telephone lines, providing support in terms that are best for each customer. Customers take more control over involvement with the service provider, but they also give the provider many more messaging and support options. Customers can set up, if desired, account hierarchies, for personal or business support, for family members, and even by communication device. Thus, the relationship created by the customer, for his or her own benefit, is *divisible.*

How divisible? A customer could set up his or her business account through a PDA, in order to receive email and monitor expenses during the day. The customer's daytime business profile would insure that the desired content comes through that device during working hours. In the evenings and on weekends, the business profile would be deactivitated; and the personal profile, with communication through his mobile phone, would be switched on. If the customer wants sports scores and times of entertainment events, those would be communicated along with other selected content from the supplier.

In the past, the closest companies came to this kind of intimacy was through cumbersome CRM systems, principally designed one way—information that the supplier's sales, marketing, and customer service groups needed about the customer, rather than information that the customer needs. When customers have the capability to build their own profiles, called *flexible hierarchies,* the best, most relevant data are available to both customer and supplier. The product of these hierarchies gives service providers the ability to know how, when, where, and why customers use their services, situation by situation. Customers can store their profiles and keep them current without having to directly involve the supplier each time a change is made.

Once customer profile management and flexible hierarchies come into more active use, suppliers will be better able to provide personalized messaging, and execute time-specific cross-sell and up-sell activities, delivered through the customer's choice of media or device. At the same time, customers will be even more active participants in managing their own services and preferences, enhancing the level of customer support.

The net result of applying these profiles on a holistic basis is more in-depth understanding of the customer, lower service costs, and higher levels of revenue and advocacy—all accomplished by giving the customer greater individual empowerment.

8

The Pivotal Emerging Data Importance of Customer Clubs, Loyalty Programs, and Communities

Customer clubs and loyalty programs, at least the ones that are successful at leveraging increased commitment and loyalty behavior on the part of customers, are evolving to become very different entities from their original, simpler definitions in the early 1980s. Some worked from the start because they used data to create the right amalgam of value and customer involvement. Newer clubs and programs are building on that success, but with more effective and broader application of customer-specific detail.

Customer communities, a relatively new source of customer insight enabled by the Internet, are a largely untapped, but potentially powerful, way of getting close to the customer and generating valuable data. The power of clubs, loyalty programs, and communities will be explored in this chapter.

Customer Data: The Engine Behind Tesco's Hugely Successful Loyalty Program

One of my key sources for the uses of information gathered by customer clubs and loyalty programs, for example, is my friend and colleague, Brian Woolf (brianwoolf.com). Brian is president of the Retail Strategy Center, Inc., and a fountain of knowledge about how companies apply, and don't apply, data generated through these programs.

Tesco, one of Europe's leading retail chains, is using its customer information for initiatives on a number of marketing and product developments. In his book *Loyalty Marketing: The Second Act,* Brian described how Tesco leveraged customer data drawn from its loyalty program to move into offering banking and financial services:

> With information derived from its loyalty card and enriched by appended external demographic data, they can readily develop profiles of customers who would most likely be interested in basic banking services as well as an array of related options, ranging from car loans and pension savings programs, to insurance for all types of needs—car, home, travel and even pets. It costs Tesco significantly less than half of what it costs a bank to acquire a

financial services customer. Without a doubt, having detailed customer information gives them a competitive edge.[1]

A couple of years ago, Tesco parlayed its offline customer data to also become the world's largest online grocery and sundries home delivery service. Additionally, Tesco uses its customer data to target and segment communications to the millions of its loyalty program members by almost infinite demographic, purchase, and lifestyle profiles. In his book, Brian notes that Tesco can create up to 150,000 variations of its promotion and reward statement mailings each quarter. These variations, as he says, "are both apparent and subtle, ranging from the product offer (i.e., which customers receive which offers at what price) to the content of the letter and the way it is personalized."[2]

Tesco is absolutely a company that knows how to leverage customer information. Their customer database contains not just demographic and lifestyle data, food spending in stores and on home delivery, but also specifics about their customers' interest in, and use of, a diverse range of non-food products and services. As Bill Gates' statement earlier in the book suggests, incisive and leveraged customer data has enabled Tesco to put distance between themselves and competitors, in both traditional and nontraditional retail markets.

The Wizard, and Thinking, Behind Tesco's Clubcard

Clive Humby, president of dunnhumby in the UK, is responsible for the Tesco Clubcard and much of the success they have achieved with it. He considers his role principally that of a mathematician, but he has a thorough understanding of how companies can use data to leverage and drive customer commitment and loyalty behavior. Tesco so completely supports Humby's ideas and concepts that they bought a controlling share in his company several years ago. He believes that customer loyalty does indeed exist or that it can be created, despite all that's been written about the fickle, or butterfly, customer:

> Everyone's heard about the death of loyalty. Yes, to a degree, loyalty schemes are dead. But that's not the same thing, as the vast majority are sales promotion programs in disguise. Sales promotion has always been tactical, smoothing out spikes and troughs, never strategic.

---

[1] Michael Lowenstein, "It's Really (Almost) All About the Data: Optimizing Loyalty Initiatives," www.searchcrm.com, February 7, 2003.
[2] Michael Lowenstein, "It's Really (Almost) All About the Data: Optimizing Loyalty Initiatives," www.searchcrm.com, February 7, 2003.

Increasingly, I believe, the customer is becoming fickle because of what we're doing to them. The customer doesn't wake up yesterday and decide to be fickle. Every day they get a bombardment of direct mail and TV offers saying "Change, Change, Change. Come to me. Come to me...." We train them to be fickle.[3]

Humby asserts that most of the fickle customers have shallow supplier commitment, i.e., they are easy to acquire but difficult to keep. They have very strong switching proclivities. One way that acquisition of these kinds of minimal commitment customers can be held in check (what we call the "Casanova Complex" of some organizations) is to make sure that customer acquisition and customer retention are kept in balance.

As stated earlier, many companies pay much more attention to winning or capturing customers than they do to keeping them. "Conquest" is a frequently used term for new customers, especially among automotive retailers. Consultants and academics have studied the strong proclivity of many companies, irrespective of size or industry, to focus on bringing in the next new customer, concentrating on having the lowest price, and compensating employees more for winning new accounts than for keeping existing customers happy and loyal.

The multi-industry continental Europe study by Professor Adrian Payne of Cranfield University cited earlier, showing that 80 percent of companies ("Acquirers") spend too much of their marketing budget on customer acquisition, also found that 10 percent spend too much on retention and that 10 percent, whom he calls "Profit Maximizers," seem to get the mix right.[4]

Why does this overemphasis and preoccupation happen? There are five reasons, according to Professor Payne:

1. Belief that existing customers will be retained; company needs to focus on acquisition
2. Companies experience high churn rates, the "leaky bucket" syndrome
3. Customer acquisition is reported regularly to analysts, shareholders and senior management; but churn rate may or may not be reported
4. The lifetime value profit impact of lost customers is not reviewed
5. Sales force and senior management compensation is often based on acquisition, not retention

---

[3] Bob Thompson, "Tesco Shines at Loyalty: An Interview with Clive Humby," www.crmguru.com.
[4] Adrian Payne, *The Handbook of CRM* (Amsterdam: Elsevier, 2005), p. 147.

Clive Humby's solution for this is simple: measure both acquisition and retention at the same time. Also, and perhaps more importantly, he believes that the acquisition team should be rewarded on customer retention, not acquisition, because it is retention and loyalty behavior that create organizational value.

He is also highly skeptical of traditional approaches to satisfaction research, particularly with new customers. In research conducted by his company, he's determined that the highest levels of supplier advocacy and commitment come just after a customer has made a switch.

So your newest customers are likely to be the most loyal, which some would consider counterintuitive. Humby explains:

> That's the point when you've just made a decision and seek affirmation by talking about it with your friends. For example, your new customer will be saying things like "I've just switched mobile suppliers and I've made the right decision, haven't I. Have you seen these new features; aren't they clever!" There's a myth that there's some sort of magical ladder. Customers come in on the bottom rung at the beginning, they go up a ladder, becoming more valuable to you and, over time, they become advocates of your brand. It just doesn't happen like that.[5]

The strong customer tendency to express high levels of satisfaction just after a switch is one of the principal results that make these kinds of survey results so very suspect. Companies rely heavily on these surveys, but they frequently lead to erroneous conclusions about loyalty:

> Too often we focus all our attention on customer satisfaction surveys that say "You just bought this: are you happy with it?" Of course they are happy with it! If it's a car, they've just spent £10,000 or more on it, so what do you expect them to say? The real question is "What about the people who didn't buy?" or what about the people who were customers and left. What do you do to find out about them? Do you contrast behaviors to really find out what is going on?[6]

So What Drives Customer Commitment and Loyalty Behavior at Tesco?

For Tesco, the ability to put customer satisfaction survey results into a proper perspective and focus on customer loyalty behavior is a key differentiator in their

---

[5] Bob Thompson, "Tesco Shines at Loyalty: An Interview with Clive Humby," www.crmguru.com.

[6] Bob Thompson, "Tesco Shines at Loyalty: An Interview with Clive Humby," www.crmguru.com.

success. Further, he questions whether artificially constructed relationships, which customers may or may not find of value, leverages true loyalty behavior. According to Humby:

> The notion of "relationships" will not deliver loyalty. Customers do not want relationships. McKinsey researchers asked customers if they want "a relationship" with their suppliers. The overall answer was "no" they didn't want CRM when it was explained to them. Most said they just wanted decent service. If you think IT can help your CRM problems that's like thinking re-decorating can save your marriage. It's how you shape your business that makes CRM work. Tesco builds its whole business around its customer data. The checkout clerks can tell you the basic store concepts of segmentation strategy and the major initiatives in the store targeted at different customer groups that week. It's not CRM as a marketing language.[7]

Humby subscribes to the concept of "reverse marketing," where identified desires and needs on the part of customers has replaced the traditional "push" we often observe coming from sales and marketing. The enterprise, reflecting the concept of divisibility, is constructed and honed around customer behavior. Instead of locating customers for existing products, or developing products and then identifying customers for them, reverse marketing enables some companies to develop products and services driven by an understanding of customer needs. Tesco is able to practice this extremely well: "The data allows us to create marketing plans for groups of customers, finding products for them rather than customers for products. Our approach is: 'We've got these customers; have we got enough offers to appeal to them?'" This statement pretty well explains Tesco's mission: to earn and grow the lifetime loyalty of their customers. And they do this through judicious gathering and interpretation of customer data.

Succeeding with Loyalty Program Customer Data

Unlike most other retailers' loyalty programs, which are, in the main, discount and frequent shopper devices that throw off masses of potentially useful but unapplied customer data, Tesco has made efficient and actionable use of this information. Humby says that the data, in effect, run Tesco's business. They use it to set pricing, plan process modification, and acquire new customers. As he concludes: "We've

---

[7] Bob Thompson, "Tesco Shines at Loyalty: An Interview with Clive Humby," www.crmguru.com.

always said that anyone can launch a points system, but a points system is just electronic sales promotion. It only becomes a loyalty mechanism when you use the data to add relevance to the customer's life."

Tesco carefully monitors their customers' purchasing patterns, overlaying customer life-stage, shopping habits, what they call "basket topology" (what products they purchase), promotional receptivity and promiscuity (migration), channels used for purchasing, brand advocacy and commitment (for Tesco), and individual customer profitability. This last element also includes the cost to serve each customer.

They know that a certain category of customers will make most of their purchases on "deal," or promotion, and then shop other chains the same way. Rather than drop them, Tesco will develop offers designed to modify the buying behavior of these customers. Other customers have such a strong image of Tesco that they will trust them with new business offerings. This has been the foundation for Tesco's move into banking and other services. The organization used customer data in acquiring customers when it introduced Tesco Personal Finance, a new suite of banking and financial services. When the company later launched a credit card through Tesco Personal Finance, the card data allowed them to so tightly promote the offer to the right profile people that Tesco became one of the UK's leading card issuers in a matter of months by volume, from a standing start. Humby sums up their effectiveness in a simple way: "It's about *relevance.*"

Relevance (and its close cousin, trust) is an important word when linking data to marketing and operational effectiveness. It will come up again within this chapter.

Relevance also refers to the customization Tesco is able to offer customers in its communication. As Humby explains:

> We send out 11 million statements with 4 million variances, so only four or five people receive the same offers. Clubcard holders get cheaper prices in exchange for the data, but money alone doesn't deliver loyalty. We track trends and create offerings like Tesco's Baby Club. 80% of all live births are registered at Tesco before the baby is born. That's loyalty. We even have a Kids' Club with permission from the parents to engage in dialogue with the kids. That is loyalty. It comes from relevance.[8]

When Tesco decided to enter the world of online grocery provision, becoming the most successful company at this form of retailing, Clubcard data

---

[8] Bob Thompson, "Tesco Shines at Loyalty: An Interview with Clive Humby," www.crmguru.com.

were used to move into this business. Because they found that many new online customers were abandoning their orders midway through completion, Tesco used Clubcard information to develop a "favorites" list, customized to each first-time customer, which mirrored their offline purchase behavior. Since navigation became so familiar and easy, click-through and order completion rates went up significantly And, impressively, these customers stayed to purchase again and again. The favorites list combined with the enjoyable online experience to reinforce relevance. Tesco, in sum, has struck gold with customer data.

. . . . and It Doesn't Matter If You're Big or Small: Green Hills Supermarket

Gary Hawkins is CEO of Green Hills, an upscale grocery retailer just outside of Syracuse, New York. Green Hills was founded by his great-grandmother, Carrie Hawkins, in 1934, offering fresh vegetables grown on their farm, until by the 1960s, it became a fully formed supermarket.

Once the store reached this size and scope, management was on a product and department basis through the early 1990s. Responding to competitive pressures during those years, sale prices were driving the supermarket down to break-even levels, or below.

Green Hills launched its frequent shopper program in mid-1991, one of the earliest food retailers to do so. From the very beginning, Green Hills saw the value of customer profile data generated through the program. Their ability to match better than 90 percent of total sales to individual customers has given them tremendous leverage. Much like the Pareto principle, they quickly discovered that the top-spending 30 percent of their customers accounted for about 75 percent of annual sales. Further, they found that their best customers shopped with them several times a week, and generated much higher gross profit margin. On the other side of the coin, the shopper program data told them that they were losing nearly 30 percent of their customer base a year.

This early insight led to some significant changes in advertising and marketing strategy. Green Hills began to see that their best customers were getting insufficient marketing value relative to their purchasing power. They learned that many of their low-end customers were purchasing only loss-leader sale items, thus generating negative profitability, while high-end customers were purchasing a wide range of products and from most departments in the store. So their good customers were subsidizing the losses caused by the poor customers.

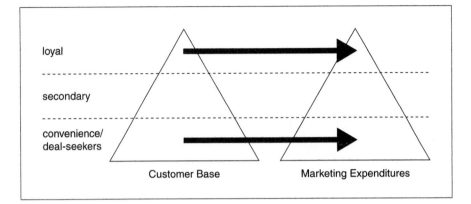

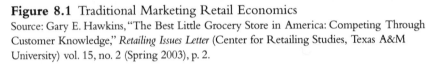

Figure 8.1 Traditional Marketing Retail Economics
Source: Gary E. Hawkins, "The Best Little Grocery Store in America: Competing Through Customer Knowledge," *Retailing Issues Letter* (Center for Retailing Studies, Texas A&M University) vol. 15, no. 2 (Spring 2003), p. 2.

The company decided to focus on optimizing the behavior of the high-end customers, recognizing and rewarding them for their loyalty. Hawkins uses the example of Thanksgiving turkeys to illustrate this new emphasis. Like most retailers, Green Hills had leveraged the sale of low-priced turkeys as a seasonal purchase volume incentive for its customers. Beginning in 1994, applying early customer segmentation data from its frequent shopper program, they began to give out turkeys to their high-end customers if they purchased at a certain threshold during the pre-holiday period, and selling them at regular prices to all other shoppers. While sales volume increased only marginally, purchases by high-end customers increased by 25 percent over the previous year; and the amount of total spending by this segment increased almost 30 percent.

As customers upped spending to earn their turkeys, they began buying products from around the supermarket, including high-margin perishables and more regularly-priced items. Overall store gross margins skyrocketed.

The learning from this promotion caused Green Hills to rethink its marketing and promotional program. There was renewed interest, and high investment, in building optimum loyalty among their best customers through enhanced services (such as higher check-cashing privileges). Green Hills' reward program also attracted other customers from the marketplace, and they provided incentives for the less frequent customers to allocate an increasing proportion of their grocery dollars there. Their overall customer retention rate rose to almost 80 percent, from the 70 percent results when they first began (Figure 8.2).

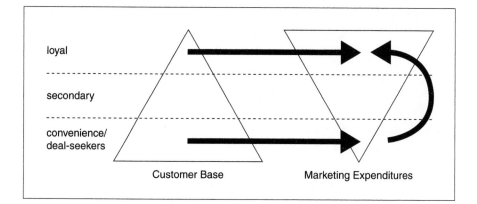

Figure 8.2 New Marketing Retail Economics
Source: Gary E. Hawkins, "The Best Little Grocery Store in America: Competing Through Customer Knowledge," *Retailing Issues Letter* (Center for Retailing Studies, Texas A&M University) vol. 15, no. 2 (Spring 2003), p. 2.

By the mid-1990s, Green Hills also began to apply two important modes of thinking and action to its customer base. First, they established quarterly purchase tier levels for their customers, enabling them to measure the number of customers in each segment and the value and percentage of total sales coming from the tiers. With this renewed approach to customer management, they were better able to concentrate marketing dollars among high spenders, cutting the waste of inefficient advertising and promotion while simultaneously increasing purchase levels among best customers several fold.

Like their larger European cousin, Tesco, Green Hills has begun offering online ordering to their customers. They will begin looking at customer-by-customer profitability, and will be utilizing technology to customize communications and pricing to individual customers.

Hawkins believes that detailed customer data is central to his company's continuing success, and offers this advice: "Retailers who incorporate customer data must view it as a business strategy—one that involves their entire organization and requires long-term commitment and perspective building." He believes that top management commitment, redirecting marketing funds to best customers, focusing on customer value delivery, and, particularly, having and using the right data are essential. As he concludes: "Gathering adequate customer data is essential. A customer-focused strategy must establish systems and processes for capturing and using the necessary information. Retailers need to collect great amounts of customer data and link large percentages of their total sales and transactions to individual customers." This is the basis for divisibility.

Community Rising

Marketers are showing increasing interest in the value of community, particularly online community, as a way of connecting with, selling to, and learning from their customers. As has been truly said, it takes a village. And that's where community begins.

To be specific, we're not talking about communities of proficiency or interest among employees within a company; nor are we talking about independent community portals, such as for people interested in grandchildren, gardening, ancient civilizations, cars, or woodworking. And we're not talking about communities organized for strictly mercantile purposes between participating members. Finally, we aren't referring to complaint and review post sites, such as epinions.com and planetfeedback.com. The communities we mean are the forums organized and managed by companies for generating feedback and sharing interest and expertise with their customers.

Further, these are predominantly online communities. Major players such as eBay have tried offline community building, even briefly publishing a magazine, but have retrenched to strictly online initiatives.

The focus on community is growing—rapidly. The editor of a prominent CRM information portal has recently written about company-managed communities. There has been a book (for which I wrote the Afterword) entirely devoted to customer communities. Online and print business periodicals are running articles on the benefits of community. There are some terrific models and community success stories, with more coming to light every day.

What *are* the benefits of customer communities, and why should marketers care, you ask? Well, most immediately, and of up-front interest to marketers, is *increased sales*. Studies by McKinsey & Company and Jupiter Media Metrix found that, from some sites, regular users of bulletin boards and feedback areas generated two-thirds of a site's sales, though they accounted for just one-third of site visitors. Further, McKinsey has determined that users who post messages to a site's forum or who contribute product/service reviews visit nine times more often than nonparticipants. They buy almost twice as often.[9] Take a breath . . . and say WOW!

There are pure-play websites, based on paid memberships, that exist almost entirely around community. One of these is Classmates.com. Connectivity is the basis of Classmates' 400 percent growth over the past two years. The company now has 30 million members, with a goal of reaching 100 million by 2005. What

---

[9] Michael Lowenstein, "The Key to Customer Communities," www.searchcrm.com, July 3, 2002.

works for Classmates.com can be applied to many other online businesses, enabling community and commerce to happily merge.

For example, retailers like eBags, online merchants of luggage and briefcases, and Orvis, the outdoor products merchant, maintain relationships with customers, and generate valuable feedback from them, through their managed communities. Orvis, predominantly a catalog marketer since its inception, began its online life strictly as an information source. For several years, it has expanded this footprint to become a fully functional online store as well. The combination enabled them to host 6 million unique visitors in 2001, double the number of the year before. Online sales now account for one-fifth of Orvis' overall revenue.

Launched early in 1999, eBags has 150 brands and over 4,000 products. It has monthly sales growth of 50 percent. eBags has focused on creating a site that provides consumer value on a personal, and purchase scenario, level.

eBags asks consumers to return to the site 30 days after making a purchase to rate the products they bought; more than 30 percent do. eBags posts all of its shoppers' opinions on price/value, appearance, durability, overall performance (good or bad), and whether the buyers would purchase the product again. Close to one-quarter of eBags' customers offer testimonials, and these are also carried on the site.

Customers of eBags are segmented according to lifestyle—business, sports interests, travel, children, life stage, outdoor activities, etc.—so that the company can target product recommendations keyed to feedback. The *My eBags* program—which includes opt-in monthly newsletters, special offers and promotions, monthly event reminders (special occasions and individual life events)—is built on in-depth research and an understanding of what customers value. The objective of this program is to make the customer's experience valuable, attractive, relevant, and personalized. Community is a central feature and theme of eBags programs.

The key issue for community participants, according to all the studies conducted, is *relevance,* similar to what Clive Humby said about loyalty programs. If there's a sense of shared interest or support, customers and visitors will chat, evaluate, and recommend—and buy. Another of McKinsey's most telling community study findings is that, even if visitors don't directly contribute to message boards and forums, they often read them.[10] This gives them enough of a connection that they are more likely to return and become purchasers and community members.

---

[10] Michael Lowenstein, "The Key to Customer Communities," www.searchcrm.com, July 3, 2002.

So, beyond sales, and potential sales, are there any other bottom-line benefits of customer community? It turns out that there are plenty. Here are just three of them.

1. *Lower Customer Service Costs.* Companies can save money by using community management software, enabling them to encourage customers to share information and participate in relevant discussions. The more sites can register members to a community, and get them to participate frequently, the more they can save money by either having online content that answers customer questions or getting another customer to answer the question. They can also benefit through mining the information from customer discussions, generating reports on customer concerns and trends.

2. *Product/Concept Beta Testing.* When companies come up with new products or concepts, they can get an early read on customer response by using their community as collaborators and jury. Customers can critique or test a proposed offering, sharing opinions and suggestions, while companies observe and mine the information. This helps companies optimize their offerings, often avoiding the missteps associated with having complete customer input prior to introduction.

3. *Customer Value Research.* Companies can conduct straight customer loyalty and customer value research by recruiting panels of forum participants. Typically, these surveys are conducted through an intranet. Results are immediate, and companies using their forum participants as panelists get response rates high enough to avoid the nonresponse bias pitfalls of other, lower response, self-completion research methods. Further, companies using their communities for value research can link results to projected, segmented customer profitability, a tremendous benefit.

Communities are not always the best research vehicle, in part because there's a tendency for only the most interested and involved individuals to participate on a regular basis, which won't keep the information fresh. To maintain vibrancy in an online community, respondents must have a strong connection to the subjects at hand and to each other, but the community sponsor should also be recruiting new participants on a regular basis so that the community does not stagnate.

The five-hundred-pound gorilla of online community, eBay, has recently taken participation to a new level. They organized a three-day community event at the Anaheim Convention Center in California. Several thousand eBayers—buyers and sellers alike—attended from around the globe. They had the opportunity to hear eBay's president and CEO, Meg Whitman, talk about the role of community, meet eBay's senior staff at forums over the three days, visit booths to help them with their trading, attend educational classes, and participate in events such as a live auction, games, and a gala.

As one community participant said in an eBay community posting, "I, for one, am thankful eBay exists. They have given us a venue. We are grateful." That endorsement represents real advocacy and commitment, the ultimate value of community.

HOG Community Heaven

Almost out of business in 1983, and with virtually no money available for advertising, Harley-Davidson took a bold and unusual step. They elected to create a community of Harley enthusiasts. Without knowing quite what the outcome would be, they began with a single chapter of Harley Owners Group, or HOG, in Milwaukee, Harley-Davidson's hometown. Starting with under 50 members in that first chapter, they used newsletters, a club magazine, and special events to build the base to 49 chapters and 60,000 members by 1985.

In the 1990s, HOG went international, spreading first to Europe then to Australia and Asia. There are now more than 1,100 chapters and 800,000 members. What has this meant for Harley-Davidson? Lots of revenue and profits. From 1984 through 1996, for instance, they spent no money on advertising, expending just $1 million in 1997, and not much more annually since then. The revenue has come from purchasing bikes, of course, but also from the tremendous variety of Harley logo gear: jackets, pants, boots, gloves, t-shirts, bike accessories, baseball caps.

Harley believes that, through its community, the company is helping to fulfill dreams. In fact, "We fulfill dreams" is the company vision. At the same time, they create a cohesive, beneficial, and motivating brand experience. This has had several results that would be the envy of any company:

- Harley owners are tremendously loyal. Very few people who own a Harley ever sell or trade it for another bike.
- Almost half of all owners have taken part in one or more rallies or riding events sponsored by HOG or Harley itself.
- A significant proportion of the company's revenues comes from selling merchandise, the living lifestyle of Harley ownership.

As John Russell, Vice-President and Managing Director of Harley-Davidson Europe, says of Harley's approach on the HOG website:

> We actively engage with our customers; we encourage our people to spend time with our customers, riding with customers, being with customers whenever the opportunity arises.

If it is important to the customer, if it's a good insight, if it's a good point of understanding and connection to the customer—it does actually make its way through into the business process and become part of what we do.[11]

Sean D'Souza, writing about the power of Harley's community, has made some general statements about the value of this form of communication and inclusion for customers:[12]

1. *The competition doesn't have a clue.* While conventional advertising and publicity are great, they cost serious moolah. And everyone, including competitors, can see exactly what you're doing. Once they get their grubby hands on your plans, they can outspend you, outsmart you and send your business into Outer Mongolia. With community, you can see who's coming through the door. And you're the doorkeeper. It gives you the chance to create Super Glue loyalty, long before your competition wises up.

2. *Communities give specific and vital feedback.* They may complain good-naturedly at times. But mostly they'll be giving you valuable feedback. They'll tell you what they want and what is passé. They'll bond with you and trust you and your judgment with each meeting. You will no longer have to guess what your customers want. They'll tell you even without your asking. What more could you ask for?

3. *No man (or woman) is an island.* You've heard that phrase before. No one likes to be an isolated case. Psychologically, we all like to be part of a group, a society, a country or a community of some sort. Give your clients something to cling to, and watch how leaders and volunteers form within the community. This will dramatically lessen your workload.

These three descriptors are clearly what has made Harley-Davidson a worldwide success. Let's look at another global phenomenon driven by the power of community.

A Really Unusual, But Extremely Powerful, Example of Online Community—Harry Potter Around the World

The Harry Potter phenomenon can be considered a prime example, as well as a metaphor, for what is possible with both online and offline targeted customer community building.

---

[11] Michael Lowenstein and Tim Wragg, "The Marketing Value of Customer Advocacy," *Admap*, December 2004, pp. 44–47.

[12] Sean D'Souza, "Can Harley's Secret Weapon Revitalize Your Marketing?" www.marketingprofs.com, February 3, 2004.

First, there are the Harry Potter books themselves. With just a few books in the series created by English author Jo Rowling, each release of a new book has created almost unparalleled excitement around the world. The interest and involvement is not limited to children. Parents and teachers have joined those enthralled by the fantasies of Hogwarts Wizardry School, Quidditch Teams, Golden Snitches, and such. The Geocities Harry Potter portal site, sponsored by Yahoo!, has been visited almost 3 million times as of 2004.

Warner Bros., in addition to offering Harry Potter gifts on its site, has made several Harry Potter movies. Warner is also considering a Harry Potter theme park, and there will be a weekly TV cartoon show based on Harry's adventures. The Potter enthusiasm extends well beyond the books, parks, TV shows, and movies to an endless array of merchandise: toys, games, costumes, keychains, mugs, stationery, party kits (balloons, candles, hats, invitations, table covers, confetti, banners, cups, treat cups, and even thank-you notes), Christmas tree ornaments, and on and on. Fritz, an online gift and collectibles site that carries famous brand names like Hummel, Lenox, Swarovski, Waterford, and Lladro has close to 30 different Harry Potter collectible items.

More impressive than the physical evidence of Harry Potter's popularity is the way fans have formed communities of interest and involvement regarding their fantasy hero and his fantasy world. There are official Potter fan sites, sponsored by companies like Warner and Scholastic. These sites feature discussion groups, trivia, and contests, plus the obligatory merchandise. Scholastic's site has discussion guides for teachers, and there are also links and content for parents.

But, there are also many unofficial fan sites, in countries as varied as the United States, Turkey, Denmark, Poland, France, Russia, Japan, Spain, Switzerland, Ireland, and Hungary. This is where, perhaps more than anyplace else, the Harry Potter community of interest is most active.

The unofficial German site (hpfc.de), founded by two teenage girls in Berlin, is especially noteworthy. Its objective is simple: to increase the fun with Harry Potter books. It offers an encyclopedia, online games, a forum for discussion, and cards to friends. Visitors become fan club members by passing an entrance exam based on their knowledge of book content. The site averages over 1 million page visits per year, with 19,000 on December 15, 2000 alone.

With all this community activity around the Harry Potter books, it's clear that it has had a profound, and positive, commercial impact, both online and offline. What are the implications and lessons of this success, and the community largely responsible for it, for both consumer and business-to-business product/service marketers? The Internet has become the world's biggest marketplace. It offers buyers scale, distribution efficiencies, more efficient communication, and enhanced access to competitive offerings. At the same time, costs and inconveniences of switching suppliers are dramatically lower. Companies that in the offline world and carrying forward to the virtual world have focused on individual customers or customer segments, must also focus on the collective, i.e., the customer community, to be successful.

The (Potential) Future of Community

The inability of most marketers to even identify, much less effectively utilize, such readily available and obvious online (and offline) relationship and data gathering techniques like community is one example of the lack of value, and noncreative approaches to customer information development. This can lead to rapid retail site customer churn.

Customers, generally speaking, can have both short-term transactional encounters and longer-lasting and firmer relationships with their suppliers. Customers are social as well as individualistic. Abraham Maslow codified this in his Hierarchy of Values when he identified higher-order needs such as Esteem, Cognition, Aesthetic, Self-Actualization, and Transcendence as human goals.

Community is likely to find its greatest future application as a research device. Using both synchronous (chats) and asynchronous (bulletin boards) communication forms of community building, research can be conducted with a few customers or thousands, facilitating both individual and social proclivities of customers at the same time. Online data collection is becoming more creative with each method. For instance, qualitative techniques such as brainstorming (idea generation, categorizing, and prioritizing), multimedia evaluation (graphics and video files, such as home interiors, kitchen appliances, and home office layouts), and quick-read polling on ideas or preferences, etc., can now be done just as in traditional focus groups and minigroups.

Companies such as Hallmark Cards are using communities to augment their suite of market research capabilities, finding that they can get both rapid feedback and more efficient research programming. They launched the company's first online community, the Idea Exchange, in 2000 and have since established three others, each with a specific and unique target market. Hallmark has determined that they can now make their innovation and creativity efforts both more focused and more productive.

Most companies, particularly on the Internet, have devoted much of their energy to only increasing transactions by appealing to more essential customer needs. Just as communities of interest can bring people together who interact, or relate, based on one or more shared values and interests (age, hobbies, business or profession, etc.), so these communities can be leveraged to facilitate buying and selling. In other words, community building is an essential element in loyalty building. Whether engaged solely as a research device or applied as a component of customer interaction, community is becoming an essential pillar of marketing and customer relationships that should be included in every program.

Virgin Student, a division of Virgin group of companies, offers a credit card and related services for 18- to 21-year-old students. They have integrated the building of an online community into their business model. Students are inherently among the more active users of online communities, and Virgin has created community content based on their frequency of usage, whether they are working full-time or part-time, by campus, by study discipline, by lifestyle interest characteristics (travel, entertainment, cooking, sports, etc.).

The Virgin student community is used to promote contests and other viral elements. In one such program, "Win A Big Red House," ten students would win free rent, at ten different houses near their schools, for an entire academic year, and for several of their friends. This contest was sponsored by Virgin Mobile. Community members were asked to post votes for nominated students, and in the initial contest, over 100,000 votes were posted. Awareness and purchase of Virgin Mobile phone service rose significantly as a result of the contest. Virgin Student has found that having an open, honest community for student-customers is essential for building their commitment to the brand.

As a final example of community's impact potential, the American Association of Retired Persons (AARP) has had an online community for several years. Each week, the association's community message boards receives over 10,000 visits and 700 posts to its message boards. In a recent survey of its forum users, AARP learned that 96 percent were likely to renew their membership in the association compared to AARP's overall renewal rate of 86 percent. Seeing the mutual value in this, AARP has increased the level of forum activity by offering enhanced community features, such as having a forum for members to share interesting experiences and memories. By the end of 2002, the number of posts had increased by 455 percent over 2001.

The challenge for community is to continually bring in new members and new ideas, and to make sure that communities do the same things for customers and prospects—create the content, engagement, and value-added relevance that leads to commitment.

Community Insight Generation Cousins

There are some qualitative and quantitative techniques that build on, or are variations of, community approaches. One of these is brand communities, and Harley-Davidson again offers an excellent example. Through HOG, Harley-Davidson conducts frequent company-sponsored events. Management blends in and rides with the members, building and developing trust and generating qualitative insight at the same time. Saturn and Jeep, through its Jamborees, do the same thing.

Customer advisory boards and panels are also an excellent way for companies to learn what customers really want. These are empanelled groups of customers brought together to evaluate concepts, products, services, and the effectiveness of operational processes. They enable companies to look at trends. Customers meet with management, often in comfortable locations, to function as a "think tank," where problems, opportunities, and emerging issues can be examined. Assignments of such boards can include:

• Validation of ideas for new product and service features
• Identification of flaws or deficiencies in current products and services
• Determination of how products and services are actually being used by customers
• Assessment of competitive products and services
• Learn about new techniques and technologies customers are considering, and how this will impact the sponsoring company's future products and services

Large companies, such as Daimler-Chrysler, IBM, Merck, The Equitable, Oracle, and Northwest Airlines, make excellent use of such boards; however, even small companies, such as Dorothy Lane Markets, a local supermarket chain in Dayton, Ohio, have standing customer advisory boards.

In some industries, such as managed health care, market forces are acting to force creation of customer advisory boards. Businesses must themselves gather a great deal of data on health plan quality before contracting with insurers, so there is need for both groups to work more closely than ever. For instance, the customer advisory board of Anthem Blue Cross and Blue Shield of Virginia includes small businesses with ten employers or less up to corporations with thousands of workers. Anthem takes the views of its customer advisory board members very seriously. They meet two or three times a year, covering all aspects of member care and benefits.

Aetna is another health-care company that actively incorporates the input of its customer advisory board in the improvement of member processes and the development of products and services. As an example of its contribution, the board recommended an electronic referral process and provided Aetna with guidance on structuring a new product.

The Bottom Line

In 2002, the Grizzard Performance Group polled 10,000 senior-level consumer and business-to-business marketing executives in U.S. companies on their organizations' customer retention marketing practices. Results of this survey showed that in pervasiveness, corporate emphasis, and effectiveness, these programs have a long way to go.

Although 59 percent reported having a customer retention program (71 percent among consumer companies, 58 percent among business-to-business companies), six out of ten companies are still devoting the majority of their resources to customer acquisition. The principal purposes of the programs, as identified by these executives, were to increase company or brand loyalty and increase the level and value of customer service. Capturing more customer information and cross-selling and up-selling based on individual customer data were much farther down the list of objectives. This result speaks volumes about how the vast majority of companies see loyalty programs.

There are major trends impacting loyalty program development:

1. Companies are having to address the fact that customers today are smarter and expect more from suppliers. They are better educated and have far more access to data, through multiple media, for comparison shopping.

2. The Internet, which has become a major channel for both information and sales, has caused many customers to change their purchasing habits, often contributing to commoditization and shallower loyalty.

3. Customer service, due to challenges such as skill levels and high turnover, as well as a trend toward offshore outsourcing, will become an increasing focus as a "barrier to exit" (see Chapter Nine for a full discussion).

4. Single-entity value programs, such as we've seen in the switching offers of telecoms or the low APR "teaser" campaigns of credit card companies, have schooled customers to be on the lookout for lower prices.

5. Free trade, and the evolution toward a global market, means that competition will only increase (in the United States) on many customer fronts.

6. Deregulation, in industries like telecom, where we've witnessed the impact of mobile telephone number portability and choice of long-distance companies, has spread to local telephone service, cable, and electrical service supply. Commodity-oriented monopolies have had to become loyalty marketers, looking to increase differentiation and perceived value.

7. Consolidation, mergers, and acquisitions are evident in many industries—telecom, banking, software, entertainment, cable, automotive—the list goes on and on. This can have a significant impact on customers, causing them to seek alternatives.

9

How Does, or Will, Customer Service Fit into the Mix?

Creating Individualized Value for Customers, Online and Offline

Although the technology for relating to customers, and providing personalized support, has significantly improved over the past few years, customer service, especially online, continues to deteriorate. At least customer service appears not to be a priority in some companies and industries.

A survey in *Marketing Business,* a publication of the Chartered Institute of Marketing in the United Kingdom, reported that when 52 UK-based food retailing companies were sent an e-mail requesting basic information, there was a disappointing range to their response.[1] Sainsbury's, one of the biggest supermarket chains in the country, like several others, did not respond at all. One took three days, and others responded but did not send adequate information. Morrison's was the only company to respond by telephone, asking if they could be of further help. There has been little, if any, improvement in the past few years.

In the United States, the news is about the same, if not worse. The customer service people of Martha Stewart, America's former domestic goddess turned entrepreneur (her own bedding line at Kmart, web site Marthastewart.com, and magazine), failed to respond to a series of e-mails by a would-be customer. That's only the tip of the iceberg. In an e-mail response study conducted by Peppers & Rogers group, only 46 percent of 65 well-known Internet retail companies answered within 24 hours.[2] More revealing, 20 percent never responded to e-mails at all. At the other end of the spectrum, almost 25 percent responded within two hours.

With the number of retail sites going out of business, or merging, and customers' growing demand for both speed and service, the pressure to handle e-mail quickly and efficiently will increase. The same applies to other forms of online customer service, and offline service as well.

---

[1] Michael Lowenstein, "Where Is Customer Service Trending?" *Customer Relationship Management,* February 2002, pp. 34–35.
[2] Michael Lowenstein, "Where Is Customer Service Trending?" *Customer Relationship Management,* February 2002, pp. 34–35.

There are ways for consumers to express their feelings about the quality and performance of e-commerce sites as well as the calls, letters, and emails to traditional brick-and-mortar suppliers. Online rating service thecustomeris-alwaysright.com identifies the overall customer service of 1-800-flowers.com as inferior. Other customer advocacy sites like Planetfeedback.com (now Intelliseek) and epinions.com post complaints about customer service by company and industry. Managed-care company Aetna/U.S. Healthcare's service rates a D+ on Planetfeedback's site, and truck and trailer rental company U-Haul, and long-distance telephone supplier MCI WorldCom, each rate a D. For these companies, complaints outpaced compliments by almost a ten-to-one ratio. On epinions, over 70 percent of the reviewers would not recommend the customer service of long-distance carriers Verizon and Cellular One. So there certainly appears to be increasing public scrutiny of products, services, suppliers, and their customer service. Is that the reality?

Well, the jury is still out on how well suppliers are paying attention to customer concerns. The American Customer Satisfaction Index, which attempts to measure the perceived quality of service delivery for industries across the United States, has found that satisfaction scores for airlines, banks, department stores, fast-food restaurants, hospitals, hotels, and telephone companies are all down. Even taking into consideration that satisfaction scores are rarely a true indicator of customer loyalty (and have no proven correlation with sales increases), this is problematical.

There are three fundamental issues involved in improving customer service, all of which impact their ability to contribute to individual customer loyalty behavior.

The first is *senior management attitude.* If companies like airlines see themselves as providers of seats for travel, and banks offering mortgages see their "product" on a commodity basis, rather than as service organizations providing strategically differentiated value, that shapes the culture, structure, systems, and virtually every process within the company. Customer service is largely viewed in those companies strictly as a cost rather than as an ambassador for positive perception, a conduit for dynamic information flow, and also as an engine for increased revenue. Customer service staff activities are typically so closely and rigorously monitored, with tightly managed performance metrics, that the measures used to assess their effectiveness very often look quite different from how employees in the rest of the company are assessed.

A recent Yankee Group report has challenged how customer service measures success, and the metrics they use to get there. The directions given to service managers—i.e., the way their priorities are set—and the way CSRs (customer service representatives) are evaluated outline the problem. Nearly half the contact-center managers surveyed by Yankee said meeting service levels was their top priority. Fewer than one-quarter indicated that driving revenue and retaining customers was their ultimate objective. So, clearly, their method of operation is at odds with providing the individualized support and value that will leverage customer loyalty and advocacy behavior.

The second issue is that customer service has become *more complicated*. It may take 15 minutes to sell a long-distance telephone service, but it takes over 200 hours to train a telephone customer service representative. Brokerage firm Charles Schwab, for example, estimates that the length of calls to Schwab has grown by 75 percent over the past five years. They have also increased the number of customer service representatives threefold. This also puts pressure on keeping these highly skilled knowledge workers.

Companies would be well advised to find methods of making CSRs more productive and contributory, while also giving them opportunity for leadership and advancement. There are many good models for having CSRs directly involved in customer relationships, as well as up-sell and cross-sell initiatives.

Finally, the *human factor,* the "heart," if you will, in relationships with customers, seems to have been drained from many customer service operations. The technological innovations that are available to customer service have only served to further remove them from direct customer involvement. It may be less expensive to have bank balances available by automated telephone menu than by a human being, but the empathy involved in answering questions and fixing problems has gone into hiding for many companies.

There are exceptions. Amazon, for one, considers every customer interaction an important opportunity—to learn. The company tracks the reason for each customer contact, on a daily, weekly, and monthly basis. There's a group within the customer service department that does nothing but analyze and anticipate problems, and also develop solutions. As an example, the number one question people used to ask Amazon was the status of their delivery. Now, on every page of their site, beginning with the Welcome page, there's a box labeled: "Where's My Stuff?" Operational changes at Amazon are truly customer driven, on an individual customer and purchase scenario basis.

The potential contribution, company-wide, represented by customer service is truly enormous. As stated, companies should begin to more actively view customer service as a profit center rather than a cost center. At Amazon, it's a reality. Customer service representatives are involved on all Amazon project and launch teams as "the voice of the customer." That's holistic and contributory, and the rightful role of customer service. It's good for the bottom line, it's good for the customer, and it's good for optimizing customer service staff loyalty.

Customer service interaction can be the source of vital information and insight, not just for handling complaints or quality control issues. It can also be a method of increasing customer loyalty. Truly customer-centric companies have learned that. Perhaps it's time for more companies to go back to the future.

We have long advocated including at least one cell of supplier staff—most often field sales, marketing, and, especially customer service—in every customer loyalty study done for our clients. The results are frequently eye-opening. What we do with staff in these studies is simply ask them to respond to the same questions asked of customers, in the way they believe customers will rate and evaluate them as a supplier. This identifies perceptual alignment and differences.

When, for instance, a client has actively pursued a total quality initiative, believing that accurate, technically advanced, complete, on-time product or service delivery, at the right price, are the ways to differentiate themselves from other suppliers and create customer loyalty, they believe that customers will reward them for it with their loyalty. Customer service and/or sales staff have been force-fed a TQ diet, and they expect that customers will:

- consider these tangible aspects of value delivery highly important, and
- not only rate the company highly but believe that these deliverables will leverage customer loyalty and advocacy

In circumstances like these, where a company has followed a path that doesn't have much impact on loyalty, the perceptions of sales and customer service staff are often significantly out of alignment with customers. Staff and customers agree that the tangible elements of delivery are well performed. Where they disagree is in the effect, or importance, of these elements.

We've frequently found that customers consider the intangible aspects of value delivery—trust, communication, interactive/collaborative aspects of service, brand equity, etc.—much more important, and more loyalty-leveraging, than the tangible aspects. They see the tangible aspects of delivery as more basic, expected, and non leveraging. For companies involved in business-to-consumer products or services, the intangible elements of delivery can represent 70 percent or more of what drives supplier choice and loyalty decisions, even for business-to-business and technical products and services.

It's equally likely to see situations where companies have made changes in their customer service protocols, such as the way in which calls or email messages are handled, without generating evidence of the effect on customers. Here again, customer service staff's perceptions may be seriously out of alignment with those of customers. Other areas of potential misalignment, or perceptual gap, include how customers and staff see change in performance over time, how they see the effectiveness of CRM or communication programs, and how they regard the level and impact of complaints.

Customer service managers or executives can reinforce a number of staff loyalty best practices—demonstrating staff trust, training staff, informing and debriefing staff, etc.—all at the same time. Here's how. Include customer-touching staff, as a sampled group (or groups), in your customer loyalty research studies. Comparing customer perceptions against staff perceptions can not only be very revealing, as we've described, but sharing these gaps with staff can create a real awareness about what is and is not working with customers.

Need more convincing? Here are three key reasons why you'll want to make staff a part of every customer survey:

1. Including staff in customer loyalty research enables staff to have a voice. This tells staff their opinions matter, which in turns helps trust to grow between the company and staff.

2. Surveying staff as part of the customer loyalty research process enables management to learn about specific process areas where there is disconnect between what staff perceives and what customers perceive. These revelations can open the door for needed changes in how customers are served.

3. Surveying staff as part of the loyalty research process helps pave the way for staff buy-in and support of new initiatives and changes, on behalf of customers, that may affect staff, directly or indirectly.

It's time for companies to be innovative and inclusive with staff. Staff want it, and customers are the beneficiaries. Another key advantage, and one not to be overlooked: In all likelihood your competitors don't have this level of customer and staff insight.

What's the Impact of Traditional and Truly Leveraging Customer Service Metrics on Retention and ROI?

As just discussed, a Yankee Group study among customer service managers showed that they considered meeting service levels their highest priority, while only one-quarter identified generating revenue and customer retention as their key goals. This often results in substantive disconnects within the organization, especially when one group, such as marketing, has a different set of customer-related metrics, goals, and objectives than customer service.

If the marketing department launches a large-scale promotional program with new customers, and neglects to adequately inform customer service or appropriately train and prepare CSRs for the tidal wave of contacts they receive, the results are inevitable: Customer service won't be able to handle all of the volume, and the CSRs will be overfocused on working to their normal metrics. So the company may 1) lose a great many new customers and/or 2) have to deal with negative word-of-mouth. Unfortunately, this type of situation occurs all too often. When customer service's activities with each customer are so different, and have so little relationship to individualized value delivery, compared to the metrics assessing their performance, this creates a tremendous disconnect. While metrics for most business units focus on revenues, costs, and profit margins, customer service is usually evaluated on hold time, call handling time, number of abandoned calls, and percentage of issues resolved without escalation, which *is* important.

The question is: What exactly do these metrics have to do with individual customer retention, leveraging of positive customer perceptions, and influence on bottom-line loyalty behavior? If the company has set enterprise-wide goals on customer retention, how does average hold time or the number of rings impact it?

Beyond these critical questions, perhaps the biggest obstacle to service productivity with individual customers, not to mention endeavoring to work with them on an issue scenario basis, is *integration*. It is all too easy to become trapped in the quicksand of abandoned calls and not see that CSRs need the tools, systems, and training to resolve customer issues quickly, and on the first call. What's so important about first-call resolution? The Purdue Center for Customer-Driven Quality has found that "once and done," the ability of an agent to effectively close out a customer issue on the first call, is perhaps the most important contributor to the service experience and a key leveraging element for positively continuing the relationship.[3] One problem, as determined by the Purdue Center, is that customer service management tends to give agents fairly narrow latitude in acting on customer issues. More serious, however, is the conflict that exists between business processes that focus principally on cost savings rather than improved customer relationships.

The reality is that the customer is the true arbiter of desired service levels. Customers have to be given the opportunity to provide feedback, hopefully immediate, on CSR knowledge and skills—especially regarding expeditious resolution—within the scope and context of the interaction, and irrespective of the channel of contact. Operationally, customers can directly contribute to the improvement of customer service ROI by generating data on call resolution.

If the objective is first-call resolution and reduced contact escalation, there are other areas that can also be impacted. These are overall productivity, vis-à-vis call

---

[3] Richard Feinberg and Wenti Xu, "It's the Solution, Stupid," Center for Customer-Driven Quality, 2004.

resolution, and associated training, development, and monitoring expenses. Monitoring, for instance, is performed by dedicated equipment and staff, and supervisors who monitor CSR calls to help determine the level of skill enhancement and training each agent requires. This is an expensive investment. To the extent that having better metrics can reduce supervisor time and monitoring resources, this goes straight to the bottom line. CSRs also prefer to function with as much autonomy as possible, so improved first-call resolution improves both their productivity and their levels of loyalty.

Most companies spend several thousand dollars a year per CSR in training and ongoing development expenses. Focusing on training for improved first-call resolution would help make CSRs more effective and productive.

The (Service) Employee Loyalty—Customer Loyalty Linkage Landscape

Apart from customer loyalty, which is (or should be) on the radar screen of every company, there is no topic that concerns organizations more than staff loyalty, commitment, and productivity. This is particularly true for customer service employees, because these groups often experience 50 percent or greater turnover per year. As we will see, this directly influences customer loyalty. Staff turnover is near 20-year highs for many companies. Two research firms, Walker Information and Hudson Institute, recently joined forces to conduct a nationwide employee loyalty study.[4] Their results confirmed that staff loyalty is in short supply:

- Only 30 percent of employees consider themselves truly loyal, committed to their organization and its goals, and planning to stay at least two years. Senior executives are included in that percentage. Looking at only non-supervisory staff, this drops to 24 percent.
- 34 percent of employees were high risk, not committed, and not planning to stay.
- 31 percent were classified as trapped. They plan to stay, but are not committed to their organization.
- Among those who felt they worked for an ethical organization, 53 percent were truly loyal. For those who didn't feel they worked for an ethical organization, the loyalty figure was nine percent.

---

[4] Diane E. Lewis, "Study of U.S. Workers Finds That Most Feel 'Trapped,'" *Boston Globe,* September 3, 2003.

Spherion, an international staff recruiting company, conducted a study that identified the at risk employees as "Emergent Workers," focused on work-life balance and flexibility, intent on managing their own careers.[5] Spherion found they are loyal as long as the company provides growth and career advancement opportunity.

The 72 percent of employees at risk or trapped represent another key, but less explored, concern for companies. The lack of employee commitment frequently translates to being out of alignment, with each other and with customers, in executing the company's mission, goals, and strategic objectives. In other words, what they are doing on the job can be counterproductive and damaging. Since the issues impacting customer loyalty and commitment to a supplier are often highly correlated with staff productivity and proaction, optimizing employee loyalty and alignment becomes doubly impactful.

Many companies don't even realize the depth of their staff retention and alignment problems. While at the senior level turnover may only be four to five percent, the real drain of talent is typically among those employees who are age 25 to 35 and have been at the same firm three to ten years. These staff members are often among the most productive and represent the highest long-term contribution potential for any company. They can also be among the most nonaligned with company vision and strategy. Yet the vast majority of organizations don't track defections, threats of defection, or misalignment among this important group. In fact, Burke, Inc., which examined the employee survey processes of Fortune 500 and mid-sized companies, found only 6 percent linked, or correlated, the results of their employee studies to customer measures; so they have almost no idea of how related and impactful they are.[6]

This "silent" defection and misalignment is particularly prevalent in large, decentralized companies with 20 to 100 divisions. On a single-division basis, the defection and misalignment numbers among staff age 25 to 35 may not seem problematic. But when viewed across all divisions of a company, the defection, potential defection, and misalignment numbers in this age group are often alarmingly high.

Firms pay a big price for staff defection. For starters, when staff defects, customers soon follow. Recent customer defection studies have shown that roughly 70 percent of the reasons customers leave can be traced back to issues related to staff turnover. And staff turnover often leads to more staff turnover. The departure of a valuable employee can send shock waves through a company culture, leaving remaining staff demoralized and disillusioned. If there was a trend toward misalignment, high staff turnover will only cause it to increase.

[5] "Fast Facts: The Impact of Emergent Workers on Employers," www.spherion.com, 2005.
[6] Jaci Jarrett Masztal, Diane M. Salamon, Gabriela Pashturro, and Lisa Steelman, "Employees Can Make the Difference!" Burke, Inc.

Replacing the departed employee is expensive. Human resource executives estimate that when all factors are considered—the recruitment fees, the defector's lost leads and contacts, the new employee's reduced productivity while learning the new job, and the time and energy co-workers spend guiding him or her—replacement costs are estimated at approximately 150 percent of the departing person's salary.

Misalignment too carries a high price tag, though it's more challenging to isolate and estimate than the loss of an employee. A lack of alignment can be seen in places like the organization's style and culture, staff communication, teamwork, and information flow, service to/focus on customers, level of training offered, productivity and efficiency, and management effectiveness.

There have been a number of landmark studies, including one conducted by Sears and another by Watson Wyatt, showing greater sales and return to shareholders when employees are loyal, aligned with goals, and committed to the company's success. This should be the shared responsibility of CEOs and the HRD department. As Marc Drizin, who heads up Walker Information's employee loyalty practice, has stated: "It's still shocking to learn how few human resource professionals are able to explain the ROI of 'doing the right thing for employees,' both on the cost side and the revenue side of the balance sheet, to their companies' management teams."[7]

Forum Corporation has conducted extensive research on what leading companies do to create an outstanding brand experience for customers.[8] Among their key findings is that there is an inextricable linkage between the customer experience and the employee experience. Especially in frontline areas such as customer service, employees have to be kept informed about business results, beginning with customer retention and loyalty levels. Management, to keep everyone aligned, have to provide a customer-focused vision for employees and also have to make sure that employees are operating and behaving in ways that benefit customers. Ultimately, Forum has found, the interests of employees and customers have to be put ahead of other stakeholders if alignment is to be optimized.

Continental Airlines is an excellent example of a company that deeply understands the relationship between customer service staff loyalty and productivity and bottom-line improvement. About a decade ago, CEO Gordon Bethune applied an incentive and tight measurement and management approach to move Continental from worst to almost-first in terms of service quality.

---

[7] Diane E. Lewis, "Study of U.S. Workers Finds That Most Feel 'Trapped,'" *Boston Globe,* September 3, 2003.

[8] Wayne A. Marks, "Uncommon Practice: What Exemplary Companies Do to Deliver an Exemplary Customer Experience," *Research Briefs,* May 2002.

This service turnaround began by conducting qualitative and quantitative research to learn about areas of perceived customer value. The company discovered that customers wanted accurate information, and highest-volume customers had a particular "need for speed" and wanted calls handled quickly. One of the principal changes that came from this learning was elimination of agent scripting. Part of agents' incentive program had been built around conformance of script usage. Insight from the research revealed that customers just want desired results, and they didn't care that agents followed a particular routine. Now Continental has the same attitude. It's the sale that counts.

Continental now measures the overall experience of each customer instead of the traditional metrics used by call centers. Agents are evaluated based on perceived quality ratings, calls handled per hour, and bookings per hour. Agents who perform well receive immediate rewards, such as being named what Continental calls its "Dream Team," where they can select their shifts and the time of their 15-minute breaks.

As for ROI, Continental has reduced its CSR turnover rate to an astonishing 1.2 percent per year, a rate many times lower than the average customer service operation, in airlines or any other industry, inside or outsourced, in the U.S. or elsewhere in the world. Continental has been named to the *Fortune* magazine "100 Best Companies to Work for in America" for several years in a row, a sure sign that the organization is focused on both employees and customers. The magazine has also named it the most admired global airline. Not surprisingly, reservation revenue is up.

Responsibilities and Opportunities in Customer Service—Customer Loyalty Alignment

Customer service representatives across the United States handle an average of 2,000 customer interactions each week. If CSRs are not aligned with the CRM strategy, indeed are not *directly involved* with creating and executing the strategy, this can represent 2,000 opportunities to put customers at risk or lose them.

Placing the customer first, or having a passionate and complete focus on customers, two of the clarion calls of CRM, have a hollow ring if CRM strategies aren't drilled down and reduced to a point where CSRs' daily efforts can have a positive impact on customer marketplace behavior. The reality is, however, that few organizations do this. Instead, they set unrealistic customer service productivity requirements, or establish perfor-mance metrics and levels that are not based on customer input or need. Further, because customer service centers haven't, until recently, begun to be seen as profit generation centers, their vision and mission, as well as their operational construct, were viewed in fairly myopic terms.

These centers of customer contact now represent the principal touch point with customers; and, beyond technology, they have the capability to generate and manage a continuous flow of customer information, and to increase customer loyalty. Getting the most out of customer contact centers will require change—for many companies, significant change.

For customer loyalty attitudes and behaviors to be optimized, one of the changes that companies will have to institute will be to start focusing on people. Hal Rosenbluth, CEO of the highly successful, multibillion-dollar travel management company, Rosenbluth International, which recently became part of American Express Travel-Related Services, said in his book *The Customer Comes Second*:

> We're talking about a change that puts the people in organizations above everything else. They are cared for, valued, empowered, and motivated to care for their clients. When a company puts its people first, the results are spectacular. Their people are inspired to provide a level of service that truly comes from the heart. It can't be faked.
>
> Companies are only fooling themselves when they believe that "The Customer Comes First." People do not inherently put the customer first, and they certainly don't do it because their employer expects it. We're not saying choose your people over your customers. We're saying focus on your people *because* of your customers. That way, everybody wins.[9]

Tremendous investments have been made on technological innovations—IVR systems, call routing, multimedia integration, and the like—yet investment in people, and processes to support them, has been stagnant, lagging behind other efforts. To deliver on the promise technology offers in customer relationships, staff performance has to be prioritized. People have to be shown what to do, given feedback about how they're doing, and rewarded if they are doing well in areas that leverage positive customer loyalty perceptions and behavior.

Meeting the objectives of an individualized customer loyalty behavior strategy means, for one thing, that targets and metrics set for CSRs must be balanced to incorporate productivity, quality of service delivered, and effectiveness of performance on behalf of customers. One of the most successful ways of accomplishing this, we have found, is through "customer first" teams, in customer service and throughout the company.

---

[9] © 1992 by Hal F. Rosenbluth and Diane McFerrin. Reprinted by permission of HarperCollins Publishers, Inc.

Tom Peters has said that, in the future: "Most work will be done by project teams. The "average" team will consist of various people from various 'organizations' with various skills. Networks of bits and pieces of companies will come together to exploit a market opportunity."[10] Such can certainly be the case with customer loyalty, customer service, and customer recovery programs. There are several advantages to networked, team-based structures as opposed to traditional hierarchies as they strive to create value for customers. They include better, more quickly shared information, greater decision agility, faster response time, and greater customer contact, as well as:

- Flattened, matrix-based organizational structures for greater efficiency
- Minimizing non–value-added functional activities, better use of staff time and talent
- Assigning ownership of performance
- Greater opportunity for self-management and a wider scope of work in each job
- Linking performance objectives, and individual and team performance to customer loyalty
- More targeted employee training and skill development

A fitting example of how customer-first teams can impact customer loyalty, customer win-back—and staff loyalty as well—comes from Baptist Health Care in Pensacola, Florida. Several years ago, Baptist Health Care ranked close to the bottom of all hospitals in national surveys in patient service performance. This situation also contributed to both declining patient populations and low staff morale.

Baptist Health Care executives were determined to turn this around. Quint Studer, then the hospital's president, said, "We had to create the type of environment where people drive by two other hospitals to get here."[11] Baptist Health Care formed ten cross-functional employee teams to examine every aspect of value delivery to patients and their families. More than 150 hospital employees now participate as team members on these original teams. Each team has membership as diverse as corporate vice presidents and cafeteria workers. Additionally, Baptist has created ad hoc and ongoing teams to address areas such as customer win-back. Up to 30 percent of Baptist Health Care employees serve on teams at any given time.

---

[10] Michael Lowenstein, "Linking Employee Loyalty to Customer Loyalty," www.thewisemarketer.com, August 2003.
[11] Michael Lowenstein, "Linking Employee Loyalty to Customer Loyalty," www.thewisemarketer.com, August 2003.

Today, Baptist Health Care's service performance ranks among the very best in national customer surveys, its market share has significantly improved, staff morale is higher, and staff loss—and the money previously spent for recruiting as a result of turnover—has dramatically declined. Baptist Health Care is now using their superior performance in patient care and services as a springboard for moving to an even higher plateau. As described by Pam Bilbrey, Baptist Health Care's Senior Vice President of Development: "We're pushing ourselves to move past the passion of service excellence to the next stage: customer loyalty."[12] A testament to the success of Baptist Health Care is the organization's recent naming to the #10 position on *Fortune* magazine's annual list of the 100 best companies to work for in America.

The array of cross-functional customer-first team possibilities is limited only by an organization's willingness to embrace the concept. Bottom-line: Customer-first teams enhance loyalty and staff productivity. Baptist Health Care is an excellent example of the success of customer-first teams. Every company should want to emulate their achievements.

Companies must also do a better job of determining just how effective service groups are at creating perceived customer value and, ultimately, optimizing customer loyalty behavior. Traditional employee satisfaction studies, just like customer satisfaction studies, are much more about measuring superficial attitudes and past events, keying largely on salaries and benefits, and the working environment, than they are about understanding how aligned staff are with customers, how productive staff are on behalf of customers, and how well supported and directed they are in providing value.

For customer-facing groups like customer service to have the same type of contribution, alignment with goals, and leadership seen in organizations like Rosenbluth International and Baptist Health Care, and for these groups to help realize the promise of customer advocacy, the three words that need to be emphasized are: *training, involvement,* and *measurement.*

The Loyalty and Financial Impact of Expressed and Unexpressed Complaints

Along with performance and loyalty metrics gathered through research, complaints are one of the best sources of customer data a supplier can have, yet most companies are getting half or less of the complaint enchilada. Their portion of the enchilada are the complaints customers post via telephone, mail, fax, and Internet.

---

[12] Michael Lowenstein, "Linking Employee Loyalty to Customer Loyalty," www.thewisemarketer.com, August 2003.

Suppliers need to have the whole enchilada, available through good research and analysis.

Nothing can be as effective as complaints at either sinking a sales, marketing, customer loyalty, customer experience, or CRM program or giving it new life. Complaints can be a positive or negative influence on customers' word-of-mouth, as well as intention to remain loyal or to defect.

At a time when product and service loyalty continues to decline, consumer advocacy groups report that more than 50 percent of the buying public have problems or complaints with the products and services they purchase. Yet it has been estimated that only about 2 to 10 percent of customers actually air their grievances to the supplier. Some industries experience notably high levels of customer complaint silence: financial services, food and beverages, pharmaceuticals, and high-tech. It's been well documented why their customers won't complain:

- They're busy, and they can't or don't want to take the time.
- They consider the complaint interaction a hassle and an annoyance.
- They see no direct value or benefit to them in making the complaint.
- They don't think the supplier will do anything about the complaint.
- They can get what they want from an alternate supplier, so they switch.

In research reported by Bain & Company, most customers who defect do not complain before doing so.[13] A typical company's complaint and defection pattern has about 22 percent of customers with poor transaction or relationship experiences. Of that group, 2 percent of customers actually complain; and, of those, about one-third each get their issues resolved, are at risk, or defect. Of those with a complaint who don't express it, about half defect and half are at risk, each representing about 10 percent of total customers. So, as we'll shortly describe, there can be tremendous impact on revenue flow and profitability.

Canadian marketing research firm Hepworth + Company, Ltd. has found that over 40 percent of the companies in their business-to-business database who had a problem or complaint never informed the supplier about it. Their reasons for not expressing their complaints were remarkably similar to those given by consumers. We've seen other studies suggesting that, depending on the industry, unexpressed b-to-b complaints may range as high as 80 to 90 percent, so this is hardly an exclusive b-to-c issue.[14]

---

[13] Frederick Reichheld, "Loyalty-Based Management," *Harvard Business Review,* March–April 1993, pp. 64–73.

[14] Michael Lowenstein, "Customer Complaints: The Whole Enchilada," www.searchcrm.com, April 1, 2002.

Even though the rate of expressed complaints is higher in the business-to-business world, the lost revenue potential of unexpressed complaints is significantly greater there because of the lifetime value of each customer. Hepworth estimates that the total amount of revenue at risk due to poor service and complaints is over 11 percent. This is 30 percent higher than the last time Hepworth conducted their study, in 1996.

Several years ago, Banc One conducted a study of the loyalty leveraging effect of expressed and unexpressed complaints on its retail customers.[15] The bank found that about half of these customers had service complaints. Of those with a complaint, only about half had expressed them. In other words, fully one-quarter of the complaint profile or reservoir was missing.

When customers do complain—through customer service operations like the Campbell Soup Company's Consumer Response and Information Center (which takes more than 300,000 calls a year), or the General Electric Answer Center, which is open all day, every day, or by other means such as e-mail, faxes, or letters, or outbound customer complaint solicitation—how the complaints are received and acted upon makes all the difference in their effect on customer perceptions and behavior.

The potential for complaints to negatively impact customers' future purchase intent and recommendation should never be overlooked. In loyalty research for one of our clients, a major manufacturer of paper and related products, it was determined that close to 40 percent of their high-volume accounts had serious performance complaints. These complaining customers were 15 percent less likely to be positive about continuing to purchase from our client than those without a complaint. Other studies show similar negative loyalty effects of complaints.

Hepworth's own business-to-business research shows that only about one-quarter of the customers who complained felt their concerns had been successfully resolved. Two reasons are that, in the minds of customers, resolution often either takes too long or requires too many contacts with the supplier. Hepworth has found that it frequently takes, for instance, three or more contacts for issues to be resolved.[16] Customers experiencing inefficient or insufficient resolution to complaints are not only less likely to repurchase or recommend from that supplier, they will spread their negativism—telling anywhere from 2 to 20 people about their experience.

---

[15] Michael Lowenstein, "Customer Complaints: The Whole Enchilada," www.searchcrm.com, April 1, 2002.
[16] Michael Lowenstein, "Customer Complaints: The Whole Enchilada," www.searchcrm.com, April 1, 2002.

With numbers like these, it's little wonder that, left poorly handled or totally unresolved, complaining customers can sabotage even the most carefully crafted marketing or customer loyalty program. The incidence of poor customer service demonstrated by many e-commerce web sites has been actively reported in the media, and also addressed earlier in this chapter. Angry customers have posted on specialty complaint sites such as uGet-Heard.com, PlanetFeedback.com, and eComplaints.com. They will even set up their own web sites so other upset and former customers have a forum for their negative experiences.

So, having seen how complaints can hurt, how can complaints complement, and even enhance, a company's customer loyalty or CRM program? There are three ways:

1. Encourage customers to contact the company with questions, comments, problems, or complaints; and make this as easy as possible.
2. Identify the root causes of all complaints, registered and unregistered, so that their sources can be addressed and corrected.
3. Enhance the effectiveness of problem and complaint resolution processes so that customers are provided sufficient contact venues.

There is a fourth method to consider when approaching complaint generation and management. And it may be the simplest and most effective of all. Most companies, in their customer value/performance research, fail to ask about complaints, either those that have been registered or those that haven't. We strongly advocate doing this. Complaints, after all, are a different category of involvement with a supplier than just low performance ratings. They're stronger. If we can identify those complaints that have been registered and how they have/haven't been resolved, and those complaints that haven't been registered and the reasons for nonregistration, this represents a complete inventory of customer complaints and sheds new light on the complaint process. Their specific potential effect on customer loyalty can then be modeled for prioritized action.

Returning to the Banc One example, those retail customers who registered their complaints—and then were handled in a positive manner by the customer service department—indicated a very high level of loyalty toward the bank. It was actually higher than those who had no complaints.

On the other hand, those customers who hadn't expressed a complaint (even though they actually had one when asked) had bank loyalty levels about two-thirds as high as those whose complaints had been handled poorly; the latter had loyalty levels only one-quarter as positive as those whose complaints had been handled well.

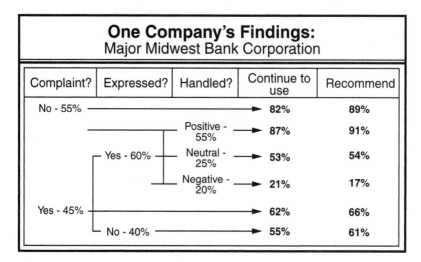

Figure 9.1 Bank Retail Customer Complaint Results

Using a simple "projective" method of looking at stated loyalty, versus actual loyalty levels, can help identify a direct financial connection with both unregistered complaints and poorly handled complaints relative to customers with no complaints and complaints that were handled well. Suppose the bank had a base of 100,000 retail customers, each with an average annual value of $10,000. Even with a discount of 25 percent between those saying they would likely remain as customers relative to those who actually did remain loyal (making the average continued use/continued average annual value percentage of 61.5 percent), the bank would have experienced a $106,267,500 annual loss (or, more accurately, missed a potential gain of this amount) on a base revenue stream of $651,000,000, derived from this unhealthy combination of poor complaint handling and failure to uncover hidden complaints:

- 100,000 retail customers, each worth $10,000. Projected revenue with 61.5 percent. Loyalty at this level is $651,000,000.
- 55,000 had no complaints. Loyalty level is 61.5 percent. Projected revenue is $338,250,000.
- 27,000 had complaints, and 55 percent were handled positively (14,850). Loyalty level is 65.25 percent. Projected revenue is $96,896,250.
- 25 percent of the 27,000 with complaints were handled neutrally (6,750). Loyalty level is 39.75 percent. Projected revenue is $26,831,250.
- 20 percent of the 27,000 with complaints were handled poorly (5,400). Loyalty level is 15.75 percent. Projected revenue is $8,505,000.

- 18,000 with complaints did not express them. Loyalty level is 41.25 percent. Projected revenue is $74,250,000.

Net revenue with this scenario is $544,732,500.

Another way to look at this is that the bank would have gained $87,142,500 ($293,625,000 compared to the $206,482,500 they did receive) if they could have gotten every customer with a complaint to express it, and if all of the expressed complaints were handled in a positive manner. Of course, a cynic might argue that companies ought to cause or create complaint situations so that they can handle them positively and generate higher levels of loyalty. In reality, that's not so far from the truth of what experience has shown.

The lesson here, as has been proven again and again, is that when customers are encouraged to dialogue with suppliers if there are performance delivery problems or concerns, that opportunity for enhanced value provision actually creates stronger relationships between them. This is especially true for frontline groups like customer service, who touch customers on an individual, experience-by-experience basis.

Having a database of the registered and unregistered complaints gives a supplier the entire spectrum of customer negativity, enabling corrective action to be much more focused and relevant. When this is combined with customer profile and contact data, and assessments of key elements of performance delivery, and metrics about intended behavior (likelihood of future purchase, likelihood to recommend, etc.) through targeted loyalty and win-back research, companies can be far more effective in optimizing customer loyalty.

Some Other Methods of Looking at Per Customer ROI Contribution of Customer Service: Linkage

The projection, or semidirect, method of looking at the revenue and profit impact of complaint solicitation and resolution, by customer and on a situation-by-situation basis, has both positives and negatives. As we've just shown, the data involved are pretty simple and straightforward; and another of its advantages is ease of interpretation for management. On the other hand, the assumptions about the yearlong worth of the customer, as we'll explore in detail in the next chapter, are just that—assumptions. Also, even given that no customer research can be considered rocket science, we are relying on statements of behavioral intent. These always have at least some shrinkage; and, unless the company is closely tracking the relationship between stated and actual purchase intent, the actual level of purchase activity will always be open to some degree of interpretation.

Fortunately, there are more exact, or direct, methods. As explained, they do require a bit more discipline, but they can help organizations make the case for relating performance and behavior likelihood metrics to actual results. A customer can be identified as "secure," or as close to truly loyal as possible, if: 1) he or she gave the highest possible ratings to research questions dealing with overall performance, likelihood to continue purchasing, and likelihood to recommend; and 2) actual purchase activity for that customer is tracked over time, and activity is related to the key question rating levels previously given.

Why are we so focused on these three metrics? Perceived overall performance has some elements of both attitude and commitment, and represents a level of attachment to the supplier resulting from positive transactions (such as customer service). Likelihood to continue purchasing and recommend are more behavioral, reflecting a maintenance or deepening of the customer's relationship with the supplier. Results for these metrics tend to lead action.

We can use these metrics to establish a customer loyalty index, or CLI, which can serve as a "placeholder" mnemonic, or guidepost, for companies for showing how well the company is achieving overall customer management goals, or objectives set, on a customer-by-customer basis. Loyalty indices can provide assistance and support in many industries and functional areas. Indeed, if a client is about to establish a new customer loyalty scheme or upgrade the elements of its service proposition (quality levels, guarantees, time specifics, contact and communication, etc.), research can be very targeted and focused on the overall performance, loyalty, and recommendation impacts of those initiatives.

Establishing a customer loyalty index before those changes are made can serve as a benchmark rather than a scorecard, and a general barometer for the effectiveness of programs and process modifications. In one instance, for example, we conducted strategic customer loyalty research for a home products retailing chain, and then created a customer loyalty index for them around overall service, future purchase intent, and likelihood to recommend scores. This was done prior to their introduction of a well-defined customer loyalty scheme.

The scheme involved the chain's best customers, identified by the variety of products and services purchased, level of expenditure, and the frequency of store visits. They received special vouchers, a priority customer care service line, private sales events, and special financing offers. Training of sales assistants and department managers in providing these customers with exemplary customer service, plus active direct response communication with these customers were also key features.

Research was conducted again following the launch and rollout of the scheme, and we were able to help determine, on a segment-by-segment and even customer-by-customer level, where the program was most effective and where it needed to be refined. Because we also obtained verbatim customer responses on an attribute-by-attribute and overall program performance basis, the research provided added depth and dimensionality to the decision making.

Our research concluded that, while other incentives were attractive, extra attention and value created in the stores, particularly with regard to time and staff effectiveness, were the principal loyalty drivers. With this insight, we helped develop new training targeted at empowering staff in helping customers. This led to the creation of new sales assistant categories, in which selected staff were given extensive training in attitude and interpersonal skills with customers. These staff members are also eligible for special reward and recognition for outstanding service. Also, we participated in store layout modification so that products were grouped more logically, and we worked with the company's IT group to streamline the checkout process.

The result has been significant improvement in the CLI scores, sales among key customer groups, and amounts spent per visit. In addition, the chain has vaulted ahead of competitors on every performance category; and loyalty-impacting complaints have dramatically declined.

Management also frequently wishes to know which aspects of value delivery, of several potential methods of upgrading or enhancing service, will be the most profitable so they can prioritize their installation. This requires the combined effect of direct linkage and projective techniques. The objective is to quantify, as much as possible, the presence (or absence) of linkage between service elements and financial results, determine how leverageable these relationships are, and then rank order the areas of activity or improvement based on projected results. Although it sounds kind of spooky and technical, this is actually fairly easy to set up.

With this "hybridized" combined technique, companies just have to dig a little deeper than the projection or direct techniques. They need to create statistical models showing the relationship between perceived performance and desired outcomes, such as higher customer retention or dollar amounts of spending. The advantage is that, in working with the statistician who builds the model, management will be looking closely at the service processes and dealing with realistic sets of expectations.

Ultimately, whether projection, direct, or blended methods are applied to help estimate the return on investment of alternative service enhancements, one thing is clear: There are multiple stakeholders, including corporate management, functional management (customer service *and* marketing *and* sales), CSRs, and the customers who will benefit.

The Future of Customer Service: Delivering Divisibility

Greg Gianforte, CEO of RightNow Technologies, who wrote the Foreword for this book, has some very definite ideas about how customer service will evolve.

As companies continue looking for ways to be more productive, efficient, and profitable, customer service will be counted upon to enhance its contribution to those goals. An increasing flow of customers, using a wider range of products and services, is an ongoing challenge for customer service groups, particularly since they are rarely given resources to match this growth.

More and more, customer service is becoming both a revenue generation and information gathering mechanism for companies, giving them both up-sell and cross-sell opportunities, plus other ways to provide value for customers. Some have even created revenue streams through offering premium customer service. Service is, as well, frequently a key attribute in building competitive differentiation and advantage, particularly in mature markets where superior service is a major factor in market leadership strategies.

Customer expectations, those elements of performance and value delivery customers consider important, are in a constant state of flux. This is particularly true with customer service, where customers tend to benchmark every company, and every contact experience, irrespective of industry. These kinds of pressures actually create an opportunity for customer service, and service operations can grow from reactive problem-solvers to proactive contributors to company revenues and equity, one customer at a time. To do so, as Gianforte believes, they will have to make significant cultural, operational, and technological change.[17]

These evolutionary changes will take customer service operations through four stages. In the first, which Gianforte calls *Rudimentary,* CSRs merely answer the phones and manually reply to emails. Service department staff haven't been trained to gather information or utilize such knowledge resources as customer databases. Additionally, service operations at this stage are evaluated using such traditional metrics as hold times and first-call resolution. These groups are looked at as a cost center within the organization, adding little value.

The second stage is *Responsive,* where customer service groups are more attentive to customer needs, through availability of more communication channels, automated contact processes, and more action-based metrics. Here too is where we begin to see contact histories and interaction databases, enabling the service

---

[17] Greg Gianforte, "The Future of Customer Service: The Road to Top-Line Impact," RightNow Technologies, 2003.

group to react more quickly and intelligently to deal with customer problems and fix service process inefficiencies. At this stage, there are more effective web self-service resources, such as chat and voice, and upgraded email response management. Business-wise, the service operation has more of a positive impact on customer perception and retention and resources are scalable so that they can better support the company's growth strategies and programs.

In the third stage, *Proactive,* the service operation monitors and captures information across all communication channels. They have detailed data about customer segments and individual customers, and they are better able to leverage customer information through personalized email messaging, operating at a lower cost-per-customer. Proactive service operations are also better positioned to support the company's value-added, competitive differentiation objectives. They apply more customer-based, service-level metrics.

The final stage is *Top Line Service.* Service operations that have reached this stage are full-time revenue producers, adding renewal and recovery to their cross-sell and up-sell activities, enhancing customer relationships and transactional experiences by applying insights from individual customer service and purchase histories. These operations do significantly more than solving problems or finding innovative solutions. They can truly address customers on a divisible basis because, by having so much detail on each customer, they can proactively make recommendations based on specific purchase and usage situations.

Gianforte cites several success factors necessary for service operations to move from Rudimentary to Top Line Service. First, service managers need to have, or develop, a clarity of vision, to understand how concepts such as divisibility can help them optimize customer relationships and revenue generation. They certainly need executive support because, for many service operations, achieving Top Line Service requires both resources and closer working relationships with other company groups, particularly sales and marketing. Continuing on the theme of interrelationships, Top Line Service operations will build cross-departmental processes and collaborations, enhancing staff abilities along the way. Finally, service groups often need the support of outside experts and technologies, such as developing advanced interactive databases.[18]

With these capabilities, service operations can be in a position to create powerful competitive advantage for their companies. These operations are direct, self-funded contributors to company growth, and are recognized as full and equal partners with sales and marketing.

---

[18] Greg Gianforte, "The Future of Customer Service: The Road to Top-Line Impact," RightNow Technologies, 2003.

10

Virtual and Real Return on Individual Customer Investment

A (Very) Brief and Simple History of Customer-Related ROI

Historically, the task of identifying profitability and return on investment (ROI), for any business initiative, has been in the hands of those financial pundits, the accountants. This goes back to the Industrial Revolution, where the need to manage and interpret the value of financial outlay and economies of scale, once companies emerged from "cottage" status, became a central focus of business.

What we've come to understand as "management accounting" (a subject many of us tried to digest in undergraduate and graduate business schools) matured during the middle and latter parts of the 20th century. Unfortunately, as business and marketplaces became more sophisticated, management accounting, as a monitoring and planning tool, became outmoded and ineffectual. This was principally because there was no standardization of costing systems and accounting practice as these dynamic changes were taking place. Also, there was the all-too-frequent likelihood that groups like sales, marketing, and customer service, though accountable for seeing that the right customers and the right relationships were maintained as they focused on outside marketplace forces, were being overwhelmed (and overmanaged) by financial groups' strict requirements and emphasis on only costing internal activities. We can still see the residue of this today in customer service, where service representatives are strictly measured on archaic, efficiency-based metrics such as average handle time (AHT) and average speed of answer (ASA).

As a result of all this, companies have tended to rely more on what can best be described as "proxy," or approximate, costs rather than actual costs, in part because they're easier to develop. We see these in RFD estimates, and their cousins, the inclusion of appended public data. These include, for instance, the *types* of products purchased, or services used. The theory here is that if customers are using higher profit products or services, they must be more profitable than those who use less profitable products and services. Of course, this approach doesn't even begin to look at costs of servicing, marketing, and communication.

Another traditional approximate cost is based on frequency of purchase, or *number,* of products used. This approach says that customers using more products or services are more profitable than those with fewer purchases and array of products and services. As many companies have learned, however, more purchases doesn't mean more profits if they're not the right products or if the customer is expensive to serve.

Some financial managers, no doubt influenced by geodemographic data analysts, have looked to customer age, income, occupation, home ownership, etc. as a proxy for profitability. Here again, cost to serve has to be considered before this has relevance.

There's even a school of costing and estimation thinking that says the more relationship and touches with a customer—i.e., the more a customer uses a company's facilities and services, and even the more transactions that take place—the greater the profitability compared to customers with few transactions. Certainly, this has proven to be a false generalization, again and again. Companies have proven they can lower costs of service, for example by outsourcing the customer contact function to India, Sri Lanka, China, or the Philippines. But these methods don't look very deeply, if at all, at impact on individual customer loyalty and advocacy behavior in the marketplace.

So where are we now? As with most understanding of customers on an individual, and even divisible, basis, determining both profitability and investment return must be based on having customer data that is as accurate and complete as possible. The several approaches to "guesstimating" just discussed have never been very effective; and even more recent attempts at customer profitability, such as by product line or individual product, have fallen short, principally because they incorporate only internal development and sales costs and not marketing or service costs.

Further, most current accounting systems are pretty parochial. They tend to focus entirely at the macro level, at the overall corporate level, such as for funding marketing programs, on the department or profit center level, or at the campaign or project level, rather than on individual customers or even key segments. Where actual direct and indirect (overhead) costs are available, they tend to be allocated, or apportioned, by customer groups as a substitute for actually compiling per customer costs. At the top of this particular accounting food chain is something called Activity Based Costing, or ABC.

With ABC, we're finally beginning to get at some semblance of understanding profits on a customer-by-customer basis. It incorporates customer lifetime value, whose merits and deficiencies we'll discuss in a bit, plus elemental predictive modeling, and charges across activity, cost center, etc. to serve individual customers. So, for example, if a retail chain wanted to identify optimum staffing levels at each store, it would look at the costs incurred across the store's customer base, what products are purchased and when, what services these customers require (and staff training and compensation investments), prospectively down to the individual customer level.

That brings us pretty current. With the advent of more advanced individual customer data software and analytics, and other business intelligence technologies, we're finally at the place where we can "get real" about ROI driven around individual customers and, perhaps, even customers on a divisible level. Customer data have become more available and more adaptive to analysis

Begin at the New Beginning. What Is Real Customer ROI? What Is Virtual ROI?

Although real customer ROI has been relatively well understood for some time, it is now beginning to be used in fairly generic ways by senior management and sales, marketing, and customer service executives in describing investments, and paybacks, with customer-related activities. Until recently, managers have had to work with highly aggregated or "proxy" RFV (recency, frequency, value or dollars spent) customer data; but now there are methods to view customer profitability on an individual basis, which we'll begin to discuss in the next section.

There are three questions that need to be asked (and answered) when calculating ROI:

1. What counts as an investment in customer-related activities?
2. What counts as a return on that investment?
3. Over what period, or periods, of time will measurement take place in making the calculation?

Customer-Related Investments

The real, or tangible, investments are pretty easy to discern. They cover, for instance, all costs of gathering, storing, managing, and applying customer data. We've discussed the absolute priority of creating a single, unified view of the customer across the enterprise, which often begins with merging, or fusing, data available from multiple sub-databases and customer touch points. Perhaps the best words to describe what we intend as the outcome of this are coherence and clarity. For companies to understand, and guide, customer behavior, customer purchase profile data must be brought together with geo-demographic household and lifestyle information, anecdotal material from sales and service, and customer research.

To begin, this will involve IT infrastructure, database development, hardware, and software. Additionally, it encompasses sales automation (activities management and reporting), contact center and service automation technology (auto-dial, AVR, one-to-one chat, complaint generation and resolution, etc.), marketing campaign and related costs (segmentation, lead generation, direct response advertising expenditures, events and promotional management, customer research etc.), and any other customer-related processes (customized production, EDI, intranets, extranets, quality assurance, etc.). These are both tangible and ongoing investments.

Another set of direct costs is people. This includes recruitment, mentoring, job and non-job training, reward and recognition programs, salary and benefits for employees. Particularly with respect to customer relationships and building customer value, these employees must have analytical, support, management, and many other skills. As in any form of skill building, this is a focus, time, and monetary investment.

Process costs must also be considered. The majority of these costs come from an analysis of existing workflow. More specifically, if a company has been addressing customers on an overall or general segmented basis, and now wishes to increase the accuracy realized in customer-specific activities and individual customer value, sales, service, and marketing processes may have to be dramatically altered. This, of course, requires both time and money investment.

Calculating Return on Investment

Return on investment is challenging enough to estimate, or calculate, on sets of activities such as communication initiatives, customer service, marketing campaigns, or loyalty programs. Although past calculations could be built around customer acquisition, customer retention and extension, and customer recovery, the task is now much more complex. When the shift in focus moves to profitability by customer, that challenge increases many-fold. Every activity—database development, web site design, market/customer segmentation, customer contact center staff training, and loyalty programs, to name a few—must now be rethought in terms of individual customer behavioral impact and return.

If the company can initially look at its customer activities on a fairly simplistic basis, such as improving customer recovery effectiveness through the contact center, this becomes slightly less daunting. Pilot programs can be conducted among customers with different attrition issues, and representing different value levels and purchase histories, to build up estimates of prospective return over time. This same step-wise approach can be applied to larger projects, such as the impact of a loyalty program on customer support, communication, cross-sell/up-sell, and referral opportunities.

ROI calculation has evolved far enough that we can apply non-traditional, or more indirect, measures and costs to those that are strictly financial in nature. These include metrics such as would be obtained from customer research (perceived overall and attribute performance, purchase and recommendation likelihood, etc.), new customers acquired, attrition and cross-sell rates, expressed and unexpressed complaint levels, number and frequency of transactions, wallet share, and even employee loyalty, alignment with customer-related objectives, and productivity.

Profits are simply the net, or remainder, of revenues minus costs. But that is where the simplicity ends. Companies must look at both cost-to-sell and cost-to-serve on an individual customer basis. They have to include both direct and indirect costs, as previously discussed. Above all, they have to recognize the likelihood that most of their customers are likely to be unprofitable. One of the pervasive mistaken beliefs of many business-to-business companies, for example, is that the biggest customers are usually the most profitable. This is false. After profit contribution analysis, companies often find that, not only are large customers not the most profitable, sometimes they're not at all profitable. They may, for example, have high service costs relative to revenue because of customized production runs, specialized inventorying and delivery requirements, and deep discounts. Just as rates of retention and wallet share may impact efficiency of service and marketing on the positive side, recognize that inefficiencies can also be created.

Time Periods

While companies often think in terms of short-term return on sales, marketing, and service activities, investments in building detailed information about customers and driving customer loyalty behavior may be long-term. In the credit card industry, for instance, it has been found that customers don't reach profitability for several years after acquisition. As demonstrated in one of my previous books, *Customer WinBack,* it's also entirely possible to generate profit from a recovered customer when that same customer was not profitable, or had yet to reach profitability, in his or her earlier life with the same supplier. So the time to reach profitability, or not, will vary significantly once this begins to be viewed on an individual customer basis.

Virtual Return on Investment

Virtual ROI comes from the softer, less tangible aspects of relationships with customers. For example, information—especially information available on both an individual customer and customer purchase scenario basis—is a tremendous asset.

Here, once the relationship has been established, we are concerned with the supplier's ability to deliver and provide perceived customer value within specific products and services over time. We are also focused on understanding the strength and vitality of the relationship, and the opportunity to build on tactically created value, or ROI that is understood on a more tangible level.

When addressing virtual ROI measurement protocols, we're principally interested in brand preferences and choices, plus performance over time. Consequently, we ask *current* customers about:

- Perception of supplier (and key competitor) performance in key areas, and importance of those areas, also including elements of reputation and image.
- Likelihood to use the supplier's products or services in the future
- Likelihood to consider the supplier as the primary source for a product or service, or exclusive source
- Likelihood to recommend the supplier
- Evidence of performance change over time
- Evidence of expressed and unexpressed complaints

Virtual ROI is where most customer loyalty researchers direct their efforts, principally because that's what senior management, sales, marketing, and related functions want. However, as indicated above, there's a great deal more to learn at this level than just degrees of satisfaction with the supplier and competitor. We can identify both improvement priorities and potential program initiatives for enhancing ties and perceived value with these customers, building real ROI.

Finally, we need to understand perhaps the most intangible elements of virtual ROI: awareness, image, and trust levels of the supplier. This is indeed the final frontier. To understand how the supplier is perceived at this level, in addition to finding out about top-of-mind awareness and salience, familiarity with/comprehension of various offerings of the supplier, and predisposition to purchase or recommend the supplier's products or services, it's vital to determine:

- How business practices, i.e., ethics, are regarded
- How the supplier is seen as an "employer of choice" by staff and/or whether they would be recommended as an employer
- The supplier's image in such areas as community involvement, public issues, the environment, etc.
- Deep feelings and emotional attachment to the company of various stakeholders

Many companies don't delve into customer perception at this depth, but deeply held emotional involvement has a great deal of loyalty-leveraging impact.

There is a growing school of thought that maintains that to achieve true partnership with customers, emotional equity will become the dominant, even exclusive focus. This, it is believed, is because businesses today have access to better, more accurate, and more timely information about their customers. Progressive, smart companies are now more able to draw conclusions about individual customer profitability; and they have the luxury, even the need, to fully understand delivery of value at the intangible level.

Emotional attachment is easiest to discern and measure in companies that emphasize service. Service, and the communication related to it, is an area where companies can customize by individual customer and specific purchase scenario. (FedEx) Kinko's, for example, configures each of its stores around customer needs. On an overall basis, Kinko's operates differently depending on whether the store is located in a suburban area along a busy highway or in a downtown business district, But, for the past several years, the company has also been organized on a local branch network basis, like the hub and spokes of a wheel. If a customer whose business involves unusual printing or business service requirements at odd hours, and the closest Kinko's is not open late, the company has assured that there will always be a Kinko's hub store open 24/7 within 15 minutes' travel time of that customer's regular Kinko's store location. These hubs will have a greater number and variety of products and services, especially for customers with higher volume, overnight, or specialized requirements. The hubs are able to access "spokes" customers' individual purchase and service sourcing histories, while the spoke location continues to provide the essential array of self-service and full-service capabilities.

There are certain business sectors, such as retail banking and auto dealerships to cite two, that tend to focus on product or service features rather than on the intangible, emotional connections, believing that making things more convenient and efficient for customers is an appropriate surrogate for building a sincere, intangible value connection. Their belief is built around a mantra of functionalism. Functionalism is absolutely relevant as one of the tangible drivers of loyalty behavior, and it is certainly important as an element, or elements, of purchase consideration. However, it has been proven again and again that it cannot replace trust, commitment, and communication as key components of profitability and virtual ROI.

Overfocusing on Customer Lifetime Value

Customer lifetime value, also known as CLV or LTV, represents the net present value of profits, coming from the investments we've just described, which creates a flow of transactions over time. Companies can look at their investments in terms of cost per sale, rate of customer retention, and also conversion of prospects. CLV is, then, used as a convenient yardstick of performance; however, it has tended to become a bit too much of a "holy grail" for corporate, marketing, and sales executives, to the extent that entire conferences and seminars are often devoted to helping optimize it.

The inherent danger of overfocusing on customer lifetime value is that companies will invest in programs that try to wring profits from only the most active, heaviest-spending customers. This neglects opportunities not only from customers who are "growable" but also former customers who could represent attractive profits, once recovered. The result of such an emphasis will inevitably be a steady increase in CLV from these customers, but, at the same time, a steadily decreasing pool of customers and ever-declining overall company profit.

When companies make decisions around CLV, either combined with ROI analysis or in place of it, they tend to have a more narrow perspective of profits relative to investment. ROI helps facilitate investment decision-making at the micro level, around individual customer life stage and customer purchase scenario. It allows, as well, for aggregated profitability estimation at the macro (corporate, department, and campaign or program) level.

ROI, simply, increases accountability. Any customer-related initiative by the overall company, or by groups like marketing, sales, and service will have "hurdle" rates established. These are minimum levels of return, against specific time periods, required to obtain funding. So, if a marketing group wants to acquire customers through certain media that have, historically, created higher customer lifetime value, the ROI approach will force a more in-depth investigation of alternative media, a determination of how many (profitable) new customers can be generated, and so on. ROI analysis can, additionally, be used to help assess returns from future customer-related investments. One of the values of more advanced ROI software and models, for instance, is that they can help make investment decisions based on the anticipated response of each customer.

Beyond basic ROI analyses, discount rates (on the future value of money or rates of customer conversion) can be applied to alternative customer-related initiatives. This enables a group, or groups, to evaluate between multiple opportunities with respect to timing of expenses and projected profits. Discount rates are often used in retail funding decisions. As an example, Gary Hawkins of Green Hills Farms looks at sales net of markdown—i.e., what the customer actually pays after price reductions—to generate true overall sales and price reductions. The price reduction, then, can be addressed as a sales or marketing expense, which it is. He's used this type of analysis to demonstrate that, whether considered customer by customer or on an aggregated basis, there's a strong tendency for the lowest-spending customers to be given the highest markdown. And he's been able to prove that, discounts and markdowns considered, the vast majority of customers cost more to serve and maintain than the revenues they generate. This will be covered in more detail a couple of sections further on.

ROI can also be adjusted to look at customer-by-customer profit from cross-sell, up-sell, referral, and even information and communication value. For instance, Bernd Stauss, professor of retailing at the Catholic University of Eichstaett in Germany, and an expert on the value of regained or recovered customers, has shown that communication benefit among lost customers—i.e., the avoidance of negative word-of-mouth and encouragement of positive word-of-mouth—can be attached to specific dollar values. Based on his research, Stauss has determined that information can add up to 10 percent onto profitability "if the use of this information leads to an optimization of internal processes, reductions of processing time, or increased productivity. Over and above this, an increase in revenue can be expected from recovered former customers if, based on complaint analysis, product (or service) variations and innovations can be achieved that turn out to be marketable."[1]

Through his studies of recovered customer profitability, Stauss has also been able to isolate the effect, or incremental sales percentage, of referrals. He has found that "likelihood to recommend" the product or service, among regained customers, translates into actual sales increases of 30 percent, compared to control groups where referrals were not gathered and followed up.

The Nitty Gritty Modeling of Individual Customer ROI

Unfortunately, reports by some of the leading research and analysis companies suggest that only about half of companies understand that it's good, and important, for them to be able to manage the customer portfolio for more profitability. When companies complain that customer-related efforts, particularly those involved with relationship management, don't meet objectives, it's often because they themselves don't apply basic measurements and models. So some tutorials from Profitability 101 are in order. The return on any investment is simple and straightforward:

$$\frac{\text{Profits} \times 100}{\text{Investment}} = \text{ROI} \%$$

---

[1] Bernd Stauss and Christian Friege, "Regaining Service Customers," *Journal of Service Research* 1 (1999): 347–361.

Beginning on the corporate level, ROI will be determined by analyzing the combined effect of all relationship (sales, marketing, service) costs, plus the other tangible (hardware, software, etc.), people, and process costs already discussed.

We now move to the next level, zeroing in on the specifics of customer relationship building and maintenance. First, our general objectives here are to optimize customer lifetime value (CLV, without being concerned yet that it's not a be-all and end-all measurement), the total number of customers (who will meet minimum profitability thresholds), and to have firm budget management of all relationship and value-building customer expenditures. Details at this level include number of prospects converted, number of customers retained, customer recovery rates, rates of referral, and so on. Next, in their quest to optimize CLV, companies will look at the amounts of profitability on the first sale once acquisition costs are subtracted, net present value (NPV) of customer segments, and—to the extent discernable—share of customer spend. Finally, companies will look at such relationship metrics as cost per sale in an effort to control sales, marketing, and service expenses. This level is where the majority of companies that are serious about ROI target their analysis, but there's much more to learn, as we'll see.

At the individual customer level, companies are focused as much on the actual dollars, and tangible cost measures, involved in optimizing ROI. For each customer, direct and indirect costs are deducted from the sales to this customer. From that, it can be determined whether a positive contribution remains to cover these fixed costs. Identifying customer-specific contribution requires detailed accounting and analysis of customer acquisition and retention. Increasingly, these analyses are incorporating intangible, soft measures and performance indicators (such as referral likelihood and the types of information provided) to help guide tactical and strategic customer-related planning. My colleague Jim Lenskold has set this up as a measurement hierarchy (see Figure 10.1) based on marketing expenditures, but this hierarchy can be expanded to any and all costs associated with building customer value and optimum return on investment:

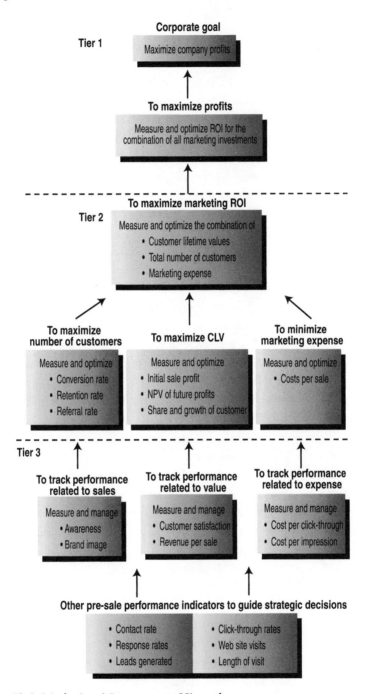

Figure 10.1 Marketing Measurement Hierarchy
Source: *Marketing Management,* June 2002, p. 33.

Let's Get Micro

As companies become more customer-centric, or begin to understand the strategic benefits of customer-centricity, applying in-depth data and advanced analytics to marry optimized relationships with optimal customer value and profitability, one thing will become increasingly clear. Individual customer profitability will become less demanding and remote and more mainstream than assessment by business unit, product, or product line.

Lenskold has identified three levels of ROI analysis that can be applied to decisions at the individual customer level—*independent, incremental,* and *aggregated*—for managing profitability.[2] It's an excellent way of addressing investment and anticipated return, on a customer and purchase scenario basis:

Independent ROI

Functional and operational managers have the ability to look at expenditures for each initiative, customer by customer and by purchase or transactional scenario, to see if they will pay out. If the ROI for the specific initiative exceeds the hurdle rate, it is cost justified unless a higher return alternative can be identified. On the other hand, results of per-customer independent ROI analyses can be compared to other initiatives, and can be rolled up and then re-examined on an incremental return basis.

Incremental ROI

When one activity is influenced by another, or there are interdependencies between activities, incremental ROI comes into play. If decisions have to be made between investments and anticipated returns from cross-sell activities with certain customers, versus the returns from leveraging referrals from the same customers, incremental ROI analysis would look at the profits from both activities as well as the positive and negative longer-term revenue implications of cross-sell relative to referral. As Lenskold describes the value of incremental ROI, it's often a method of protecting against averaging out the results of multiple customer initiatives, some high-performing and some low-performing.

Aggregated ROI

This is the total revenue (real and virtual) for all customer-related activities for an individual customer or an identified specific customer purchase scenario. Aggregated ROI is a strategic perspective, connecting the decision processes, making them more interdependent. It could represent, for example, all of the

---

[2] James Lenskold, "Marketing ROI: Playing to Win," *Marketing Management,* June 2002.

recovery efforts, including discounted offers directly related to previous purchase activities, among customers who purchased specific products and services. This comparison would be made to offer content, and prospective conversion rates, revenue, and profitability levels for acquiring new customers.

Bernd Stauss and Christian Friege demonstrated this a few years ago when looking at costs per order, gross and net contributions per order, and net investment contribution for new enrollees in a continuity book program relative to recovered former customers.[3] In their test, which looked at a one-year payback of these alternatives, the net ROI among recovered former customers was 214 percent, versus only 23 percent for converted customers from external lists. If the company was focused on a return period of the first 12 months, the decision became pretty straightforward.

A Dose of Reality: Most Customers Are Not Profitable

Martha Rogers has defined a company's customers as *MVCs* (Most Valuable Customers), *MGCs* (Most Growable Customers), *Migrators*—i.e., customers whose value is unknown but who can move up or down and who are not particularly loyal—and *BZs* (Below Zeros), those customers who actually detract from the bottom line. The most valuable customers, those who spend more time and money with a retailer or service provider anyway, are also those more likely to use their loyalty cards or otherwise participate in loyalty/frequent shopper schemes. Migrators are likely to go where the best offer resides. Below Zeros are the occasional or infrequent buyers who don't see any real value in what they're getting, and so provide little reward or payoff for a company's frequency-building efforts.

Companies have to concentrate on creating benefit for MVCs with each transaction or element of communication. For instance, with customers who purchase online, MVCs have to be treated differently, i.e., immediately recognizing them; providing personalized greetings; and quickly providing targeted content and offers that match both their purchase profiles and, where possible, their specific purchasing scenario for that visit. Especially when customers are members of a loyalty program, sites must be as easy to navigate and place orders, and be as multifunctional, as possible. If the company has both online and offline presence—i.e., is a bricks-and-clicks supplier such as Office Depot—the goal is to have seamless integration for customers across all touch points.

---

[3] Bernd Stauss and Christian Friege, "Regaining Service Customers," *Journal of Service Research* 1 (1999): 347–361.

For every household spending additional money with a retailer as the result of a loyalty promotion or program, there are several times more for whom the same retailer invests marketing and/or communication funds with non-commensurate, even negative return. Companies involved in loyalty and continuity programs seem much more concerned and impressed with top-tier results than in looking at the overall picture. They recognize that better customers visit the store more often, spend more on each visit, spread their purchases over a greater number of items and store departments, are less immune to the pull of competition, and have lower processing costs. Also, they "cherry pick," i.e., purchase special sale items, less frequently.

While it is recognized that leading retailers can capture over 90 percent of their total sales and 75 percent of their transactions through these frequent buyer programs, most retailers, even knowing this, don't look at the data to discern customer life cycles, nor do they conduct detailed customer purchase and profitability analyses. Many are just beginning to learn what can be done with this information, and the impact customer data can have on investment and return.

Gary Hawkins, in his dual role as president of consulting firm Hawkins Strategic and CEO of Green Hills Farms, a specialty grocery store in Syracuse, New York, has integrated customer data from multiple streams to help exploit opportunities created on an individual customer basis. His company can create advertisements and promotions on both a customer and scenario level, offering Pepsi products to loyalty Pepsi buyers, for example, tied to the customer's life stage, rate of consumption, scenario need (party, Super Bowl, etc.). They can offer consumer-specific ads through its kiosks on the sales floor, and then also electronically deliver special offers at the point of sale. This is one- to-one marketing and relationship building, and then some.

Hawkins first identifies his customers based on their place within the life cycle—new customers entering the base; active customers; customers declining in activity; and lapsed, or former, customers. Recognizing that half of the new customers didn't return after the first purchase, he developed approaches to understand their individual needs and also enhanced communication and value approaches to these customers. As a result of close analysis of the customer base, they have leveraged the information to design, layout, and physical renovations of the store, and also used it as the base for extensive employee training.

Like Tesco on a much grander scale, Green Hills Farms measures exact customer profitability, built from item level purchases up. They provide customer-specific communication and pricing on an individual basis, and it pays off. The top 1 percent of their customers have represented 20 percent of sales over a five-year period, and the top 10 percent represented two-thirds of their sales. Their annual retention rate exceeds 80 percent. As Hawkins concludes: "Competing through customer knowledge—herein lie the true opportunities in retailing."[4]

Is Divisible, Scenario-Based ROI Feasible or Possible . . . And If It Is, Will Anybody Use it?

This would seem, on the surface, a fairly open question were it not for the fact that 1) the tools and technology are already available and affordable and 2) a number of companies are already evaluating performance, and making decisions, on a customer-by-customer and scenario-by-scenario basis.

In the credit card industry, for example, data mining techniques have advanced to the point that companies can look at individual customer opportunities through "propensity modeling." Historic purchase data can be aggregated with individual demographic and lifestyle information, plus current supplier performance assessments and virtual ROI measures to create campaign or contact "scorecards," the propensity or likelihood that a customer will react to specific offers and can include discriminators, attributes with strong causal relationship or decision-making leverage for that offer. Credit card companies can thus create "opportunity matrices," alternative returns, by customer and period, aggregated into segments based on likely response. So they can select customers for each campaign, or a campaign for each customer, calculate the potential by customer, plan the specific sets of activities, and look at alternative investment opportunities.

Let's go a little deeper. Companies have access to more detailed analytics than ever before: customer life cycle value analysis (CLCV), microsegmentation, lifetime value (LTV) modeling, cross-sell/up-sell/referral models, customer contact optimization, merchandise analysis, predictive attrition and churn models, credit risk scoring, and new customer acquisition/payback. And that's just the tip of the iceberg.

With proper customer insight and analysis, individual customer- and scenario-based decision making enable companies to encourage multichannel purchasing, where only single channels are the normal buying mode. They can look at segments of potential multichannel customers by comparing them to the scenario dynamics of similar customers, and then design communication and marketing approaches that will leverage the desired behavior. Similarly, moderate purchasing customers can be migrated to higher value and more frequent purchase activity by

---

[4] Gary E. Hawkins, "The Best Little Grocery Store in America: Competing Through Customer Knowledge," *Retailing Issues Letter,* Spring 2003, p. 5.

matching their scenario-based market baskets, and then promoting products and services, by microsegment and individual, relative to similar customers' purchase scenarios. Some companies refer to this as *affinity analysis,* because the emphasis is on identifying similarities and differences between moderate purchasers and high purchasers so that moderate purchasers can be up-sold and cross-sold.

Finally, when companies look at number and type of transactions over a specific period of time, they can get down to the trends of customer behavior, including seasonal activity. They can then develop very individual models of communication and value building. The one impediment that appears to remain is speed. Even though the business intelligence software exists for planning at the customer scenario level, companies often can't get the information to user groups in a timely fashion because they are relying on a single IT infrastructure to support all major functions—transactions, information, and reporting. This creates informational bottlenecks and gridlock. One study on business intelligence application usage, in fact, reported that 60 percent of companies of various sizes, and across a range of industries, were experiencing such problems when trying to generate reports from live database systems.[5] So long as situations like this continue, companies will be challenged to yield positive ROI from systems designed to provide individual customer, and customer scenario, guidance.

Agreeing on Customer ROI Metrics

For companies to have more consistency regarding customer and divisible, or scenario-based customer ROI, there will have to be greater agreement and unanimity on principles and metrics. We believe there are several easy-to-follow rules that can be followed:

1. Define the customer behavior objectives.

On a customer-by-customer basis, what is the company trying to achieve? Greater purchases of certain items or services? More frequent purchases? Cross-sales? Referrals? Participation in loyalty, or new product/service research? More self-help customer service? Most ROI initiatives sink or fail on discipline-related objective-setting. Whether it's returns from promotional programs, marketing campaigns, process upgrades, new product and service development, communications initiatives, loyalty schemes, or other customer-focused activities, setting

---

[5] Appfluent Technology, "Real-Time Business Intelligence Not Yielding ROI," www.thewisemarketer.com, November 12, 2002.

budgets and objectives at the same time, with all involved parties participating, assures that everyone is on the same page.

If, for example, the company computes ROI begins by looking at the activity of the customer base, as in the total number who made purchases in the past year, stick with that. Begin the analysis by looking at the annual revenue divided by the total number of active customers to get average revenue per customer. Then a basic behavioral framework might be added based on a combination of research results (key metrics such as overall performance, likelihood to continue purchasing, and likelihood to recommend) and per-customer sales to identify customers who might be classified (as in the landmark model developed by Dick and Basu in 1994) as:

- *Advocates,* or those who are truly loyal (high performance/high continued purchase and recommendation)
- *Accessible* (high performance/low to moderate continued purchase and recommendation)
- *Trapped* (low to moderate performance/high continued purchase and recommendation)
- *At Risk* (low to moderate performance/low to moderate continued purchase and recommendation)[6]

The company can then make a simple calculation of prospective margin loss among customers who are less than truly loyal. So, if the company wishes to project what rate of return they might achieve with a focused initiative among customers who are not fully committed, the break-even requirements can be determined as a starting point to see if the effort will be worthwhile.

For customers identified as Advocates, the principal course will be to maintain and grow the relationship. For those who represent themselves as Accessible, some form or forms of intervention and re-establishment of trust will have the greatest likelihood of returning them to positive advocacy. For those who are Trapped, the company will need to research their issues and concerns on an individual basis, perhaps by focused research or outbound Customer Service contact, to stabilize them. Finally, if customers are At Risk, the profitability of each must be assessed; and then, if profitable, investment can be made toward intervention and stabilization.

2. Establish highly specific, measurable objectives.

It's not nearly enough to use general terms in setting goals, such as increasing share of customer. Ideally, there will be specific objectives for each customer, such

---

[6] Alan S. Dick and Kunal Basu, "Customer Loyalty: Toward an Integrated Conceptual Framework," *Journal of Marketing Science* 22 (1994): 99–113.

as increasing the range of products and services purchased by a certain percentage. If this is considered too detailed, these objectives should be established on a microsegment basis.

3. Put consistent, systematic approaches in place for collecting relevant data.

Without a constant flow of customer profile and transaction data, plus performance and loyalty research that is as real-time as possible so that benchmarks can be established, setting specific objectives is a waste of time and effort.

Most companies' use of antiquated, satisfaction-based approaches to this research is one of the biggest challenges to having action-based ROI metrics. What is needed is a set of metrics that looks at positive behavioral levers (high attribute performance ratings, perceived overall performance, likelihood to continue purchasing and anticipated volumetric levels, and likelihood to recommend), and negative levers (low attribute performance ratings, areas of expressed and unexpressed complaint, decline in perceived performance over time).

4. Weight influence of each behavior leverage factor.

We have often defined perceived value as an equation, namely the combination of benefits represented by tangible and intangible elements in a product or service purchase decision, minus whatever the customer has to invest, or give up, to get those benefits. This is different for each element and for each customer. For example, if the elements inherent in choosing to purchase from one supermarket or another include prices, purchase specials and incentives, security, product variety, product freshness, speed of checkout, store cleanliness, friendliness of store personnel, proximity to my home, amount of parking, etc., then the weight, or importance, of each of these factors for each customer must be taken into consideration. For example, an upwardly mobile, busy-lifestyle woman with young children may place a great deal more value on speed of shopping and transactions, the array of ready-prepared foods, and also on the availability of gourmet products when she entertains. A retired couple might put more emphasis on basic products, such as soups, and more bulk-oriented buying.

5. Create a mnemonic, index, or scorecard.

Management somehow is always more comfortable dealing with a "magic bullet" number or simple set of metrics. Although the objective is actionability, quantifiable measures, with high weightings relative to specific or customer group goals, can be assigned. Lower weights can be set up for objectives that have a more marginal relationship to the measurement.

6. Review regularly, take two aspirins, and call me in the morning.

Customers, and marketplaces, are highly dynamic entities. Plans, indices or score-cards, and performance results should be reviewed with as great a frequency as feasible. To make certain that this review process is given the priority it deserves, customer revenue and profitability goals should somehow be tied to employee incentives and recognition—not just for sales, as is most often done, but for everyone. For example, MBNA has set up global quarterly customer retention goals for the entire company; and progress against these goals and the indices and metrics used to track them can be seen everyday on monitors installed through-out all of their buildings. The entire corps of MBNA employees, reflective of their customer-centric culture, receives incentive compensation if these objec-tives are met.

The Landscape for More Active Use of Per-Customer ROI

In Chapter Eight, in the discussion of customer clubs and loyalty programs, the results of a definitive 2002 study among 10,000 senior-level consumer and business-to-business marketing executives showed how their companies approached retention marketing. It was found that while 59 percent had retention programs of some sort, capturing more customer information was a lower-level priority.

Perhaps the most disappointing and challenging finding, however, was that segmentation and ranking of customers by profitability was considered the least important objective of these programs. While 77 percent of those with programs segmented customers based on gross sales (and 58 percent segmented them based on demographics, psychographics, or geography), only 47 percent segmented them by net profit, and a mere 24 percent segmented their customers on lifetime value.

As concluded by W. Michael King, group vice president of the Grizzard Performance Group, the company that conducted the study: "Many businesses don't understand that their retention program should center around the experi-ences and preferences of their most profitable customer segments, not the entire database. Building brand preference among individual customers without regard to the value that customer brings to the company is a risky way to allocate resources, at best."[7]

---

[7] W. Michael King, "Customer Retention Marketing: What's Working," *Performance Report,* no. 20, Fall 2002.

Finally . . . What Is the Financial Worth of Creating an Individual, Divisible Experience for Your Customers?

Walker Information, examining the ROI of retail customers' in-store experience in 2003, found that truly loyal consumers—i.e., those who trusted the retailers and could report positive transactional and service experiences irrespective of need and purchase situation—reported that, on future spending alone they were *15 times* more likely to increase spending with a store than customers who are at high risk of defection.

For example, Walker found that in consumer electronics, 51 percent of customers are planning to increase their spending. Among customers reporting true loyalty as a result of their "bank account" of positive experiences, this figure jumped to 76 percent; but, among high risk customers, it dropped to a shocking 4 percent. In home improvement stores, individual store share of wallet climbs from 71 percent for the average customer to 80 percent for the truly loyal customers, and drops to 50 percent among the high risk group.

The takeaway is clear. Companies must understand how value is created for each customer, at each purchase scenario, to optimize loyalty and financial return.

11

(NOT) BACK TO THE FUTURE

The Critical Disconnect Between Suppliers, Their Customers, and Their Customers' Experiences . . . and How Data Changes Disconnect to Connect

In 2003, Strativity Group, a New Jersey-based customer relationship consultancy, conducted an important study among close to 200 executives in the U.S., Europe, Asia, and Africa.[1] What made the study so valuable was that it focused on the degree to which businesses thought they were earning their customers' loyalty. In addition, the study revealed just how far companies have to go in addressing and relating to customers on an individual, much less divisible, basis.

Among the disturbing results:

- Sixty percent felt that their relationships with customers are not well defined or structured.
- Forty-two percent said that their company will acquire any customer that is willing to pay; and in business-to-business services, this was close to 70 percent.
- Only 37 percent felt that their company has the tools to service and resolve customer problems and complaints.
- Only 36 percent of the European executives believed that their company deserved their customer's loyalty vs. 54 percent of the U.S. respondents.

What these results demonstrate is a critical breakdown in customer-by-customer experience management. There is a significant shortfall in the ability to define, and deliver, the value customers are seeking in a supplier relationship. Still, 58 percent felt that their company is committed to the customer (61 percent in the U.S. and 46 percent in Europe). As demonstrated in Chapter Six, statements and initiatives toward creation of commitment to customers often mask a lack of fundamental understanding of what customers truly want in the relationship. This is reflected in that Strativity Group finding that 55 percent of executives felt that their company does not conduct a true dialogue with its customers.

---

[1] "Why Businesses Say They Don't Deserve Loyalty," www.thewisemarketer.com, March 10, 2004.

Ultimately, perceived value is the strongest motivator of loyalty. It's principally about relationship—as the customer defines it—rather than transactions. Successful companies such as Southwest Airlines, Commerce Bank, Microsoft, and Starbucks strive to make each sale so habitual and pleasant that it's almost like an eagerly awaited book or magazine subscription. Southwest Airlines does it by making the flying experience nonroutine and comfortable. Commerce Bank does it with extended service hours and extraordinarily well-trained staff. Starbucks does it with a European café-like ambience and newer technologies such as stored value cards, linked to the customer's primary credit card. The credit card automatically reloads the Starbucks card when the value falls below a predefined level.

Companies such as Starbucks are leveraging the streams of customer data from various sources to upgrade communication and deepen the relationship. In moving toward creating a truly divisible engagement, companies like Starbucks can identify individual customers, track their behavior, tailor promotions and services to them, and otherwise customize each interaction and visit occasion. This enables them to focus on loyal customers, becoming less and less dependent on inconsistent and occasional customers who need to be courted to obtain each additional transaction. By concentrating their efforts on the more engaged and active customers, those whose reasons for returning are well understood, companies can proactively build processes and design communications vehicles required to deliver optimum value to their best, longest-term, and most valuable (and positively communicating) customers.

Understanding the Critical Relationship Between Employee Commitment and Customer Commitment

One of the most revealing findings from the Strativity Group study was that only 36 percent of the executives believed that their company invests in people more than in technology (38 percent in the United States and 10 percent in Europe).[2] There is a direct linkage between employee loyalty, productivity, and commitment to the customer and that customer's commitment to the supplier, as borne out by two of the key study findings:

- Eighty percent of the executives who believed that they have the tools and authority to serve the customer agreed that their company is committed to customers (vs. 38 percent among those who strongly disagree).

---

[2] "Why Businesses Say They Don't Deserve Loyalty," www.thewisemarketer.com, March 10, 2004.

- Ninety-five percent of those who strongly agree that the role of the customer is well defined within their organization agreed that their company is truly committed to customers (vs. 45 percent among those who strongly disagree).

Much of what drives customer commitment stems from the degree to which the company's culture—and the training, focus, and motivation of their staff—is concentrated on the creation of value for customers. Where there is a great deal of customer attrition and churn, it's often because there is only reactive dialogue between customers and employees, ineffective customer data sharing and application between groups, accompanied by low levels of staff training, poor career pathing, and resultant high employee turnover. Structurally and operationally, companies are not committed to customers; and customers are keenly aware of the disconnect between their needs and what the company and its employees are willing to deliver.

In his landmark *Men Are from Mars, Women Are from Venus* books on male-female communication and relationships, couples therapist John Gray has concluded that men and women speak fundamentally different languages. The emotional needs, communication styles, and modes of behavior men demonstrate are frequently not understood or appreciated by women; and the reverse is also true. As a result, the language differences between men and women can be so great, Gray asserts, that each gender can seem to come from a separate planet.

According to Gray, a good part of this difference stems from the fact that men want to be trusted, accepted, and appreciated while women want to be understood and respected. Gray believes that men often act as if they are right, invalidating a woman's feelings. In reaction, women may disapprove but not disagree with male efforts at creating relationship value and solving problems; and they also "keep score" differently, looking for a continuous flow of consideration rather than occasional bursts.

Gray's ideas are a very useful metaphor for helping interpret the interaction between customers and the suppliers who provide them with goods and services, trying to earn their loyalty. Gray explores how male-female language and behavior differences can cause attrition and defection in loyal relationships. Males, in this context, are like suppliers, seeking to be trusted and to earn loyalty. Females are like customers, seeking to be heard and validated. To better understand this disconnection between suppliers and customers, several years ago we conducted original research among purchasing agents and sales/marketing managers to better understand the essential male-female language and behavior differences between customers and suppliers.

Our sample included a statistically valid cross-section of purchasing agents in both business-to-business and consumer product and service companies. Purchasing agents were selected because, while others often influence purchases and may even be instrumental in decision making, it is the purchasing agent who usually has the most day-to-day contact with suppliers. We also included sales and marketing managers. This is because sales managers from business-to-business and consumer product and service can provide a landscape perspective of the entire selling and support process. Finally, marketing managers were included because they are frequently responsible for their company's communication efforts.

One of the first things we wanted to know from the purchasing agents was whether they saw their suppliers as *commodity-oriented,* providing competitive prices and basic service and support, or *customer-oriented,* working to deliver optimum value and benefit. Customer-orientation, which emphasizes relationships and high customer commitment, correlates very closely with customer loyalty.

Only 43 percent of the purchasing agents said their suppliers were customer oriented, compared to 73 percent of the sales managers and 71 percent of the marketing managers who thought that purchasing agents would consider them customer oriented. This significant difference was a telling clue to the degree of misinterpretation and misperception between customers and suppliers. The two groups are not speaking the same language, struggling to make one another understood.

We asked each group to assess the importance and performance of close to 20 elements, or attributes, of delivery. These included product/service quality, communication, timeliness, problem solving, service support value, supplier flexibility/adaptability, billing, and pricing, to name a few—a complete spectrum of the tangibles and intangibles a supplier provides to the customer.

Like the results from our first question, these findings were no less sobering and revealing. With minor exceptions, the sales and marketing managers rated attribute importance similarly to purchasing agents. The real story was in the attribute performance ratings. Other than pricing, need anticipation, and communication channel availability, purchasing agents consistently gave high attribute ratings less often than sales and marketing managers. Many of these differences were in relationship and communication areas, critical in leveraging customer loyalty.

One of the things that particularly struck us was just how low purchasing agents rated their suppliers. For example, under 10 percent gave "Excellent" ratings on communication, follow-up, service support, supplier dependability, and flexibility/adaptability attributes. These are attention-getting results. In the aspects of delivery that really matter to purchasing agents, sales and marketing managers seem not to be speaking their language.

Almost two-thirds of the purchasing agents told us that they the number of suppliers they use for any given product or service has decreased over the past two or three years. Only about 10 percent reported that their supplier list had increased. Further, only about half said that, if any suppliers were warned of possible termination, the suppliers responded aggressively to re-establish the relationship and delivery of value. Apparently, the language purchasing agents use to communicate this may not be well enough understood for threatened suppliers to respond with any greater enthusiasm.

On the other side, about half of the sales and marketing managers reported segmenting their customers according to long-term value; so many of them had no idea how to apply resources to customers based on their worth. In addition, about half of the marketing managers and 30 percent of the sales managers could not identify an annual customer loss percentage. Equal percentages of both groups didn't know the percentage of lost customers they were able to win back. We found these figures close to amazing.

Probably the most unsettling statistic in our research, especially in view of the rate at which purchasing agents reported trimming back their corps of suppliers, was the fact that almost two-thirds of the sales and marketing managers said their companies had no way of identifying customers at risk for defection. How can they intervene to save a valued customer if they can't even determine which one is most likely to leave? To be proactive, companies not only have to have loyalty processes and programs in place, they have to communicate with, and respond to, customers in language they understand.

A New Day Isn't Comin' . . . It's Here

When times were simpler, companies created value and commitment among their customers by understanding individualized, customer-by-customer and purchase-by-purchase needs. Today, whether the transactions are offline or online, it's still the relationship and relevance between customer and supplier that count.

Companies can create detailed profiles around what customers care about, or don't care about. Programs and processes can be successful, largely because customers have helped formulate them, directly or indirectly.

Offline, targeted messaging, effective mixing and application of media, use of loyalty programs and communities to generate relevant data, leading-edge approaches to understand customer perceptions and behavior, and more enlightened incorporation and leveraging of customer service—all of these will, for progressive companies, help to increase engagement and commitment.

Online, new technologies will facilitate stronger supplier relationships and enhance retention effectiveness:

- Tracking and reporting technologies give companies the tools to show how customers interact with content, bringing into play their preferences, opinions, and lifestyle specifics.
- Customer insight can be "fused" with demographics and purchase profiles to help companies marry the right audience, with the right message, at the right time.
- New metrics enable companies to go beyond click-throughs to assess the degree of interaction between the customer and site content, indicating the strength of the customer-supplier relationship and which customers have the highest value potential.
- Advanced database management and data mining software facilitate the timing of messages, and design of content, to stage in the customer life cycle.

Companies can, in addition, utilize new web-based technologies to distribute incisive, in-depth information on individual customers, down to specific purchasing situations. Outbound, companies can create endless variations of content such as e-newsletters, reinforcing customers' experience of the supplier or brand. And, in addition, this informational and promotional content has built-in measurement and reporting capabilities. The supplier can see what customers read, and in what order, what has been bookmarked, what has been passed along to someone else, etc. It's the online equivalent to having a detailed, accurate monitor on what a customer did when shopping at a retail store.

Just as companies can develop profiles of engagement and purchasing patterns offline, e-commerce companies can create databases of customer online experiences, leveraging those experiences to customize communication with that customer. Customer preferences can be established through direct and indirect feedback, plus profiling; and then the supplier can respond with meaningful content and offers on an ongoing basis. From this, commitment and barriers to exit can be created.

A Company That Makes "Customer Divisibility" a Reality—Today and Tomorrow

Michael Price, General Manager of Price Automotive Group, has been mentioned several times in this book. His company, representing seven automotive dealerships in Delaware and the Eastern Shore of Maryland, does "customer divisibility" about as well as any company in the world. What Michael has accomplished proves that companies of any size, and in any industry, can optimize the loyalty and commitment of customers and the loyalty and commitment of employees.

Here are some of the achievements of his flagship dealership, Price Toyota, in New Castle, Delaware:

- Sixty-seven percent of their business is repeat or referred.
- 13.5 vehicle sales are made per representative per month.
- Ninety-seven percent of their customers are A or B credit scored.

All of these results are significantly above industry norms or standards. For example, average representative monthly sales levels are 9.5 vehicles per month, so reps at Price Toyota sell about 50 percent more than the average.

Price's success is driven by closely monitored process management at each customer life stage, always with the objective of optimizing perceived customer value. This is built on a solid foundation of insight into customer needs and expectations coupled with flexible, innovative approaches to delivering benefits. Further, the dealership is able to customize, and value-enhance, the individual and lifetime experiences of each customer.

One of the key early customer learnings at the dealerships had to do with the purchase transaction process. Customers tend to equate a long, drawn-out vehicle purchase transaction with personal vulnerability, filled with negatives and potential added, unwanted expense; and, beyond two hours, future purchase intent and recommendation likelihood scores decline rapidly. Simply stated, speed equals trust, at least insofar as buying a vehicle is concerned. The shorter the transaction time, the greater the customer's level of trust in the dealership. Price has reduced the transaction time for most customers to under two hours, with the finance and insurance (F & I) element compressed to under 25 minutes. Among the more than 75 percent of customers who complete their purchases in under two hours, 100 percent plan to repurchase at the dealership, 97 percent plan to service their vehicles there, and 67 percent have already referred.

Price's dealerships have adopted a "one-price" approach to sales, in which the best vehicle price is offered to the customer up-front in the transaction, eliminating the necessity of negotiation, a part of the sales process which most vehicle buyers report detesting. The dealerships offer 15 high-perceived-value benefits to customers, including a 72 hour buy-back/exchange policy, service and parts discounts, no charge towing, and $300 extra for their Price vehicle at trade-in. These are some of the tangible elements of value. The real differentiators for Price dealerships are the approaches to creating intangible, emotionally-based value.

Price understands that, particularly at the beginning of the customer's life with the dealership, traditional sales processes had to be redesigned and realigned to address each customer's needs. This means that the processes had to match what customers want, eliminating obstacles and perceived negatives. Sales reps, for instance, are carefully trained to guide customers through the purchase and to offer quick, responsive support. They are on salary rather than commission. Also, the dealership has defined the critical profit-driving linkage between employee and customer loyalty, and so special emphasis is placed on making certain that sales reps—and all Price staff—feel that they are part of a team, that they are directly contributing to the dealerships' successes, and that they are appropriately compensated without having to push customers for each additional dollar. As a result, Price experiences very low employee turnover.

Vehicle owner research has clearly proven that loyalty to the dealership is leveraged at least as much by cumulative service experiences as the sales and delivery processes, so Price puts equal weight on service performance. Its value guarantees are offered through a Preferred Customer Card, which provides such benefits as five no-charge diagnostic service certificates, four no-charge oil service certificates, free roadside assistance, mobile service for light repairs, and free loaner cars if the vehicle isn't fixed right the first time. Price also offers extended service hours, a child safety program, and a service menu that has been greatly simplified for easier write-up.

At the center of what make Price's dealerships work so well is customer data. They actively utilize local market information, and study trading area family demographics so they can target the right customers. They obtain detailed lifestyle data—hobbies, interests, etc.—on each prospect, and this helps them focus on niches with similar profiles. Within each identified niche, they can locate, and market to, prospective customers who are likely to be most receptive to their value proposition.

The customer base is continually monitored to help gauge profiles of ideal prospects. Post-sales communication and service experiences are monitored to identify any potentially neutral or negative situations that need to be stabilized or turned around. Price does some basic predictive churn modeling to help identify when their customers will be ready to make the next vehicle purchase.

Price actively believes in customer engagement, providing service reminders and otherwise customizing the post-sale communication for each owner. Uniquely, Price is also concerned about customer loss, and invests in customer win-back. They identify when and why a customer would have stopped servicing his or her vehicle at the dealership and have methods in place to re-establish the relationship. Few other dealerships do this.

The Price BDC and Its Multilayered Customer Divisibility Role

If there's a single, data-driven function within Price that makes customer divisibility come alive, it's the BDC, or Business Development Center, a hybridized cross between proactive customer service and individual customer account manager. At Price, the BDC does virtually everything with respect to developing and coordinating the continuous delivery of value throughout the customer's life cycle.

At prospecting, sales, and delivery processes, the BDC has several coordinating responsibilities:

- Track, confirm, and help close phone appointments for sales reps
- Train new sales representatives in prospect telephone skills
- Manage all lead calls that come from the Internet or factory
- Generate daily work plans for each sales representative, in both electronic and paper formats
- If a sales rep leaves Price's employment, the owner who was sold by the departed rep is assigned and transitioned to another rep

Through the BDC, Price carefully tracks each prospect visiting the dealership to continuously upgrade their methods of reaching these desired customers. Uniquely, they extensively follow up with each lost prospect with calls, a thank-you card, or a model brochure, and a brochure about the dealership. Lost prospects are placed in a follow-up queue; and, if they do not buy within three weeks, they are placed on a separate, long-term follow-up queue. As a check on what the BDC is doing, sales managers or sales reps call each unsold prospect within 24 hours; and, using the daily work plans the BDC has developed for sales reps, they can coordinate communication and disposition efforts.

Once the vehicle is delivered, the BDC follows up with each customer. On an ongoing basis, the BDC manages owner communication. Price dealerships maintain a communication frequency rate of four to five times a year, and it is the BDC's responsibility to extend benefits or notifications of value to every customer in the base. They are, in effect, the ongoing relationship manager for the dealerships.

The communication strategy is built around the term of each customer's lease or loan. Price has software that incorporates up to 21 factors behind each owner's historic purchase patterns, and so can custom design which rewards should be offered and when. Toward the end of the loan or lease term, the rate of communication builds, with a focus on reminding owners of the value they receive from the dealership. Price offers such benefits as service coupons, an emergency valet key (which customers must have cut at the dealership), cards (anniversary, holiday, birthday) with gift certificates, invitations to test-drive new models that fit their profile (with a dining gift certificate), notifications of safety updates for their vehicles, and communication about Price's referral rewards program. In other words, like Tesco, all of Price's communication to owners is built around *relevance*.

The BDC follows up, by telephone, all service transactions within 24 hours. They also serve as a listening post, conducting ad hoc service research. A particular focus is the proactive collection, analysis, and reporting of any flaws in the service process, especially complaints. When they receive a positive response, a "thank you" post card is sent to the owner. If a problem is reported, it is usually resolved within a day or otherwise tracked until it is closed out. Service advisors make separate follow-up calls within 72 hours to reinforce their relationship with the owner, and they are first made aware of any negative issue the BDC would have uncovered.

If owners order special parts, the BDC sets up the appointment, prioritizes the parts order, calls the owner when the part has been delivered, and sends a follow-up card confirming the appointment. For those situations where owners stop getting their vehicle serviced at the Price dealerships, after nine months the BDC sends a win-back letter, plus two special incentive coupons.

At the back end of the customer life cycle, it is the BDC that helps to predict, target, and market to owners at the right time—i.e., when they are ready to repurchase, based on the end date of their lease or loan, their historical buying and brand loyalty pattern, etc. If a lease is renewed, they manage follow-up with each customer.

The BDC also serves as the dealership's overall process improvement team leader and coordinator, conducting multidepartment meetings among teams, using the feedback they've generated from owners to improve processes. Customer anecdotal and dimensional data, however, is the core of what makes the BDC so effective in these multiple roles. They have customer follow-up logs, generate problem resolution reports, and create daily follow-up work plans.

Any change of a customer's status can be picked up by a member of the BDC staff. If, for example, an unsold prospect asks to be recontacted in six months because his daughter will be graduating college at that time, the BDC will note this in the prospect's profile. Then they send a follow-up letter indicating when they will be back in touch. The BDC creates a customized communication strategy for that prospect, often including attractive offers made through timed mailings. The communication campaign is guided by a special software package, which can update each prospect and customer's lifestyle every 90 days.

As Michael Price concludes, the key to his success with the BDC is "awareness of ever-changing customer personal situations, enabling us to completely customize the objectives for every contact." In very few words, what Michael has described is customer divisibility.

Tesco's Unretailer-like Customer Data Gathering Approaches

It's not an overstatement that Tesco, as an organization, knows more about how its customers think about the company and the supermarket buying experience, and they've leveraged it farther, than any retailer in the world. In addition to leading-edge mining and modeling Clubcard loyalty program data to learn about customer wants, needs, and response to new products and services, Tesco utilizes some other infrequently applied approaches (at least by most retailers) to gather anecdotal and dimensional customer insight.

For instance, each of Tesco's senior managers and executives spends at least one week per year working in the stores, performing various service functions and observing customer behavior. This is actually a formal program for upgrading customer-related in- store processes. One such example of this was a proposal, and eventual action, to have barcodes printed on both sides of cases of beer, enabling customers to move more quickly through checkout lines.

Tesco also conducts more qualitative and quantitative customer research than most of its peers, focusing on taking negatives out of the store experience and building in more value. In one of its surveys, Tesco learned that mothers shopping with children, one of the chain's major constituencies, disliked the candy displays at or near checkout lines. Most chains find these impulse item displays attractive sources of revenue, and, irrespective of customer concerns or complaints, they resist removing them. Tesco, however, proactively generates customer complaints, and they considered the elimination of such displays a testable proposition. What they found was that the increased loyalty among moms doing their grocery buying with kids more than offset lost sales.

Intelligently designed qualitative research can also provide valuable insight, and Tesco has utilized it well. Consumer panels and juries have helped the company develop specialty clubs for young mothers, children, and a healthy lifestyle, with customers providing direction on Internet and offline communication content, events, and other viral approaches.

Revisiting the Harrah's Customer Data Machine

Aspects of Harrah's use of data to optimize their divisible approach to customers have been presented earlier in the book. The Harrah's numbers are indeed staggering: 25 million slot machine customers use personalized frequent-gambler cards, called Total Rewards, every time they gamble, to earn free meals, trips, hotel rooms, and other goodies and prizes. In return, Harrah's continuously adds to and hones its extensive database, which now has 90 separately identifiable demographic/lifestyle segments. This enables Harrah's to devise personalized, customized incentives for customers to play slots at any of the company's close to 30 gaming properties across America (26 properties in 13 states), encouraging strong brand equity and cross-sell and up-sell activities between properties at the same time.

The Pareto Principle is alive and well at Harrah's. Just over one-quarter of their customer base generate over 80 percent of their revenues.

Slots players, once considered the "great unwashed" customers of casinos, have long since eclipsed all other forms of gaming in terms of value. For Harrah's, these customers now account for over 80 percent of the company's operating profit. This has been strong incentive for the organization to build ever more sophisticated data mining, modeling, and communication programs around them.

Beginning with several key pieces of customer information—gender, age, place of residence, machines and amounts played—Harrah's can predict, with a high degree of accuracy, which customers will be the most valuable and over what time period. This is important because, through years of tracking, Harrah's has learned that the 30 percent of their customers, mostly locals who don't stay at their hotels, and who spent between $100 and $500 on slots per visit to one of their casinos, accounted for 80 percent of company revenue and almost 100 percent of profits. (Note: This mirrors an evaluation by the New Jersey Casino Control Commission, showing that, in the 25 years of legalized gaming in Atlantic City between 1978 and 2002, slots went from 44 percent to 74 percent of total gambling revenue.)[3] Thus there is strong return on investment for cultivating long-term value and positive relationships, especially with slots players rather than "high-rollers."

Chief Operating Officer Gary Loveman, a former Harvard University business professor, identifies age and distance from the casino as key predictors of frequency for Harrah's, coupled with the kind of slot machine played and how many coins are played at each machine.[4] The perfect player, Loveman's profiles have shown, is a 62-year-old woman who lives within 30 minutes of a casino and plays

---

[3] Amy S. Rosenberg, "Slot Players Cashing in on Clout," *Philadelphia Inquirer,* March 7, 2003, p. A14.

[4] Philip Bligh and Doug Turk, "On Customer Loyalty," *Customer Relationship Management,* June 2004, pp. 49–51.

dollar video poker. Harrah's has identified such customers as having substantial disposable cash, a good deal of available time, and the kind of access to casinos that make it an entertainment and leisure-time option. The company's models and algorithms identify this kind of individual as a prospective frequent player, and until her individual identity begins to crystallize, she would be marketed to on that basis. As Harrah's learns more about her based on what she does, promotion content, frequency, and method become increasingly more refined, built around the 90 lifestyle segments mentioned above.

As noted, distance from a casino is one of the key variables. If a customer has attractive potential characteristics but lives farther away, the communication package will typically also include time-sensitive discounts or comps on rooms and transportation. Closer-in prospects and customers receive food, entertainment, and cash incentives. Every communication and promotional variable is actively tracked, by customer, for return on investment and level of response.

The company is also focused on divisibility as an unstated but well-executed conceptual strategy. Harrah's has learned that its customers have long memories so experience optimization, for example, is operationally emphasized. Research has revealed that if a customer's recent experiences at Harrah's were highly positive, they increased their spending with company casinos by 24 percent over the next year. Conversely, if experiences were disappointing, spending decreased by 10 percent during the same period.

One notable mark of how successful Harrah's has been at applying customer microsegmentation and divisibility concepts for optimum effect is that more than half of the revenue from the company's three Las Vegas casinos comes from its customers outside of Nevada. The company has a record of several years of quarter-to-quarter double-digit compounded growth in revenue and profit. Truly impressive.

Using Customer Data to Create a Moving Experience

There's nothing like a real-life story to exemplify the power of using the right customer data, at the right time, to create value on a divisible—and long-term—basis. Erik Peterson, CFO of Go Direct Marketing, a Canadian consulting firm, recounts this experience:

> It was ten years ago and I remember the experience vividly. As soon as they opened the cabin door, I rushed out of the plane and hurried downstairs to my usual car rental counter. I hadn't bothered to book ahead, but so what, I was first in line. I had been doing this same three-day trip every other week and by now the rental agency knew my face, which right now was full of hope.

Sadly, they had nothing. Reluctant but having no option, I moved down the aisle to the friendly green spaces of National Car Rental and yes, they had a car for me. I gave the National rental agent my license and my Amex Gold Card. She filled in the blanks on the rental agreement and asked if I wanted the extra insurances. Usually, I took the extra coverage—this trip was two hours into the mountains and I always worried about steering round a bend into an elk or a mountain goat.

Then the agent said "Oh but you are already insured through your Gold Card, so you don't need our coverage." These were words worth a meaningful fifteen dollars a day—words I'd never heard from my usual rental agency in the previous twenty months of travel. Impressed with her integrity, and underimpressed with theirs, I became an instant convert to National and over a ten-year period gave them approximately $10,000 of business. For nothing more, or less, than a customer experience created from fifteen words of advice.

It was not technology that made me a loyal customer; it was respect for the customer as demonstrated one-to-one by a customer-friendly car rental agent. And it was of value to National Car Rental because:

- it cost the company nothing
- it was different from, and better than the competitive experience
- it was effortless

National Car Rental's bright shiny signage, their reputation-boosting mass media, their established position in the airport, all raised my awareness of what they did and how they did it. I also knew, or assumed I knew, their value proposition would be pretty much the same as the other car rental people. Closing the sale was through face-to-face contact with another human being. Her honest off-the-cuff remark ("Oh but you are already insured through your Gold Card, so you don't need our coverage") moved me from trial to repeat in about ten seconds.

Why didn't my former rental agency see me as a recapture target? They weren't looking my way, they didn't see me heading off to a competitor, their lack of system was a symptom of a lack of strategy. Their focus was on selling, not retention.

Too many sales are made by people and businesses who think that's their sole reason for being. Just sell it and get on with the next sale, they think. This unworthy ethic could prevail in a world of kinder competition, scarcer capacity, and price parity. Today, the best customer experiences surprise, delight and can be replicated—they nurture the next transaction.[5]

What's instructive about Erik Peterson's example is not that it happened, but that it's possible to repeat it again and again, for companies in any business and of any size, simply through the better application of known customer data.

Three Other Quick Examples of Powerful Customer Data Application

Here are three *small* companies that are very *big* on gathering the kind of information to help keep their customers coming back and spending more.

1. Dorothy Lane Markets

A small chain of three supermarkets in Dayton, Ohio, Dorothy Lane uses some pretty nontraditional but highly effective ways of learning what their customers want. Each night, for instance, senior store employees call five customers who shopped that day for feedback about their experience. Every week, store managers send handwritten letters to customers inviting them to ask questions, offer suggestions, and make their concerns known. They use the information not only to improve their operations but also to reward their best customers with innovative gifts: free bouquets of flowers, invitations to concerts, charitable donations, and the like. Dorothy Lane tracks customer purchases so closely it can send highly targeted offers to its customers. Four to six customized communications go out, usually in postcard form, every month.

2. Capitol Concierge

Busy employees in more than 80 buildings in the Washington, DC metropolitan area call on the live, personal assistants at Capitol Concierge (and its online sister company, VIPdesk) to help them with their daily chores and "to do" lists. Dedicated to "customer chemistry," Capitol Concierge first develops a detailed, multipage profile on each customer. Then staff members use every customer interaction to get in-depth information. Hiring the right employees, training them in the art of active listening (becoming like detectives, particularly in identifying the needs of top customers), helping them stay focused, and rewarding them for the

---

[5] Erik Peterson with Virginia Green, "Customer Experience Management: What Does It Really Mean?" RMG Connect, Vancouver, British Columbia, Canada.

behavior are all-important. Beyond merely creating an informational database, Capitol Concierge believes in one-by-one, face-to-face feedback collection. Resolving a customer problem or complaint, for example, is an opportunity to learn. Capitol Concierge also regularly conducts short phone surveys, organizes customer focus groups, makes monthly contact calls, and, like Dorothy Lane Markets, uses a customer advisory board to help improve service processes.

3. Ticket City

When people think about buying tickets and event packages for concerts, sports, and theatre shows on the Internet, Ticket City wants everyone to think of them first. A small, e-tail-based company located in a suite in Austin, just off the University of Texas campus, they advertise their toll-free number, 1-800-SOLD-OUT, almost everywhere imaginable. Orders were coming from three distinct sources—phone, click-throughs on promotional links, and directly through their web site. However, the company didn't know which channel customers used to learn about them. SO, to make the best use of marketing and advertising dollars, they had to find out. Though not wanting to overload customers with intrusive questions, when orders are placed through every touch point, Ticket City finds out how customers learned about them, if they are new customers, and other questions designed to help the company understand how they can provide better customer value.

The bottom line is that any motivated company, irrespective of size or industry, can use in-depth data to optimize customer loyalty. Creating situation-based messages and experiences, customer by customer, can be achieved today and will be even easier in the one customer, divisible future.

AFTERWORD

Why Active Advocacy Rules in a Divisible Customer, Word-of-Mouth World

Trying to determine who the greatest athletes have been over a span of the last 100 years is an exercise best left to the sports pundits (and people with nothing more important to occupy their time). Differences in training, diet, equipment, and facilities make such comparisons almost impossible. Similarly, over the past 25 years, so much has changed about the way marketers communicate with, and sell and market to, their customers that comparing eras, media, message content, and levels of effectiveness are pretty much an academic exercise.

Today, marketers must be aware that customers are so overwhelmed with messages and the availability of product and service information that they've gone, in large measure, to alternative, less traditional methods of helping them decide what and where to buy. At the heart of seeking sources for decision input is trust. This is an era where spam, pop-up ads, telemarketing, and other forms of targeted advertising and promotion, indeed most forms of electronic and print advertising, receive low trust scores in customer research. Beyond permission e-mail, brand websites, and the like, customer trust is highest for word-of-mouth. How high? Over 90 percent of consumers, as identified in a 2004 Forrester study, said they trust word-of mouth, compared to less than half of that for most other forms of advertising and communication.[1]

While, since 1977, the aggregate value of advertising as a decision making influence has remained about the same, word-of-mouth has doubled in leveraging power to the point where it is the dominant communication device in our society. Through its studies, NOP World Roper Reports has learned that over 90 percent of customers identify word-of- mouth as the best, most reliable source of ideas and information about products and services, about the same percentage who find it the most trustworthy source. As a result, no matter how well suppliers believe they understand their customers' needs and behaviors on a divisible basis, they must have both a strategy and array of tactics that help customers create influence and personal leverage on a peer-to-peer, situation-by-situation basis. This is truly divisibility in its purest form.

---

[1] Pete Blackshaw, "Quantifying Word of Mouth," www.marketingprofs.com, October 19, 2004; Patricia Odell, "Live from Forrester Consumer Forum: Consumers Feel Assaulted by Ads," *PromoXtra*, September 21, 2004.

What this means is creation of *active advocacy*, a state of deep-rooted, emotional engagement between a customer and supplier that goes beyond satisfaction, beyond delight, beyond loyalty, and even beyond commitment. Advocacy represents the highest level of involvement, engaging with suppliers in an emotional bond well beyond the typical relationship between supplier and customer, and having them actively talk about their experiences to friends, relatives, and colleagues.

Advocacy is not merely a new way of thinking about customers on a divisible level. Arguably, if the name of the game is value optimization, learning about how customers think about suppliers, brands, products, or services, and then carrying their experiences and consideration forward as proactive advocates, this is, or will become, the *only* way to think about them. It will help companies learn about how emerging trends, image, performance, and reputation relative to competitors, problems and complaints, response to new product or service ideas, and even rumors and back-fence Internet gossip can impact customer advocacy behavior.

The following data shows comparisons of behavior over time of customers who gave high ratings on typical satisfaction and recommendation likelihood questions. The top line is the actual performance of consumers who were identified, using a proprietary series of questions, as active brand advocates.

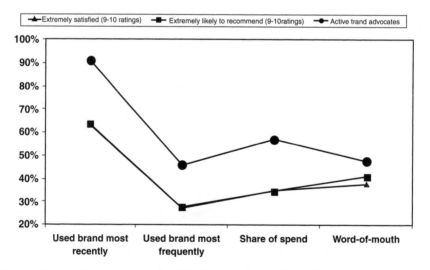

Figure A.1 A Comparison with Highly Satisfied and Highly Likely to Recommend Customers
Source: Customer Management Center of Excellence, NOP World, 2004.

What's abundantly clear is that, compared to customers who were highly satisfied or even highly likely to recommend (as those who promote this metric as the single number that can be used to understand the drivers of growth), those who were active brand advocates used products more recently, more frequently, and with higher share of spend than either of those two groups of customers. Moreover, even though measurement of word-of-mouth is very much in an embryonic stage of marketing sophistication, active advocates were higher on this measure as well.

In the all-too-near future, having the tools to address and treat customers on a divisible basis in the traditional ways will likely not be enough to assure competitive superiority. It will take active customer advocacy. Advocacy incorporates every link along the relationship chain between suppliers and their customers—from the employees connecting with customers at each touch point, to the touch processes themselves (both messaging and individual experience), the corporate structure and culture, and even the way intermediate and senior management consider customers. The percentage of customers who are active brand or supplier advocates will become the new, and most sustainable and reliable, measure of success, guiding all customer-related activities.

INDEX

A

Abacus Direct, 23–24
Accenture study, 28–29
Accessible, 90–92, 183
Accurint, 27–28
Active advocacy, 204
Activity Based Costing, 168
Adam's Mark, 15
Adapting the customer's perspective
    Bearing Point study, 65–66
Advanced linking software
    Innovative Systems, 11
Advocacy, 203–205
Advocates, 183
Aggregated ROI, 178–179
Amazon, 147
Ambivalent non-users, 95
American Airlines
    frequent flier program, 62–63
American Association of Retired Persons
    (AARP), 141
American Customer Satisfaction Index, 146
Analytical sieve, 42
Annenberg Public Policy Center
    University of Pennsylvania, 26
4anything.com, 22
At Risk, 183
At risk customer, 74
Attitude, online experience, 69
Authority, 105
Automatic Call Distribution (ACD), 1
Automotive industry, 33
Available non-users, 95
Average handle time (AHT), 167
Average users, 95

B

Banc One, 159–160
Baptist Health Care, 17, 156
Basex, 58
Basu, Kunal, 90, 183
Bearing Point study, 65

Behavior leverage factor
    weight influence of, 184
Berry, Jon, 34
Bethune, Gordon, 153
Blockbuster Entertainment
    data mart, 48
Blogs, 35, 120–121
Blue Martini, 15
Bonded Sender
    IronPort, 58
Brand, 53
Brand communities, 141
Brin, David
    death of privacy, 27
British Airways, 17
British Telecom
    study on database errors, 10
Business Development Center (BDC)
    Price, 195–197
Buzz
    customer divisibility, data privacy, and viral
        marketing, 34–36
    internet chat room-created, 34–36

C

Campbell's Soup Company
    Consumer Response and Information
        Center, 159
CanSpam law, 2002, 58
Capitol Concierge, 16, 39, 201–202
Carlzon, Jan, 110
Casanova Complex, 21–22, 127
Cendant Corporation, 25
Chartered Institute of Marketing, UK, 73,
    145
Churn modeling, 181
    predictive, 114–120
Cialdini, Robert, 105
Classmates.com, 134–135
Comments and complaints, 7f, 8
Commerce Bank, 49, 99–100
Commodity-oriented supplier, 190
Communities, 125–144

Rudimentary stage
customer service, 165
Russell, John, 137–138

S

Salespeople, 34
Scandinavian Airline System, 110
Scarcity, 105
Scorecard, 184
SeaBridge Software, 111–112
Segmentation, 8, 18
Seisint
creation of Matrix, 27–28
Selling and sales force automation, 31
Senior management attitude, impact on customer service, 146–147
Senior management support, 12
Shallow users, 95
Short message service (SMS) technology, 63–64
Simplicity, online experience, 69
Smith, David, 43
Sobey's Inc., 89
Southwest Airlines, 67–68
Spam, 21, 57–58
Spherion, 152
Starbucks, 188
Strativity Group, 187
Strongly unavailable non-users, 95
Strugglers, 8
Superquinn, 16–17
Supplier persuasion, 105–108
Suppliers
disconnect with customers, 187–205
Suspect stage of life cycle, 74
Sweepstakes programs, 22

T

Target
RFID, 118
Targeting messages and managing experiences, 53–71, 73–85, 87–108
TARP, 39
Telegraph, 3
Telephone, 3
Ten Golden Rules of Customer Plus—Delta, 39–41
Terrorism
data privacy and, 24

Tesco, 54, 125–131
clubcard, 126
clubcard customer charter, 28–29
customer commitment and loyalty behavior, 128–129
RFID, 118
unretailer-like customer data gathering approaches, 197
Text messaging, 21
The Modeling Agency, 116
Third party information, 7f
Ticket City, 202
Timing, customer data, 43–44
T-Mobile, 76
Top line service stage, customer service, 166
Touch processes, 54
customer life cycle, divisibility, and messaging applied to, 81–83
Training, effects on data quality, 12
Transparency, online experience, 69
Trapped, 90–92, 183
Truly loyal, 90–92
TRUSTe, 27, 58
Tucker, Robert, 127

U

Under-achievers, 8
Undesirable prospective customers, 33
Union Bank of Norway, 50
Unstructured data, 8–9
US Airways
customer commitment, 87–88
USA Today/RIT award for customer service, 17

V

VIPdesk, 16
Viral marketing, 21–36
customer divisibility, data privacy, and buzz, 34–36
ongoing challenge, 30–33
Virgin student, 141
Voice Over Internet Protocol (VoIP), 71

W

Walker Information, 88, 151, 186
WalMart
database of customer transaction records, 28

About TEXERE

Texere, a progressive and authoritative voice in business publishing, brings to the global business community the expertise and insights of leading thinkers. Our books educate, enlighten, and entertain, and provide an intersection where our authors and our readers share cutting edge ideas, practices, and innovative solutions. Texere seeks to cultivate, enhance, and disseminate information that illuminates the global business landscape.

www.thomson.com/learning/texere

About the typeface

This book was set in 10.5/12pt Bembo.